QUALITY ENGINEERING
IN PRODUCTION SYSTEMS

McGraw-Hill Series in Industrial Engineering and Management Science

Consulting Editor

James L. Riggs, *Department of Industrial Engineering, Oregon State University*

Also available from McGraw Hill

Schaum's Outline Series in Mechanical and Industrial Engineering

Each outline includes basic theory, definitions and hundreds of solved problems and supplementary problems with answers.

Current List Includes:

Acoustics
Basic Equations of Engineering
Continuum Mechanics
Engineering Economics
Engineering Mechanics, 4th edition
Fluid Dynamics
Fluid Mechanics & Hydraulics
Heat Transfer
Introduction to Engineering Calculations
Lagrangian Dynamics
Machine Design
Mechanical Vibrations
Operations Research
Strength of Materials, 2nd edition
Theoretical Mechanics
Thermodynamics

Available at Your College Bookstore

QUALITY ENGINEERING IN PRODUCTION SYSTEMS

Genichi Taguchi

International Consultant

Elsayed A. Elsayed

Professor and Chairman,
Department of Industrial Engineering,
Rutgers University

Thomas C. Hsiang

Director of Statistical Services
Universal Foods Corporation

McGraw-Hill Book Company

New York   St. Louis   San Francisco   Auckland   Bogotá   Caracas
Colorado Springs   Hamburg   Lisbon   London   Madrid   Mexico   Milan
Montreal   New Delhi   Oklahoma City   Panama   Paris   San Juan
São Paulo   Singapore   Sydney   Tokyo   Toronto

This book was set in Times Roman by Publication Services.
The editors were John Corrigan and John M. Morriss;
the cover was designed by John Hite;
the production supervisor was Friederich W. Schulte.
Project supervision was done by Publication Services.
R. R. Donnelley & Sons Company was printer and binder.

QUALITY ENGINEERING IN PRODUCTION SYSTEMS

1 2 3 4 5 6 7 8 9 0 DOC DOC 8 9 3 2 1 0 9 8

ISBN 0-07-062830-0

Library of Congress Cataloging-in-Publication Data

Taguchi, Genichi, (date).
    Quality engineering in production systems.

    (McGraw-Hill series in industrial engineering and
    management science)
    Bibliography: p.
    Includes index.
    1. Quality control—Statistical methods. 2. Pro-
duction management—Quality control.   I. Elsayed,
Elsayed A.   II. Hsiang, Thomas C.   III. Title.
IV. Series.
TS156.T33   1989   658.5'62   88-8882
ISBN 0-07-062830-0

ABOUT THE AUTHORS

Dr. Genichi Taguchi is an international consultant in the field of quality control and assurance. He has served as Director of the Japanese Academy of Quality from 1978 to 1982. He was awarded the Deming Prize in 1960 in recognition of his contributions in the development of various techniques for industrial optimization while he was on staff at Electrical Communication Laboratories of Nippon Telegraph and Telephone Public Corporation. From 1964 to 1981, he served as a professor at Aoyamagokuin University. Since 1981, he has served as a full time consultant to various companies such as AT&T, Bell Communications Research, Ford, Xerox, and many companies in the United States, Japan, Taiwan, and the People's Republic of China. Throughout the many years of his career, Dr. Taguchi has developed methods for on-line and off-line quality control which form the basis of his approach to a total quality control and assurance in a product's development cycle. Dr. Taguchi received his Doctor of Science from Kyushu University in 1962.

Dr. Elsayed A. Elsayed is Professor and Chairman of the Department of Industrial Engineering, Rutgers University. His research interests are in the areas of quality and reliability engineering, production planning and control, and automated manufacturing systems. Dr. Elsayed held teaching and research positions at Cairo University, University of Windsor, and University of Utah. In 1987–1988, he spent his sabbatical with AT&T Bell Laboratories conducting research on reliability modeling and analysis of semiconductors. He served as a consultant to Bell Communications Research, Sea-Land, Personal Products, AT&T, and other manufacturing companies. He is a coauthor of "Analysis and Control of Production Systems," Prentice-Hall, 1985. He is a senior member of IIE, ASME, SME, and ASEE and is listed in Who's Who in the East, and Who's Who in Engineering. Dr. Elsayed received his Ph.D. in industrial engineering from University of Windsor in 1976.

Dr. Thomas Hsiang is the Director — Statistical Services of Universal Foods Corporation, Milwaukee, Wisconsin, where he plays an integral role in training, consulting, and developing the implementation of all needed elements of the Total Quality Effort throughout the company. He previously held positions in Quality and Statistics with various divisions in Bell Canada, AT&T, Bell Laboratories, and Bell Communications Research, where he served as a manager, teacher, and consultant in using statistics for the improvement of quality and productivity. He also taught at the Department of Statistics, Rutgers University, as an adjunct professor. He has had numerous publications in quality and statistics. He was co-winner of the Best Paper Award of the 1982 American Society for Quality Control Congress. A native of Szechuan, China, Tom was educated in Taiwan and Canada, earning his B.S. (1965) in Chemical Engineering from Tunghai University; M. Eng. (1967) in Chemical Engineering from McMaster University; and M. Math (1969) and Ph.D. (1971) in Statistics from the University of Waterloo. Tom is a member of the American Statistical Association (ASA) and the American Society for Quality Control (ASQC), and he is a registered Professional Engineer.

CONTENTS

PREFACE

The traditional role of quality control is basically to eliminate from production lines those parts that do not conform to specifications, and to inspect and test–finish products for defects. Given this definition, quality control is almost limited to inspecting and testing on a detailing or sampling basis.

The increased emphasis on "higher quality" products at lower costs, combined with the competition from overseas for U.S. markets, has magnified the importance of quality control. Consequently, quality control activities have been redefined to ensure the quality of the product during every phase of its life cycle. This book describes quality control from an engineering standpoint. It is intended to amplify the concept of "on-line" quality control as applied during production.

Chapter 1 provides a comprehensive discussion on the value of product quality and the relationship between product quality and price. The chapter also introduces the concept of an Overall Quality Control System, including its components and applications.

Chapter 2 covers a "loss function" approach as a measure of quality, and its use in determining product specification, target values of product characteristics, and desired tolerance(s) relevant to each target value.

The aim of Chapter 3 is to discuss tolerance design as well tolerancing for each of three basic types of variable characteristics.

Chapter 4 presents "on-line feedback quality control" and also illustrates the use of the "loss function" for the design and evaluation of a feedback control system.

Approaches for "on-line process parameter control" for variable characteristics are examined in Chapter 5.

Chapter 6 provides approaches for an on-line quality control system for attribute characteristics, including techniques for determining the optimal diagnosis interval and its effect on the quality loss per unit of production.

Chapter 7 considers different methods for improving the parameters of the production, diagnosis, and adjustment processes to minimize the total quality loss.

Chapter 8 discusses the use of preventive maintenance as a means of improving the parameters of the production process to reduce the quality loss of production.

Examples are provided throughout this book to reinforce and illustrate the concepts, methods, and approaches involved. The end of each chapter contains problems to facilitate practice.

This book is intended primarily for those involved in the research, development, and manufacturing phases of a product's life-cycle, including design engineers, production and manufacturing engineers, quality engineers, and applied statisticians. It is also intended for senior undergraduate students and first year graduate students in industrial-, production-, manufacturing-, and systems-engineering disciplines. Students should have a familiarity with basic statistical quality control.

Although we have included a few results of our own research, this textbook is not solely the work of the three authors, and the many references throughout the book reflect our indebtedness to others. We have attempted to give appropriate credit to everyone involved. We would like particularly to acknowledge the Japanese Standards Association for permission to use certain material in Chapters 6 and 7.

The interest in this book was originated by Thomas Hsiang when he worked for Bell Communications Research, Inc. (Bellcore) as the District Manager—Quality and Reliability Engineering at the Quality Assurance Operations Center. During his tenure, Genichi Taguchi and Elsayed A. Elsayed served as consultants to the Quality Assurance Operations Center. We are grateful to Bellcore for the continued editorial, technical, typing, and drafting support. In particular, we wish to express our thanks to Pete Pence and Norm Sherer for their support during the initiation of this work; Jen Tang for his technical review; Loinel Howard, Jr., and Jim Falk for their assistance and coordination in making the publication of this book possible; Donald Rector and Pamela Richardson for their editorial work and Christine DeHanes for her managerial efforts in the professional typing, editing, formatting, and drafting of this work.

Additional thanks are due to Professor Yu-In Wu for technical discussions, to John J. Gordon (formerly with AT&T Technologies, Inc.) for editorial efforts and to Wayne B. Clark and Universal Foods Corporation for interest and support of this endeavor.

We would also like to thank Anne Duffy and John Corrigan of McGraw-Hill for their efforts in facilitating the review of the book and bringing the project to fruition. Our great appreciation to the following reviewers who provided many useful comments and suggestions: Jeya Chandra, The Pennsylvania State University; Frank Kaminsky, University of Massachusetts; J. Bert Keats, Arizona State University; Hau Lee, Stanford University; Joseph Mize, Oklahoma State University; Ronald Snee, Dupont Company; and Dennis B. Webster, The University of Alabama.

Finally, we reserve the greatest thanks for our families for their encouragement and support.

Genichi Taguchi
Elsayed A. Elsayed
Thomas Hsiang

QUALITY ENGINEERING
IN PRODUCTION SYSTEMS

CHAPTER
1

QUALITY
VALUE
AND
ENGINEERING

Prior to World War II, the quality of Japanese-made products was poor. Prices were low, and it was difficult, if not impossible, to secure repeat sales. A simple comparison between the quality of products made in the United States and Japan at that time can be illustrated by the following example: Assume that a product made in Japan was one-half the price of a similar product made in the United States. If losses incurred by the customer through use of the Japanese-made product were nine times its purchase price, and if losses incurred by the customer through use of the U.S.-made product were equal to the price of the U.S.-made product, then the total loss to the customer because of the purchase of the Japanese-made product would be $2\frac{1}{2}$ times the loss caused by the purchase of the U.S.-made product. This would suggest that the U.S.-made product was $2\frac{1}{2}$ times superior in quality to the Japanese-made product, according to the following calculations:

	U.S.-made product	Japanese-made product
Purchase price	P	$0.5P$
Losses due to product use	P	$9(0.5P)$
Total cost to customer	$2P$	$5P$

The trade-off between quality and price is an important subject. Product quality is affected by its tolerance design; we therefore present a detailed methodology of tolerance design in Chap. 3.

To further illustrate the importance of trade-off between product quality and price, we quote an expression used by many executives, "The quality of our product is excellent, but the price is too high." As indicated earlier, there must be a balance between quality loss and product price. The price represents the loss to the customer at the time of purchase, and poor quality represents an additional loss to the customer during the use of the product. A goal of quality engineering should be to reduce the total loss to the customer.

Applying the quality-price trade-off, we need to predict quality loss at the product design, process design, and production phases. A product is usually priced at several times the unit manufacturing cost (UMC). Therefore, UMC becomes a very important factor in the trade-off analysis. In terms of quality loss, a monetary prediction is necessary. Many companies still use percent defective as a measure of quality level. Defective products, however, are usually not shipped. Only the products that are shipped cause quality problems to consumers. For this reason, the loss caused by unshipped defective products should be considered as a cost, not a quality loss.

In this book, quality loss is defined as the loss a product costs society from the time the product is released for shipment. Losses such as failure of function, harmful effects, pollution, operating costs, and maintenance costs are all included. Chapter 2 explains how to evaluate quality loss in terms of monetary units, assuming product tolerances are correct. The concept of loss function is also introduced. Chapter 3 discusses a method for specifying tolerances; it is intended especially for product designers. However, tolerance is so important that production engineers and production personnel also need a good understanding of its meaning. Chapters 4 through 8 deal with various on-line quality control and engineering aspects in production, including preventive maintenance.

It is important to note that company-wide activities are needed to improve quality and productivity. These activities are

1. Product planning
2. Product design
3. Process design
4. Production
5. Service after purchase

The remainder of this chapter provides an overview of the various activities that constitute an overall quality system.

1.1 AN OVERALL QUALITY SYSTEM

The following sections describe a company-wide quality control system. The overall system involves the quality concept and quality cost through all phases of a product's life cycle. The life cycle begins with product planning and continues through the phases of product design, production process design, on-line production process control, market development, and packaging, as well as maintenance and product service. This section discusses the concept underlying an overall quality control system, that is, *what* constitutes an overall quality control system, and *how* it affects the quality of the products produced.

From the standpoint of value received, product quality is determined by the economic losses imposed upon society from the time a product is released for shipment. A typical example is loss caused by *functional variation:* the deviation of one of a product's principal functional characteristics from the specified "nominal (target) value" of the product design specification. If process design and quality control engineering are not capable of sufficiently reducing deviation by process adjustments, then inspection may be an economically useful alternative.

Product design engineering may in itself operate as a primary factor in major losses by including tolerances that result in assembly misfits or special production processes that are unnecessary. Similar examples can be found in other phases of the product life cycle, such as market development, packaging, or product maintenance.

Ideally, an integrated system of overall quality control, in which all activities interact to produce products with minimum deviations from target values, will minimize quality costs and make the most economic use of human and other company resources. This system, which aims to achieve controlled production of products with superior quality, can be called an *overall quality system*.

As discussed earlier, quality loss, in broad terms, is defined as the losses imposed on society from the time a product is released for shipment. The discussion in this book is specifically concerned with the losses caused by deviation in a product's functional characteristics from their specified nominal values (desired target values).

The two types of undesirable and uncontrollable factors that can cause deviation from target values in a product's functional characteristics are known as external and internal noise factors. Operating environment variables (such as temperature or humidity) are examples of external noise factors. There are two categories of internal noise factors. They are

deterioration, such as the wearing out of parts caused by friction and the loss of spring resilience, and

manufacturing-process imperfections, such as variations in machine setting

The broad purpose of the overall quality system is to produce a product that is *robust* with respect to all noise factors. Robustness implies that the product's functional characteristics are not sensitive to variation caused by noise factors.

In order to achieve robustness, quality control efforts must begin in the product design phase and be continued through production engineering and production operation phases. During the product design and production engineering phases, these three steps must be followed:

1. System design
This step depends on the product phase during a life cycle. For example, during the research and development phase, system design involves the development of a prototype design and determination of materials, parts, components, and assembly system. In the production engineering phase, the determination of the manufacturing process is involved.

2. Parameter design
In this step, the levels (values) of controllable factors (design parameters) are selected to minimize the effect of noise factors on the functional characteristics of the product.

3. Tolerance design
This step applies if the reduction in variation of the functional characteristic achieved by parameter design as described above is insufficient. Narrow tolerances are then specified for the deviations of design parameters in relation to the levels determined by the parameter design.

These three steps have been widely used in many industries for improving the quality of products. Quality control activities at the product planning, design, and production engineering phases will be referred to as *off-line* quality control or quality engineering, whereas the quality control activities during actual production will be referred to as *on-line* quality control.

Taguchi and Wu (1979) summarize these activities for a typical manufacturing facility in Table 1.1. An asterisk (∗) as in the fourth column of the table indicates that the external noise can be controlled at that step in the product's life cycle. A plus (+) indicates that it is not preferable to control the external noise

TABLE 1.1
Functional quality engineering activities

Quality control activities	Product phase	Steps	External noise	Internal noise	Variation among units (tolerances)
Off-line	Product design	System design	∗	∗	∗
		Parameter design	∗	∗	∗
		Tolerance design	+	∗	∗
	Production engineering	System design	+ +	+ +	∗
		Parameter design	+ +	+ +	∗
		Tolerance design	+ +	+ +	∗
On-line	Production operation	Process control	+ +	+ +	∗
		Feedback	+ +	+ +	∗
		Inspection, etc.	+ +	+ +	∗

Key:
  ∗ = possible
  + = not preferable
  + + = impossible

at that step. A double plus $(+ +)$ indicates the impossibility of controlling the noise at a step.

1.2 QUALITY ENGINEERING IN PRODUCT DESIGN

As indicated earlier, product design has the greatest impact on product quality. It is essential to consider all aspects of the design (including factors built into the product) that affect the deviation of functional characteristics of the product from target (nominal) values. It is also necessary to consider methods to reduce the undesirable and uncontrollable factors (such as noise) that cause functional deviations.

The three steps—system design, parameter design, and tolerance design— are applied to a design of a product as described below.

1.2.1 System Design

System design denotes the development of a basic prototype design that performs the desired and required functions of the product with minimum deviation from target performance values. It includes the selection of materials, parts, components, and the assembly system. For example, the design of an electrical circuit for a television set that converts an input of 100-V alternating current to 115-V direct current requires a search for the technically best circuit that is specifically relevant to this design. An automatic control system might be included in the design of the circuit so that a target value of the desired voltage (115 V) is set, and then continuous measurements of the output power of the circuit are taken. If there are deviations between the measurements and the target value, the automatic control system should change the relevant parameter in the circuit. For instance, it may change the resistance value of a rheostat so that the difference between the target value and the measured output voltage is reduced to zero.

In brief, the system design of such an electric circuit requires an appropriate circuit design.

1.2.2 Parameter Design

Once the system design is established, the next step is to ascertain the optimal levels for the parameters of each element in the system so that the functional deviations of the product are minimized. As an illustration of parameter design, consider the design example of the electric power circuit for a television set with the capacity to convert an input of 100 V AC to an output of 115 V DC. After the selection of a prototype circuit (system design), it is necessary to determine the optimal levels of the circuit parameters.

Consider an example where 100 V is supplied to the prototype circuit but an output of only 80 V is obtained. To reduce the gap of 35 V (difference between the target voltage and that actually measured in the prototype circuit), the parameter h_{FE} (transistor gain) of a transistor used in the circuit is set at a different level.

The effect of h_{FE} on the output voltage is shown in Fig. 1-1. Since the value of h_{FE} varies considerably during its life in the circuit, choosing its level to be A' in order to reduce the gap will result in a circuit with significant exposure to output voltage deviation from the target value. As shown in Fig. 1-1, when a low-grade transistor is used ($h_{FE} = A'$), the value of h_{FE} would be likely to vary as much as 30 percent of the mean value, resulting in variations in the output voltage as large as the interval $Y_1 - Y_0$.

Therefore, the level of h_{FE} should be chosen at A_0, because variations about A_0 will have minimal or no effect on the output voltage. This choice will reduce the difference between actual and nominal (target) voltage to 20 V, which must be eliminated by changing another circuit parameter. Assume a resistor used in the circuit has a linear effect on the output voltage and that an increase of 1 kΩ in resistance decreases the voltage by 5 V. The gap will be diminished by choosing a value of the resistor 4 kΩ larger than that currently present in the circuit.

Determination of the optimal levels of parameters is an off-line process and is usually accomplished by using an experimental design approach. The end result of this design step is to determine the optimal combination of levels of parameters and all components of the prototype, that minimizes or diminishes the effects of various noises while keeping performance as close as possible to its nominal (target) value.

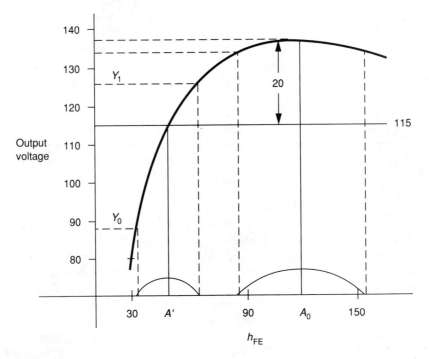

FIGURE 1-1
Effect of h_{FE} on the output voltage.

1.2.3 Tolerance Design

Once the system design is completed and the optimal values of the parameters of the elements (components) are obtained, the next step is to determine the tolerance of each individual parameter (factor) by trading off quality loss and cost. In effect, it is necessary to define allowable ranges for deviation in the parameter value. Obviously, the narrower the range of deviation, the more costly the product becomes, as a result of increased manufacturing cost. On the other hand, the wider the range of deviation, the larger the deviation in product function from a specific target value. The tolerance design step determines the most economical tolerances: those that minimize product cost for given tolerable deviation from target values. In Chap. 3, approaches are examined for optimal tolerance design, taking into consideration losses caused by deviation from nominal values given by the parameter design as well as costs of different grades of components.

1.3 QUALITY ENGINEERING IN DESIGN OF PRODUCTION PROCESSES

When the design and fabrication of the prototype with optimally determined tolerances and specifications are completed, product manufacturing proceeds with three design steps. These are similar to the three steps of the product design phase, namely system design, parameter design, and tolerance design. These steps are now explained in terms of how they are applied to the design of production processes.

1.3.1 System Design

System design (as related to production processes) determines the manufacturing processes required to move a workpiece from partial completion to a more advanced stage of completion. During the manufacturing processes, energy is added to the workpiece in order to change its shape, remove material from it, or change its physical properties or function. There are generally many manufacturing processes that can perform the same function on a workpiece. For example, metal removal can be performed by using turning operations, milling operations, or shaping operations.

The main objective of system design is to determine the manufacturing processes that can produce the product within the specified limits and tolerances at the lowest cost. This system design function is usually performed by manufacturing, production, and industrial engineering.

1.3.2 Parameter Design

Parameter design in production process design determines the operating levels of the manufacturing processes so that variation in product parameters is minimized. Typical examples of variations in the operating levels of the manufacturing processes include temperature variation, raw-material variation, input-voltage variation, and tool-condition variation. These variations, as well as several unidentified noise factors, can cause nonuniformity in the production processes, resulting in out-of-specification products or nonuniform production output. The nonuniformity of the production processes can be minimized by determining optimal levels for the parameters of the processes. Operating levels can then be shifted to points where the effects of process variations on the product are minimal.

The parameters that affect the performance of the production process are established during the "test setup" run. Consequently, production process design is classified as an off-line quality control process, and experimental design approach is used to determine the optimal levels of the parameters for the process.

1.3.3 Tolerance Design

Once the optimal operating conditions for each element of the production process have been determined, the allowance ranges for changes in operating conditions and other variables are determined. As mentioned earlier, the narrower the range of the operating conditions, the smaller the variation or nonuniformity of the product, with a necessary increase in production-process cost. Thus, the objective is to find optimal ranges of the operating conditions that minimize the sum of variation cost and cost of the product. This is the on-line feedback control system design problem explained in this book.

1.4 QUALITY ENGINEERING IN PRODUCTION

On-line quality control as explained in this book deals with the daily activities to control process conditions by observing either quality characteristics of products or process parameters. The methods used in such activities are extensions of engineering methodologies called feedback control, feed-forward control, and calibration. It is known that all processes will drift if control is not applied. Therefore, the purpose of on-line quality control is to produce uniform products by adjusting processes according to information about the process and/or the product produced. Based on this information, a solution to minimize quality loss or cost can be devised.

One observation is usually enough to control the process for each period, even in attribute cases. A typical example of using one observation to control a process is the error control of a watch. The error control of a watch can be accomplished by periodically checking the error with the standard time signal and correcting it when the magnitude of error exceeds some control limits.

The error of the watch is a function of the controlling methods. One does not need to take a sample of the error of time, but it is necessary to predict the error for the controlling method devised. Consider an example where there are two watches, and the quality of one is good, while that of the other is poor. The good-quality watch has an error of 30 seconds a year, while the poor-quality watch has an error of 30 seconds a day. If the poor-quality watch is calibrated daily, and the good-quality watch is calibrated yearly, there would be no difference in the quality of the two watches. Quality is a function of not only design, but of the control system.

Without controlling the process, it is not possible to control a product's quality. How often should we observe the process or product, and what are the optimal control limits? To answer this question we have to start with the prediction of quality level, which becomes a most important step in on-line quality control. Chapters 4 through 8 discuss the quality prediction and control issues in more detail.

1.5 QUALITY ENGINEERING IN CUSTOMER SERVICE

Despite tight controls applied in the design and production steps, some defective products find their way to customers. Such defective products may create problems in subsequent processes or may result in liability claims by consumers once the product reaches the market. Appropriate postmanufacturing service must be provided for cases where consumer claims are justified.

The sales department of the manufacturer has an obligation to provide adequate service to customers with justifiable claims. This service should take the form of repairing or replacing the defective products and compensating for damages that the customer may have incurred.

1.6 SUMMARY

This chapter introduced a definition of quality as the loss incurred due to deviations of product characteristics from their target values, and also introduced the concept of the overall quality system. Three basic steps were discussed to achieve robustness of the product and the production processes, namely system design, parameter design, and tolerance design. These steps constitute what we refer to as off-line quality control.

We conclude this chapter by emphasizing that quality of products or performance of processes must continuously be improved so that the deviations of the product characteristics from the target values are minimized.

PROBLEMS

1.1. Quality is viewed differently by different people. How would you view it if you were
    (*a*) a customer?
    (*b*) an engineer who is responsible for a product line?
    (*c*) an applied statistician in a manufacturing company?
    (*d*) the president of a manufacturing company?
1.2. Propose a new definition of quality and an appropriate measure for it.
1.3. Describe the elements of a total quality system in a manufacturing company. What would the differences be in a service company?

1.4. There are three basic steps to be applied in each phase of the product life cycle; these steps are system design, parameter design, and tolerance design. Show how these steps can be applied for the manufacturing processes of a product.

1.5. What are the main differences between off-line and on-line quality engineering systems? Can some of the activities of these two systems overlap? If so, can you determine the areas where each system must be restricted?

1.6. The receiving department of a manufacturer inspects incoming parts. The inspection is limited to measuring the principal dimensions of the parts. If the dimensions of a measured part do not meet the required specifications, the part is either discarded or returned to the supplier; if the requirements are met, the part is accepted. The inaccuracy of the measurement process may cause the acceptance of parts that do not meet the specifications or the rejection of good parts. What are the parameters of the measurement process? Design off-line and on-line quality control systems that ensure the quality of the process.

1.7. Assume that the inspection department in Prob. 1.6 uses GO and NO-GO gauges to check the dimensions of the incoming parts. Define the parameters of the measurement process under this environment. How do the off-line and on-line quality control systems differ from those you developed for Prob. 1.6?

1.8. Variation in product quality is usually attributed to three factors: (i) the fabrication equipment, (ii) the material, and (iii) the operator. Describe examples for each of the above factors that may result in variations of product quality.

REFERENCES

Burgam, P. M. "Design of Experiments—the Taguchi Way." *Manufacturing Engineering*, vol. 94, no. 5 (May 1985), pp. 44–47.

Crosby, P. B. *Quality is Free.* New York: McGraw-Hill, 1979.

Feigenbaum, A. V. *Total Quality Control.* New York: McGraw-Hill, 1983.

Garvin, D. A. "What Does 'Product Quality' Really Mean?" *Sloan Management Review*, vol. 26, no. 1, pp. 25–43.

Gingerich, J. Z., and J. W. Peery. "CAD/CAM and Quality." *Quality Progress*, 1984.

Juran, J. M. *Quality Control Handbook.* New York: McGraw-Hill, vol. 17, no. 6 (1979), pp. 8–9.

Shewhart, W. A. *Economic Control of Quality of Manufactured Product.* New York: Van Nostrand, 1931.

Shewhart, W. A. "Statistical Methods from the Viewpoint of Quality Control." Department of Agriculture, Washington, D.C., 1939.

Taguchi, G. "Off-line and On-line Quality Control Systems." *Proceedings of the International Conference on Quality Control,* vol. B4 (1978), pp. 1–5.

Taguchi, G. "Quality Engineering in Japan." *Proceedings of CAD/CAM, Robotics and Automation International Conference*, February 1985, pp. 9–12.

Taguchi, G. *Introduction to Quality Engineering.* Tokyo: Asian Productivity Center, 1986.

Taguchi, G., and Y. Wu. *Introduction to Off-line Quality Control.* Tokyo: Central Japan Quality Control Association, 1979. (Available from American Supplies Institute, 6 Parklane Boulevard, Suite 511, Dearborn, MI, 48126.)

Wyckoff, D. D. "Dynamic Aspects of Quality Management." Working paper, Harvard Business School, 1984.

CHAPTER 2

LOSS FUNCTION AND QUALITY LEVEL

This chapter focuses on evaluating the quality level of manufactured products. Chapter 3 discusses methods for specifying tolerance. On-line quality control activities during production are discussed in Chaps. 4 through 8.

The concept of percent defective has been widely used as a measure of quality level. Usually, however, the percentage of defective products in shipped goods is small. Also, there are not many manufacturers who ship defective products. Even in developing countries a manufacturer usually screens products to ensure that only nondefective units are shipped. When defective product units are not shipped, the consumer is not directly affected except in increased cost. Therefore, the incidence of defective product units should not be considered a quality problem, but a cost problem. How to evaluate the quality level of products shipped to consumers is the problem of concern.

In the past, percent defective, process capability index (C_p index, defined as the tolerance interval divided by 6 times the square root of the mean squared deviation from the target—see Eq. 2.1), and warranty cost have been used as measures of quality level for shipped products. There are manufacturers in the United States and Japan who require suppliers to produce items with a process capability index (C_p) of more than 1.00. However, one major weakness of the process capability index is that there is no apparent immediate basis for specifying the optimal value of C_p. This index is a poor measure of quality level because management and engineers cannot comprehend the actual significance of its values; for example, what is the actual improvement when C_p changes from 0.9 to 1.2? Percent defectives or warranty costs are understandable because they are monetary-related measures. Still, warranty cost is useless for taking action in production processes because of time lag, and it cannot measure the loss in market share. We need appropriate methods for predicting quality before shipping or during production. Therefore, we introduce a monetary evaluation of the quality of products, assuming that tolerances are correct.

2.1   THE LOSS FUNCTION

Consider a comparison between the quality of color television sets produced by two factories belonging to the same manufacturing company. One factory (A) is located in America, and the other factory (B) in Japan. Suppose the comparison was based on color concentration, which relates to the color balance of the television sets. Although both factories used the same design, the television sets produced in the American factory had lower quality, and consumers consequently preferred products made in Japan.

Figure 2-1 shows the differences in quality characteristic (i.e., color concentration) distributions. The figure shows that the quality distribution of the Japanese-made television sets (shown by the solid curve) is approximately a normal distribution with a target value at the center; its standard deviation is about 1/6 of the tolerance, which in this case equals 10.

In quality control, the index of tolerance divided by 6 standard deviations is called the process capability index, denoted by C_p.

$$C_p = \frac{\text{tolerance}}{6 \times (\text{standard deviation})} \qquad (2.1)$$

The process capability of the Japanese-made television sets is therefore 1.

On the other hand, the quality distribution of the American-made television sets (shown in Fig. 2-1 by a dotted curve) has less out-of-specification products than the Japanese-made products and is quite similar to the uniform distribution for those products that are within the tolerance limit. Since the standard deviation of the uniform distribution is given by $1/\sqrt{12}$ of the tolerance, the process capability index for these sets is given by

$$C_p = \frac{\text{tolerance}}{6 \times (\text{tolerance} / \sqrt{12})} = 0.577 \qquad (2.2)$$

and is worse than that for the sets made in Japan.

Loss is always incurred when a product's functional quality characteristic (denoted by y) deviates from its target (nominal) value (denoted by m), regardless of how small the deviation is. Figure 2-2 shows a simplified relationship between quality loss and the amount of deviation from the target value. As shown in this figure, quality loss caused by deviation equals zero when $y = m$; the loss increases when the value of the functional characteristic moves in either an upward or downward direction from m. When the value of the functional characteristic

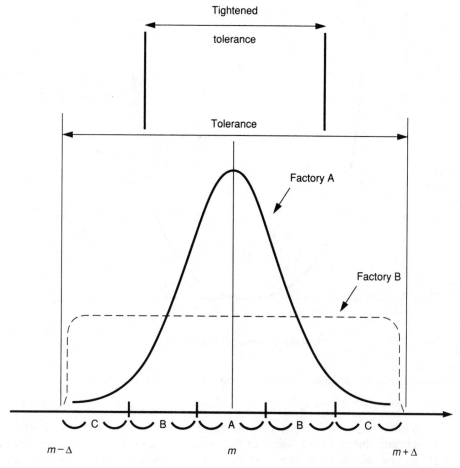

FIGURE 2-1
Distribution of color concentration.

exceeds either one of the limits $m + \Delta$ or $m - \Delta$ (where Δ is defined as the tolerance and 2Δ is the tolerance limit), the quality loss is equal to the cost of the product's disposal or manufacturing.

2.1.1 Derivation of the Loss Function

Assume the loss due to a defective part (because of discarding, repairing, or downgrading) is A. Then denote the loss function by $L(y)$ and expand it in a Taylor series about the target value m:

$$L(y) = L(m + y - m)$$

or $$L(y) = L(m) + \frac{L'(m)}{1!}(y - m) + \frac{L''(m)}{2!}(y - m)^2 + \cdots \quad (2.3)$$

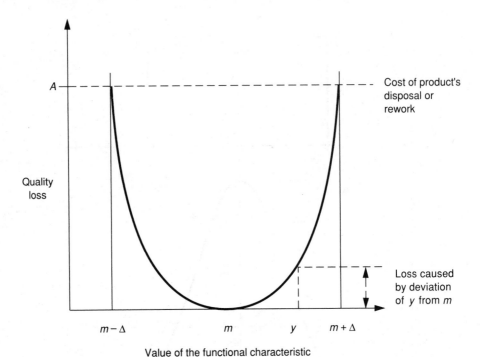

FIGURE 2-2
Relationship between quality loss and deviation from the target value (m).

Because $L(y) = 0$ when $y = m$ (by definition, quality loss is zero when $y = m$), and the minimum value of the function is attained at this point (Fig. 2-2), its first derivative with respect to m, $L'(m)$, is zero. The first two terms of Eq. 2.3, then, are equal to zero. When we neglect terms with powers higher than 2, Eq. 2.3 reduces to

$$L(y) = \frac{L''(m)}{2!}(y - m)^2 \qquad (2.4)$$

or
$$L(y) = k(y - m)^2 \qquad (2.5)$$

where k is a proportionality constant.

The use of quadratic loss function, minimum mean squared error, and minimum mean squared deviation criteria has been fairly extensive in the statistical and control theory literature (e.g., Athan and Falb, 1966, Box and Jenkins, 1976). More recently, Jessup (1985) discussed the rationales behind the quadratic loss function in relation to the value of continuing improvement. He used several practical examples to show the losses caused by variation in process output and the effects of different patterns of variation on the long-term economic performance, equivalent to the "loss to society" approach as advocated and explained in this book.

When the deviation of a product's functional characteristic is an amount Δ from the target value m, the loss equals A. Then Eq. 2.5 gives

$$A = k\Delta^2$$

or

$$k = \frac{A}{\Delta^2} \tag{2.6}$$

In the following, the loss function is applied to the television set example.

Example 2.1. Assume that the cost of repairing a failed television set in the factory is \$2 per unit. Compare the losses caused by deviations from the target value for two television sets, one produced in Factory A and the other produced in Factory B, as described earlier in Fig. 2-1. Recall that the tolerance interval ranges from $m - \Delta$ to $m + \Delta$, where $\Delta = 5$.

Solution. In order to calculate the losses caused by deviation from the target, we need to determine the constant k of Eq. 2.5. Since $\Delta = 5$ and $A = \$2$, the following result is obtained from Eq. 2.6:

$$k = \frac{A}{\Delta^2} = \frac{2.0}{(5)^2} = 0.08$$

The expected loss caused by deviation in the production of the television set in Factory A is obtained by taking the expectation of $L(y)$ in Eq. 2.5. Thus,

$$L = k\nu^2 (\$/\text{unit}) \tag{2.7}$$

where ν^2 is the mean squared deviation from target m. For Factory A, $\nu = 10\%$, and

$$L = 0.08 \left(\frac{10}{6} \right)^2 = \$0.222/\text{unit}$$

The loss caused by deviation in the production of the television set in Factory B is also

$$L = k\nu^2$$

but now $\nu = 10/\sqrt{12}$ and

$$L = 0.08 \left(\frac{10}{\sqrt{12}} \right)^2 = \$0.667/\text{unit}$$

A summary of losses caused by deviation for television sets produced in both factories is given in Table 2.1. The table indicates that the losses caused by deviation for television sets produced in Factory B are three times those for the same type of television set produced in Factory A, despite Factory B's zero fraction defective.

2.1.2 Uses of the Loss Function

The loss function approach can be used in evaluating the effect of quality improvement. For example, assume that Factory A has improved the process

TABLE 2.1
Quality comparison between two manufacturers of television sets

Manufacturer	Target	Mean squared deviation v^2	Expected loss per unit, L	Number defective
Factory A	m	$\dfrac{100}{36}$	$0.222	0.27%*
Factory B	m	$\dfrac{100}{12}$	$0.667	0.00%

*This is obtained by using the standard normal distribution (see Appendix A).

so that a new standard deviation from target of $^{10}\!/\!_8$ is attained. What would be the losses caused by deviations from the target value?

With the use of Eq. 2.7 and $k = 0.08$, as obtained in Example 2.1, the following is obtained:

$$L = kv^2$$

$$L = 0.08\left(\frac{10}{8}\right)^2 = \$0.125$$

The loss per unit of production would decrease from $0.222 (current process) to $0.125, resulting in $0.097 savings per unit.

Let us see how the loss function is related to the process capability index C_p. For the current process and the improved process discussed above, Eq. 2.7 gave

$$L_1 = kv_1^2 \quad \text{(loss with current process)} \tag{2.8}$$

$$L_2 = kv_2^2 \quad \text{(loss with improved process)} \tag{2.9}$$

Divide Eq. 2.8 by Eq. 2.9 to obtain

$$\frac{L_1}{L_2} = \frac{v_1^2}{v_2^2} \tag{2.10}$$

But

$$C_{p_1} = \frac{\text{tolerance}}{6v_1} \tag{2.11}$$

and

$$C_{p_2} = \frac{\text{tolerance}}{6v_2} \tag{2.12}$$

Then substitute Eqs. 2.11 and 2.12 into Eq. 2.10, to obtain the following:

$$\frac{L_1}{L_2} = \frac{C_{p_2}^2}{C_{p_1}^2} \tag{2.13}$$

Equation 2.13 implies that the losses caused by deviation are reciprocally proportional to the squares of the C_p indices. If the loss and the C_p index at the beginning of a process are known, then the loss after changes in the process capability can be determined thereafter by using the C_p index at the desired production period and substituting it into Eq. 2.13.

2.1.3 Economic Consequences of Tightening Tolerances as a Means to Improve Quality

As illustrated in the following example, the loss function approach can be used to determine the economic impact of tightening the tolerance to improve product quality. In order to reduce the difference in quality and process capability indices between television sets produced in Factories A and B (Example 2.1), the management of Factory B tightened the tolerance from $m \pm 5$ to $m \pm 5 \times \frac{2}{3}$. The cost of repairing an out-of-specification unit is still \$2. What is the economic impact of tightening the tolerance?

With the original tolerance, the expected loss is $L = k\nu^2 = \$0.667$, as shown in Table 2.1. The expected loss after tightening the tolerance is

$$L = k\nu^2 = 0.08\left(\frac{2}{3} \times \frac{10}{\sqrt{12}}\right)^2 = \$0.296/\text{unit}$$

If improvement of the process was obtained by repairing the failed units (units outside the new tolerance $m \pm 5 \times \frac{2}{3}$) at a cost of \$2 per unit, then the average cost of repair is as follows:

Average cost of repair per unit = percent of production that needs repair to meet the tightened tolerance × repair cost per unit

$$= 0.333 \times 2 = \$0.667$$

A summary of the results of this example is shown in Table 2.2. In this case, tightening tolerance is an uneconomical alternative because the expected total loss of tightening tolerance and repair ($0.667 + 0.296 = \$0.963$) is greater than the expected loss using the original tolerance (\$0.667).

TABLE 2.2
Quality improvement by tightening tolerances

	Tolerance	Percent defective	ν	k	ν^2	Expected quality loss per unit
Original	$m \pm 5$	0.00	$\dfrac{10}{\sqrt{12}}$	0.08	$\dfrac{100}{12}$	\$0.667
Tightened	$m \pm 5 \times \dfrac{2}{3}$	0.00	$\dfrac{10}{\sqrt{12}} \times \dfrac{2}{3}$	0.08	$\dfrac{44.44}{12}$	\$0.296

2.1.4   The Loss Function for Similar Products (or for a System with Independent Components)

Products having similar functions can be collectively evaluated, regardless of their sizes and specifications, by using the loss function approach. For example, suppose that resistors of k different types are supplied to an assembly plant. The quality of the supplied resistors can be measured by

$$\text{Expected quality losses } L = \left(\frac{A_1}{\Delta_1^2} v_1^2 + \frac{A_2}{\Delta_2^2} v_2^2 + \cdots + \frac{A_k}{\Delta_k^2} v_k^2 \right) \qquad (2.14)$$

where $2\Delta_i \; (i = 1, 2, \ldots, k)$ = tolerance limit of type i resistor
$A_i \; (i = 1, 2, \ldots, k)$ = price (loss) per unit of type i resistor
$v_i^2 \; (i = 1, 2, \ldots, k)$ = mean squared deviation of the resistance of type i resistor

When a product has several measurable functional quality characteristics, the total losses caused by deviations can be estimated by using Eq. 2.15 following, where k represents, in this case, the number of measurable functional quality characteristics of the product.

$$\text{Losses due to deviations } L = \sum_{i=1}^{k} \frac{A_i}{\Delta_i^2} v_i^2 \qquad (2.15)$$

Equation 2.15 provides an index of the total quality of the product because it takes into consideration all the functional quality characteristics of the product.

Example 2.2.   A manufacturer of gauge blocks requires that the blocks meet certain flatness (surface roughness) standards for the measuring ends as well as having a specified length between the ends of each block. The loss caused by unacceptable flatness is $50, and the loss caused by unacceptable length is $20. These losses represent the cost of repairing (if possible) the defective blocks. The specifications of a 1-in gauge block follow:

Length 1.00000 ± 0.00010 in
Surface roughness $0.00020 \; \mu m$ or less

The following length measurements were taken:

| 1.000010 | 1.000020 | 0.999990 | 0.999995 | 1.000010 |
| 1.000005 | 1.000020 | 1.000000 | 0.999998 | 0.999990 |

Also, the following surface roughness measurements were taken:

| 0.00010 | 0.00020 | 0.00015 | 0.00005 | 0.00003 |
| 0.00010 | 0.00006 | 0.00018 | 0.00010 | 0.00020 |

What are the expected total losses caused by deviations?

Solution. Expected loss caused by length deviations (L_1):

$$L_1 = \frac{A_1}{\Delta_1^2}\nu_1^2$$

$A_1 = \$20$

$\Delta_1 = 0.00010$

$$\hat{\nu}_1^2 = \frac{1}{10}[(1.000010 - 1.000000)^2 + (1.000020 - 1.000000)^2 + \cdots$$

$$+ (0.999990 - 1.000000)^2] = 1.2 \times 10^{-10}$$

where $\hat{\nu}_1$ is the estimate of the mean squared deviation.

$$L_1 = \frac{20}{(0.00010)^2} \times 1.2 \times 10^{-10} = \$2.4$$

Expected loss caused by surface roughness deviations (L_2):

$$L_2 = \frac{A_2}{\Delta_2^2}\nu_2^2$$

$A_2 = \$50$

$\Delta_2 = 0.00020$

$$\hat{\nu}_2^2 = \frac{1}{10}[(0.00010)^2 + (0.00020)^2 + \cdots + (0.00020)^2]$$

$$= 1.7 \times 10^{-8}$$

$$L_2 = \frac{50}{(0.00020)^2} \times 1.7 \times 10^{-8} = \$21.2/\text{unit}$$

Expected total loss $= L_1 + L_2 = \$23.6/\text{unit}$

2.1.5 The Loss Function and Justification of Improvements

The loss function can also be used to justify improvements of the process, as illustrated in the following example.

Example 2.3. Assume that Factory A wishes to improve the quality of its television sets by reducing deviations from the target value so that the new standard deviation will be 10/8. This improvement can be technologically achieved at an additional cost of $0.05 per unit of production. Should the factory improve its process? (Assume that no inspection is performed.)

Solution. Total loss per unit of the current process (see Table 2.1):

$$L = k\nu^2$$

$$= 0.08 \left(\frac{10}{6}\right)^2 = \$0.222 \tag{2.16}$$

Total loss per unit after improving the process:

$$L = 0.08 \left(\frac{10}{8}\right)^2 = \$0.125$$

Additional cost of improvement = \$0.05/unit

Additional cost plus loss per unit = 0.05 + 0.125

$$= \$0.175 \tag{2.17}$$

The net gain resulting from improvement in the process capability is obtained by subtracting Eq. 2.17 from Eq. 2.16, and equals \$0.047 per unit of production. If the production rate of this factory is 100,000 units per month, then the expected savings will be \$4700 per month, or \$56,400 annually.

2.1.6   The Loss Function and Inspection

The loss function approach can be used effectively to determine whether 100-percent inspection can be justified or not. It should be noted that the objective of inspection is to screen or repair defective products that cannot meet the given specifications. Therefore, inspection cannot be used to improve the quality of items within the specifications. The improvement of the process can only be accomplished through improved manufacturing techniques or product design, not through screening or 100-percent inspection.

Example 2.4. Consider the case where the diameter of a stainless-steel bar is $m \pm 5\mu m$. The cost of repairing a defective bar is \$6, and the cost of inspection is \$0.03 per unit. Would a 100-percent inspection of items be justified? The estimated standard deviation of the process is 10/6.

Solution. The expected loss without inspection is

$$L = k\nu^2$$

where

$$k = \frac{A}{\Delta^2} = \frac{\$6.00}{5^2} = \$0.24$$

Therefore

$$L = 0.24 \left(\frac{10}{6}\right)^2 = \$0.667/\text{unit}$$

Assuming that the characteristic of the product follows a normal distribution, the proportion of the products falling outside the specification $m \pm 5$ is 0.27 percent, as indicated in Table 2.3. The variance after screening defective products by using 100-percent inspection (ν_{out}^2) is obtained using the procedure shown below.

After the total inspection, the out-of-specification products shown by the hatched area in Fig. 2-3 are removed. The probability density function of those items that have passed the screening (acceptable items) is given by dividing the probability density function of the normal distribution by Q, the proportion of acceptable items.

Let $f(y)$ be the density function of the normal distribution, which is given by

TABLE 2.3
Distribution of quality characteristic and its loss[†]

Specification: $m \pm 5\mu m$, loss by unit defective $(A) = \$6$, loss function $L = 0.24v^2$ dollars

Case	Mean	Standard deviation	Screening	Variance v_{out}^2	Fraction defective discovered	L(dollars)	Outgoing fraction defective (%)
1	m	$\dfrac{10}{2}$	no	$\left(\dfrac{10}{2}\right)^2$	0.00	6.000	31.73*
2	m	$\dfrac{10}{2}$	yes	$0.539^2 \times \left(\dfrac{10}{2}\right)^{2*}$	31.73*	1.743*	0.0*
3	m	$\dfrac{10}{4}$	no	$\left(\dfrac{10}{4}\right)^2$	0.00	1.500	4.55*
4	m	$\dfrac{10}{4}$	yes	$0.880^2 \times \left(\dfrac{10}{4}\right)^{2*}$	4.55*	1.162*	0.00*
5	m	$\dfrac{10}{6}$	no	$\left(\dfrac{10}{6}\right)^2$	0.00	0.667	0.27*
6	m	$\dfrac{10}{6}$	yes	$0.986^2 \times \left(\dfrac{10}{6}\right)^{2*}$	0.27*	0.648*	0.00*
7	m	$\dfrac{10}{8}$	no	$\left(\dfrac{10}{8}\right)^2$	0.00	0.375	0.01*
8	m	$\dfrac{10}{16}$	no	$\left(\dfrac{10}{16}\right)^2$	0.00	0.094	0.00*
9	m	$\dfrac{10}{\sqrt{12}}$	no	$\left(\dfrac{10}{\sqrt{12}}\right)^2$	0.00	2.000	0.00**
10	$m - 2.5$	$\dfrac{10}{6}$	no	$2.5^2 + \left(\dfrac{10}{6}\right)^2$	0.00	2.167	6.68*
11	$m - 2.5$	$\dfrac{10}{12}$	no	$2.5^2 + \left(\dfrac{10}{12}\right)^2$	0.00	1.667	0.14*
12	$m - 2.5$	$\dfrac{10}{16}$	no	$2.5^2 + \left(\dfrac{10}{16}\right)^2$	0.00	1.594	0.00*
13	$m - 2.5$	0	no	2.5^2	0.00	1.500	0.00
14	$m - 5.0$	0	no	5.0^2	0.00	6.000	0.00

† Based on Taguchi (1981)
* Normal distribution
** Uniform distribution
(no mark) Applicable to any type of distribution

$$f(y) = \frac{1}{\sqrt{2\pi}\,\sigma} e^{-(1/2)[(y-\mu)/\sigma]^2} \qquad -\infty < y < \infty$$

where μ and σ are the mean and standard deviation of the normal distribution, respectively. The proportion of acceptable items, Q, is the area under the normal curve bounded by $m - 5$ and $m + 5$.

$$Q = \int_{m-5}^{m+5} \frac{1}{\sqrt{2\pi}} \times \frac{6}{10} e^{-(1/2)(6/10)^2(y-m)^2} dy$$

$$= 0.9973$$

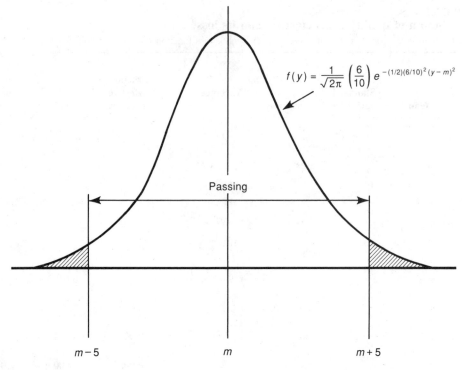

$$f(y) = \frac{1}{\sqrt{2\pi}} \left(\frac{6}{10}\right) e^{-(1/2)(6/10)^2 (y - m)^2}$$

Passing

$m - 5$ m $m + 5$

FIGURE 2-3
Normal distribution and specification.

Therefore, the variance of the passed items, ν_{out}^2, is

$$\nu_{out}^2 = \frac{1}{0.9973} \int_{m-5}^{m+5} \frac{1}{\sqrt{2\pi}} \times \frac{6}{10}(y - m)^2 e^{-(1/2)(6/10)^2(y-m)^2} dy$$

Using integration by parts, ν_{out}^2 is obtained as

$$\nu_{out}^2 = \left(\frac{10}{6}\right)^2 \times (0.986)^2$$

The expected total loss in the case of 100-percent inspection, L, is therefore

$$L = \text{inspection cost per item} + (\text{loss of a defective found in the inspection} \times \text{fraction defective}) + k\nu_{out}^2$$

$$= 0.03 + 6.00 \times 0.0027 + 0.24 \times (0.986)^2 \times \left(\frac{10}{6}\right)^2$$

$$= \$0.694/\text{unit}$$

Since the loss in the case of 100-percent inspection is higher than the loss when no inspection is performed (0.667/unit), 100-percent inspection is not justified.

One might conclude that in this case 100-percent inspection is useless in improving quality, because the fraction defective is only 0.27 percent. It is different, of course, when the purpose of 100-percent inspection is to find serious defectives.

In the case of a normal distribution with a standard deviation that is $\frac{1}{4}$ of the tolerance, the loss without inspection, L, is

$$L = 0.24 \times \left(\frac{10}{4}\right)^2 = \$1.50/\text{unit}$$

The proportion of the product falling outside the specification is 4.55 percent (see Table 2.3), and the variance of the outgoing items is $(0.88)^2$ times that of the original value. The total loss in the case of 100-percent inspection when σ equals 10/4 becomes

$$L = 0.03 + 6.00 \times 0.0455 + 0.24 \times (0.88)^2 \times \left(\frac{10}{4}\right)^2$$

$$= 0.03 + 0.273 + 1.162$$

$$= \$1.465/\text{unit}$$

This result is an improvement of $0.035 per item. If there are 200,000 items produced each month, the amount of improvement is $7,000 each month.

Assuming that the standard deviation is $\frac{1}{2}$ the tolerance and the production output still follows a normal distribution, the portion of the product falling outside the specification is 31.7 percent. Even if all the products are inspected and the defective ones screened out, the standard deviation of the outgoing quality is reduced to only 53.9 percent of the original value ($\sigma =$ tolerance/2). Therefore, the loss caused by variation (using the values given above) is

$$L = 0.24\left(0.539 \times \frac{10}{2}\right)^2 = \$1.743$$

Not only is this worse than the loss of $0.667 for $\sigma = $ 10/6 and no inspection, but it is also worse than the loss of $1.50 for $\sigma = $ 10/4 and no inspection, with 4.55 percent defective products. Thus, the solution to the quality problem is, in this case, through improvement of the process and not through 100-percent inspection.

Table 2.3 shows a summary of the expected losses caused by variation for different probability distributions. These expected losses do not include the cost of inspection or loss caused by defective products found by inspection. Cases 1 through 6 demonstrate how screening reduces total losses for the given parameters. A detailed analysis of Case 2 follows, in order to illustrate how the results of the table are obtained.

Since $\qquad\qquad\qquad\qquad L = kv^2$

then
$$6.00 = k\left(\frac{10}{2}\right)^2$$

and
$$k = 0.24$$

The probability density function of all units produced is

$$f(y) = \frac{1}{\sqrt{2\pi}}\left(\frac{2}{10}\right)e^{-(1/2)(2/10)^2(y-m)^2}$$

The percentage Q of units falling within the specification limits $m \pm 5$ is obtained as follows:

$$Q = \int_{m-5}^{m+5} \frac{1}{\sqrt{2\pi}}\left(\frac{2}{10}\right)e^{-(1/2)(2/10)^2(y-m)^2}dy$$

One can substitute $t = \frac{2}{10}(y - m)$ in the above equation to obtain

$$Q = \int_{-1}^{1} \frac{1}{\sqrt{2\pi}}e^{-(t^2/2)}dt$$

$$= 0.6827$$

The fraction defective is $1 - 0.6827 = 0.3173$.

When inspection is performed, the conditional mean squared deviation of the passed (i.e., acceptable) items, ν_{out}^2, is

$$\nu_{out}^2 = \frac{1}{0.6827}\int_{m-5}^{m+5} \frac{1}{\sqrt{2\pi}} \times \frac{2}{10}(y - m)^2 e^{-(1/2)(2/10)^2(y-m)^2}dy$$

$$= \left(\frac{10}{2}\right)^2(0.539)^2$$

The expected loss is

$$L = 0.24 \times \left(\frac{10}{2}\right)^2(0.539)^2 = \$1.743$$

2.2 QUALITY EVALUATIONS AND TYPES OF TOLERANCES

This section illustrates the evaluation of the quality level of products by using the loss function approach for three types of tolerances. The three types are listed below:

1. The-Nominal-The-Best (N type)

2. The-Smaller-The-Better (S type)

3. The-Larger-The-Better (L type)

2.2.1 The-Nominal-The-Best (N Type)

This type of tolerance is required for many products, parts, elements, and components when a nominal size (or characteristic) is preferred. Dimensions, clearance, and viscosity are typical examples of this type of characteristic. Also, the basic size of a screw thread or the diameter of a gear are the nominal (target) sizes from which large variations are undesirable. Bilateral tolerances are usually used in this type of application. The term *bilateral tolerance* means that the tolerance, as related to a basic dimension, is given in two directions—plus and minus.

Quality evaluations for bilateral tolerances are presented for situations in which the plus and minus tolerances are of equal amount, as well as when the plus and minus tolerances are unequal. Examples follow.

2.2.2 N-Type Tolerance When the Plus and Minus Tolerances Are of Equal Amount

As mentioned above, the bilateral system of tolerances allows variation in both directions from the target value. If one desires to specify an equal variation in both directions, then a combined plus-or-minus symbol ($\pm$) is used with a single value, as shown in Fig. 2-4.

Under an N-type tolerance, the manufacturer should aim for the target value for production, and the variation should be reduced to a minimum. The following example illustrates how the quality level of a product is evaluated for an N-type tolerance with equal variation around the target value.

Example 2.5. A manufacturer of ball bearings used in gas turbines requires that tolerances of the diameter and hardness of each ball be as follows:

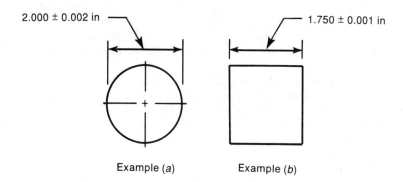

2.000 ± 0.002 in   1.750 ± 0.001 in

Example (*a*)   Example (*b*)

FIGURE 2-4
Examples of bilateral tolerances with equal variations.

Tolerance of diameter $m_1 \pm 0.6 \, \mu m$

Tolerance of hardness $m_2 \pm 2.0$ (Brinell hardness)

where m_1 and m_2 are the target values of the diameter and the hardness, respectively. The production rate is 80,000 balls per day at a cost of 30¢ per ball. Defective balls cannot be reworked and are scrapped. The following deviations from the diameter and the hardness target values were recorded.

Deviations from the target diameter:

0.3	0.0	−0.1	0.0	0.3	0.2	0.1	−0.2	0.6	0.4
−0.2	0.1	0.0	−0.4	0.5	0.4	−0.2	0.0	0.0	0.2

Deviations from the target hardness:

−1.0	−1.6	−0.4	−1.0	0.6	0.4	−1.2	−1.3	−0.2	−0.4
−0.4	0.5	−0.3	0.6	0.6	−0.9	−0.7	−0.9	−0.7	−1.3

Based on the diameter and hardness measurements recorded above, determine the quality levels of the production process for the diameter and hardness attributes of the balls.

Solution. By the analysis in this chapter, the loss caused by deviation from the target value is estimated as

$$L = \frac{A}{\Delta^2} \nu^2 \tag{2.18}$$

where A = cost of a defective product

         2Δ = tolerance limit

         ν^2 = mean squared deviation of the produced values (y's) from the target value (m)

The quantity ν^2 is usually estimated based on available data. The usual estimate of ν^2 has been referred to as $\hat{\nu}^2$ and is obtained as follows:

$$\hat{\nu}^2 = \frac{1}{n}\left[(y_1 - m)^2 + (y_2 - m)^2 + \cdots + (y_n - m)^2\right] \tag{2.19}$$

where n is the number of measurements available, and y_i is the value of measurement i.

Equations 2.18 and 2.19 are used to determine the quality level of the diameter of the balls. Actually, this quality level (expressed in dollars) is the loss attributable to deviations of the particular characteristic involved (in this case, ball-bearing diameter) from its specified target value.

$$A = 30¢$$

$$\Delta = 0.6$$

$$\hat{\nu}^2 = \frac{1}{20}\left[(0.3)^2 + (0.0)^2 + (-0.1)^2 + \cdots + (0.2)^2\right] = 0.075$$

The quality level of the diameter of the balls, as measured by the loss function, is

$$L = \frac{30}{(0.6)^2} \times 0.075 = 6.25¢$$

Similarly, the quality level of the hardness of the balls, as measured by the loss function, can be obtained as follows:

$$A = 30¢$$

$$\Delta = 2.0$$

$$\hat{\nu}^2 = \frac{1}{20}[(-1.0)^2 + (-1.6)^2 + (-0.4)^2 + \cdots + (-1.3)^2] = 0.704$$

$$L = \frac{30}{(2.0)^2} \times 0.704 = 5.28¢$$

The difference between the quality levels relating to the required hardness and diameter of the balls becomes evident when the yearly production rate is considered, assuming 250 working days per year.

$$\text{Difference in quality levels} = (0.0625 - 0.0528) \times 250 \times 80,000$$

$$= \$194,000 \text{ per year}$$

As shown above, the loss function approach can be used to compare the quality levels of the various processes underlying the different attributes.

It should be noted that the mean squared deviation of y from the target value m, as given by Eq. 2.20 below, is decreased by reducing either the variance of y or the term $[E(Y) - m]^2$. The reduction of variance can be achieved by using both off-line and on-line quality control approaches.

$$\text{Mean squared deviation} = E(Y - m)^2$$

$$= \text{var}(Y) + [E(Y) - m]^2 \qquad (2.20)$$

where $E(Y)$ is the expectation of Y, and var(Y) is the variance of Y.

Let $\bar{y}$ be the estimated expectation of Y. No adjustments of the process are needed when predicted $\bar{y} = m$; however, if predicted $\bar{y} \neq m$ then an amount of adjustment equal to $\bar{y} - m$ can be made on y. If the amount of adjustment is denoted as $\bar{e}$, then

$$\bar{e} = (\bar{y} - m)$$

$$= \frac{1}{n} \sum_{i=1}^{n} (y_i - m)$$

$$= \text{predicted deviation from target} \qquad (2.21)$$

In other words, if predicted $\bar{y}$ does not equal m, as shown in Figure 2-5, the process should be adjusted (if possible) so that predicted $\bar{y}$ coincides with m, to obtain a significant decrease in the mean squared deviation.

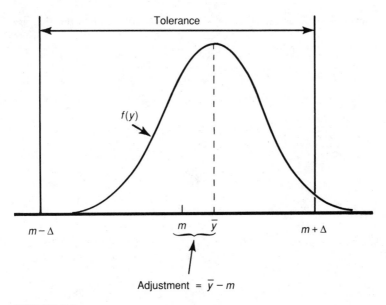

FIGURE 2-5
A process without adjustment.

Example 2.6. Consider the ball-bearing manufacturer in Example 2.5. Examination of the diameter data shows more positive deviations than negative ones, whereas the hardness data show more negative deviations than positive ones. Assume that the manufacturer can shift the means of the data to the target values. What are the quality levels of the diameter and the hardness after the adjustments?

Solution. The process should first be adjusted so that the value of every diameter is adjusted by an amount $\bar{e}$, the predicted deviation of the diameter from the target value. The new deviation (after adjustment) from the target value is

$$\text{Deviation after adjustment} = y - m - (\bar{y} - m)$$

$$= (y - \bar{y}) \tag{2.22}$$

Let the sum of squared deviation after adjustments of the diameter of the balls be denoted as $\hat{\nu}_d^2$. Then

$$\hat{\nu}_d^2(\text{after adjustment}) = \frac{1}{n-1}\left[\sum_{i=1}^{n} y_i^2 - \frac{\left(\sum_{i=1}^{n} y_i\right)^2}{n}\right] \tag{2.23}$$

$$\hat{\nu}_d^2 = \frac{1}{19}\left[0.3^2 + 0.0^2 + \cdots + 0.2^2 - \frac{2^2}{20}\right]$$

$$= 0.0684$$

The denominator $n - 1$ is used instead of n in the above equation because one degree of freedom is used to estimate the mean. The quality level of the diameter after the adjustment is

$$L = \frac{30}{(0.6)^2} \times 0.0684 = 5.70¢$$

Thus, the annual improvement is

$$(0.0625 - 0.0570) \times 80,000 \times 250 = \$110,000$$

Similarly, by using Eq. 2.23 and denoting the squared deviation after adjusting the hardness of the balls by $\hat{v}_h^2$:

$$\hat{v}_h^2(\text{after adjustment}) = \frac{1}{19}\left[(-1.0)^2 + (-1.6)^2 + \cdots + (-1.3)^2 - \frac{(-9.6)^2}{20}\right]$$

$$\hat{v}_h^2 = 0.499$$

The quality level of the hardness after the adjustment is

$$L = \frac{30}{(2.0)^2} \times 0.499 = 3.74¢$$

The annual improvement resulting from this adjustment is

$$(0.0528 - 0.0374) \times 80,000 \times 250 = \$308,000$$

Also, a comparison of quality levels between the diameter and the hardness after the adjustment indicates that the quality level of the hardness is 5.70/3.74, or 1.5 times better than that of the diameter.

The above procedure can also be used to evaluate the quality levels of the same product when provided by different suppliers.

Example 2.7. An automobile manufacturer requires that the steering knuckle for disk brakes be made of two separate parts, the knuckle and the spindle. They must be assembled by shrink-fitting the spindle into the knuckle, thereby achieving a more desirable stress distribution. The specification of the diameter of the spindle is $m \pm 20\mu$m. The loss caused by a defective spindle is \$24. The manufacturer observed the deviations shown in Table 2.4 from three different suppliers. What are the quality levels of their spindles? If adjustments could be made, what would the quality levels be after adjustments?

Solution. By using Eq. 2.18 we obtain the suppliers' losses before adjustments are made as follows:

$$k = \frac{A}{\Delta^2} = \frac{24}{(20)^2} = 0.06$$

and

$$L = 0.06\hat{v}^2$$

where

$$\hat{v}^2 = \frac{1}{n}\left[(y_1 - m)^2 + (y_2 - m)^2 + \cdots + (y_n - m)^2\right]$$

A summary of the suppliers' losses before adjustments is given in Table 2.5.

TABLE 2.4
Suppliers' observed data

Supplier	Deviation from target										Price per unit
1	−5	8	5	−4	3	−2	5	4	0	1	$36
	−2	0	3	8	−4	−6	2	5	−3	0	
2	−6	−3	−5	−6	−7	−5	−3	−7	−7	−6	$36
	−5	−4	−8	−6	−3	−8	−6	−5	−4	−9	
3	−7	18	0	15	−16	−7	−10	−9	−17	−3	$32
	−8	−10	12	−10	−6	−9	10	4	16	−13	

Adjustments could be made so that $\bar{y}_1 = \bar{y}_2 = \bar{y}_3 = m$. The mean squared deviations after adjustment for Suppliers 1, 2, and 3 are obtained using Eq. 2.23 as follows:

$$\hat{v}_j^2 = \frac{1}{n-1}\left[\sum_{i=1}^{n} y_i^2 - \frac{\left(\sum_{i=1}^{n} y_i\right)^2}{n} \right] \qquad j = 1, 2, 3$$

Thus,

$$\hat{v}_1^2 = \frac{1}{19}\left[(-5)^2 + (8)^2 + \cdots + (0)^2 - \frac{(18)^2}{20}\right] = 17.67$$

$$\hat{v}_2^2 = 2.98$$

$$\hat{v}_3^2 = 122.26$$

The suppliers' losses, if adjustments could be made, are given in Table 2.6. The above data suggest that the manufacturer should choose Supplier 2 as the source for the spindles if Supplier 2 is able to keep the distribution of spindle diameters centered at the target value m.

2.2.3   N-Type Tolerance When the Plus and Minus Tolerances Are Not Equal

The most general case of the bilateral tolerance system is where the tolerance limits are set at unequal distances from the target value m. This is usually written

TABLE 2.5
Suppliers' losses before adjustments

Supplier	$\hat{v}^2$	$L = 0.06\hat{v}^2$
1	17.60	$1.06
2	34.75	$2.08
3	122.40	$7.34

TABLE 2.6
Suppliers' losses after adjustments

Supplier	$\hat{v}^2$	$L = 0.06\hat{v}^2$
1	17.67	$1.06
2	2.98	$0.18
3	122.26	$7.34

as $m_{+\Delta_2}^{-\Delta_1}$, where Δ_1 and Δ_2 are the lower and the upper limits of the tolerance, respectively. The loss caused by deviation of a data point y from the target value is shown in Fig. 2-6 and is expressed as

$$L(y) = \begin{cases} \dfrac{A_1}{\Delta_1^2}(y - m)^2 & \text{if } y \le m \\[2mm] \dfrac{A_2}{\Delta_2^2}(y - m)^2 & \text{if } y > m \end{cases} \tag{2.24}$$

where A_1 is the loss caused by y being below the lower limit of tolerance, and A_2 is the loss caused by y being above the upper limit of tolerance.

When n observations are taken, the expected loss L is obtained as

$$L = \frac{1}{n}\left[\frac{A_1}{\Delta_1^2}\sum{}'(y - m)^2 + \frac{A_2}{\Delta_2^2}\sum{}''(y - m)^2 \right] \tag{2.25}$$

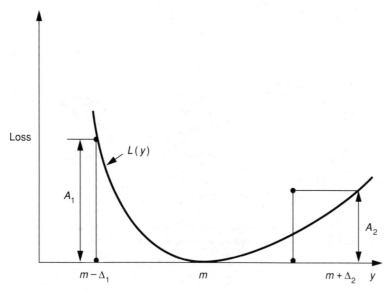

FIGURE 2-6
Loss due to deviations from m.

where $\Sigma'(y - m)^2$ is the sum of the squared deviation for y_i smaller than m, and $\Sigma''(y - m)^2$ is the sum of the squared deviation for y_i larger than m.

Example 2.8. An automobile manufacturer requires that the clearance between the cylinder and the piston of a six-cylinder engine be $3^{-2}_{+7}\,\mu m$. Defect loss for each cylinder and piston assembly is $200, and the monthly production is 50,000 units. Data showing deviation from the target value for the first two months of production are shown below. What are the quality levels during these two months? What is the improvement, if any, of the quality level?

Month	Deviations											
1	−2	3	0	4	5	−2	3	−2	0	−1	−1	−3
	0	4	3	−2	0	1	0	5	6	2	−1	
2	3	2	0	1	−1	−1	0	−2	3	0		
	6	−2	4	3	0	−2	0	−1	2	4		

Solution. The quality level of the production during Month 1 is determined by using Eq. 2.25:

$$A_1 = A_2 = \$200 \qquad \Delta_1 = -2 \qquad \Delta_2 = 7$$

$$L_1 = \frac{1}{23}\left\{ \frac{200}{(-2)^2}[(-2)^2 + (-2)^2 + (-2)^2 + (-1)^2 + (-1)^2 + (-3)^2 + (-2)^2 \right.$$

$$\left. + (-1)^2] + \frac{200}{7^2}[3^2 + 4^2 + 5^2 + 3^2 + 4^2 + 3^2 + 1^2 + 5^2 + 6^2 + 2^2] \right\}$$

$$= \frac{1}{23}\{1400 + 612.24\} = \$87.50$$

The loss during Month 2, L_2, is

$$L_2 = \frac{1}{20}\left\{ \frac{200}{(-2)^2}[(-1)^2 + (-1)^2 + (-2)^2 + (-2)^2 + (-2)^2 + (-1)^2] \right.$$

$$\left. + \frac{200}{7^2}[3^2 + 2^2 + 1^2 + 3^2 + 6^2 + 4^2 + 3^2 + 2^2 + 4^2] \right\}$$

$$= \frac{1}{20}\{750 + 424.49\} = \$58.70/\text{unit}$$

The losses resulting from variation on the lower limit are greater than those of the upper limit in each month. The improvement of quality level per unit during Month 2 is

$$87.5 - 58.7 = \$28.80$$

which results in an improvement of

$$28.8 \times 50,000 = \$1,440,000 \text{ per month}$$

2.2.4   The-Smaller-The-Better (S Type)

A The-Smaller-The-Better type tolerance involves a nonnegative characteristic, whose ideal value is zero. A typical example of such a characteristic is impurity. Wear, shrinkage, deterioration, and noise level are also examples of this type.

Under The-Smaller-The-Better (S-type) tolerance, the characteristic value is $y \geq 0$, the target value is $m = 0$, and the upper tolerance limit is Δ. The quality level (loss function) is estimated as

$$L = \frac{A}{\Delta^2} v^2 \tag{2.26}$$

where A is the loss caused by exceeding the upper tolerance limit.

Example 2.9. A manufacturer of gauge blocks requires that the flatness of the surface of each block be within 12 μm. Obviously, the smaller the deviation in the flatness of the block, the better the block. The loss caused by out-of-tolerance conditions is $80. Two machine tools, M_1 and M_2, are used in manufacturing the blocks. The flatness data given below were obtained by measuring two blocks each day for two successive weeks. Compare the quality levels of the two machine tools.

Machine	Flatness data (μm)									
M_1	0	5	4	2	3	1	7	6	8	4
	6	0	3	10	4	5	3	2	0	7
M_2	5	4	0	4	2	1	0	2	5	3
	2	1	3	0	2	4	1	6	2	1

Solution. This is a The-Smaller-The-Better (S-type) case with an upper tolerance limit $\Delta = 12$ μm and $A = 80.

The quality level of machine M_1 is

$$L_1 = \frac{A}{\Delta^2} \hat{v}_1^2$$

where

$$\hat{v}_1^2 = \frac{1}{20}(y_1^2 + y_2^2 + y_3^2 + \cdots + y_{20}^2)$$

$$= \frac{1}{20}(0 + 5^2 + 4^2 + \cdots + 7^2)$$

$$= 23.4 \ \mu m^2$$

Hence,

$$L_1 = \frac{80}{12^2} \times 23.4 = \$13$$

The quality level of machine M_2 is

$$L_2 = \frac{A}{\Delta^2} \hat{v}_2^2$$

where
$$\hat{\nu}_2^2 = \frac{1}{20}(5^2 + 4^2 + \cdots + 1^2)$$

$$= 8.8 \ \mu m^2$$

giving
$$L_2 = \frac{80}{12^2} \times 8.8 = \$4.90$$

Therefore, the quality level of machine tool M_2 is better than that of M_1 by \$8.10. A daily production of 2000 pieces will result in a difference of \$4,050,000 per year (250 working days).

2.2.5   The-Larger-The-Better (L Type)

There are cases where The-Larger-The-Better is applicable to characteristics such as the strength of materials and fuel efficiency. In these cases, there are no predetermined target values, and the larger the value of the characteristic, the better it is.

Under this type of tolerance, the characteristic value is $y \geq 0$, the lower tolerance limit is Δ, and the target (or ideal) value is $m = +\infty$. A is the loss caused by falling below the lower tolerance limit (i.e., $y < \Delta$). The quality level of this type of characteristic is obtained by transforming the L-type tolerance to an S-type tolerance as follows:

Let

$$z = \frac{1}{y} \tag{2.27}$$

The characteristic $z \geq 0$ has an S-type tolerance with the target value $m = 0$ and the upper specification limit $1/\Delta$. The loss function of the characterisitic z is

$$L(z) = \frac{A}{(1/\Delta)^2}z^2 \tag{2.28}$$

Equation 2.28 is put in terms of the desired characteristic, y, by substituting Eq. 2.27 in Eq. 2.28. Thus,

$$L(y) = \frac{A\Delta^2}{y^2} \tag{2.29}$$

or
$$L = A\Delta^2\hat{\nu}^2 \tag{2.30}$$

where
$$\hat{\nu}^2 = \frac{1}{n}\left(\frac{1}{y_1^2} + \frac{1}{y_2^2} + \cdots + \frac{1}{y_n^2}\right) \tag{2.31}$$

In effect, the loss function (quality level) associated with a The-Larger-The-Better type of tolerance is obtained by taking the reciprocals of the measurements and treating them as The-Smaller-The-Better type.

Example 2.10. The strength of an adhesive is usually determined by the kilograms force (kgf) needed to break apart specimens joined by the adhesive. Two types of adhesives, S_1 and S_2, which cost $50 and $60 per unit weight, respectively, are to be compared. The lower specification limit Δ is 5 kgf for the breaking force. The out-of-specification units are discarded, resulting in a loss of $70 per unit. The annual production rate is 120,000 units. Sixteen units were tested for each type of adhesive, and the following data for the breaking force were obtained:

Type of adhesive	Breaking force (kgf)							
S_1	10.2	5.8	4.9	16.1	15.0	9.4	4.8	10.1
	14.6	19.7	5.0	4.7	16.8	4.5	4.0	16.5
S_2	7.6	13.7	7.0	12.8	11.8	13.7	14.8	10.4
	7.0	10.1	6.8	10.0	8.6	11.2	8.3	10.6

Compare the quality levels of S_1 and S_2.

Solution. In this case, the larger the force, the better the adhesive. The quality level of S_1 is obtained by using Eq. 2.30.

$$L_1 = A\Delta^2\hat{\nu}_1^2$$

$$A = \$70$$

$$\Delta = 5\,\text{kgf}$$

$$\hat{\nu}_1^2 = \frac{1}{16}\left(\frac{1}{10.2^2} + \frac{1}{5.8^2} + \cdots + \frac{1}{16.5^2}\right)$$

$$= 0.0228$$

$$L_1 = 70 \times 5^2 \times 0.0228$$

$$= \$39.90$$

Similarly, the quality level of S_2 is:

$$L_2 = A\Delta^2\hat{\nu}_2^2$$

$$\hat{\nu}_2^2 = \frac{1}{16}\left(\frac{1}{7.6^2} + \frac{1}{13.7^2} + \cdots + \frac{1}{10.6^2}\right)$$

$$= 0.01139$$

$$L_2 = 70 \times 5^2 \times 0.01139$$

$$= \$19.90$$

Considering the cost per unit of S_1 ($50) and S_2 ($60), the savings that result from the use of S_2 instead of S_1 are

$$(50 + 39.90) - (60 + 19.90) = \$10 \text{ per unit}$$

and the annual savings are $1,200,000.

The loss function can be used to evaluate the quality level of production during different intervals of time. This evaluation might suggest recommendations for quality improvement or changes in the production process.

Example 2.11. The tensile strength data, in kilograms per millimeter squared, of thread samples collected every day for two consecutive months of production are as follows:

Month	Tensile strength data (kg/mm^2)							
First month	15.2	10.3	12.4	13.6	14.5	12.8	13.2	11.4
(23 work days)	14.6	12.5	13.8	14.0	12.5	14.0	13.6	14.2
	14.6	12.3	15.4	13.7	13.0	12.7	15.0	
Second month	13.6	15.0	14.3	12.6	14.3	15.0	14.6	13.2
(22 work days)	11.5	12.6	13.6	12.0	13.1	12.1	15.1	13.7
	14.2	13.6	14.1	12.8	11.7	10.2		

Compare the quality levels of the two months assuming the lower specification limit is 10.0 kg/mm^2. Defect loss is $0.5 per linear meter, and the monthly production is 200 million meters.

Solution. This case involves The-Larger-The-Better (L-type) tolerance. The quality levels are determined by using Eq. 2.30 and 2.31.

The quality level during the first month of production, L_1, is estimated as

$$L_1 = A\Delta^2\hat{\nu}_1^2$$

where
$$A = \$0.5$$

$$\Delta = 10.0$$

$$\hat{\nu}_1^2 = \frac{1}{23}\left(\frac{1}{15.2^2} + \frac{1}{10.3^2} + \cdots + \frac{1}{15.0^2}\right)$$

$$\hat{\nu}_1^2 = 0.005682$$

Therefore,
$$L_1 = 0.5 \times 10^2 \times 0.005682 = \$0.2841$$

Monthly loss $= 0.2841 \times 200 \times 10^6 = \$56,820,000$

The quality level during the second month of production is found similarly:

$$L_2 = A\Delta^2\hat{\nu}_2^2$$

$$\hat{\nu}_2^2 = \frac{1}{22}\left(\frac{1}{13.6^2} + \frac{1}{15.0^2} + \cdots + \frac{1}{10.2^2}\right)$$

$$\hat{\nu}_2^2 = 0.005809$$

$$L_2 = \$0.2905$$

Monthly loss $= 0.2905 \times 200 \times 10^6$

$$= \$58,100,000$$

The quality level of the first month is better (L_1 is lower) than that of the second month of production by an amount

$$58,100,000 - 56,820,000 = \$1,280,000$$

As demonstrated above, the quality level should be evaluated periodically. It should be used as an indicator of the performance of the production line and considered an important index.

Quality-level calculations can be used to evaluate suppliers or products having similar functions, or to evaluate the quality level of a product having several characteristics of the same or of different tolerance types. Suppose that k types of products are produced. The quality level of the production line is given by the sum of the losses that correspond to the specified tolerances. For example:

$$L = \frac{A_1}{\Delta_1^2}\hat{v}_1^2 + \frac{A_2}{\Delta_2^2}\hat{v}_2^2 + \cdots + \frac{A_k}{\Delta_k^2}\hat{v}_k^2 \qquad \text{(for N and S types)}$$

$$L = A_1\Delta_1^2\hat{v}_1^2 + A_2\Delta_2^2\hat{v}_2^2 + \ldots + A_k\Delta_k^2\hat{v}_k^2 \qquad \text{(for L type)}$$

where A_i = loss caused by a defective component of type i ($i = 1, 2, \ldots, k$)
$\hat{v}_i^2$ = mean squared deviation of type i component
Δ_i = tolerance limit of an individual component of type i

2.3   DETERMINATIONS OF TOLERANCES

This section explains a method for determining tolerances of the quality characteristics. The determination of tolerance is illustrated in the following example.

Example 2.12. Consider the production of high-voltage transformers. During the life of this kind of transformer, output voltage might change because of the deterioration of transistors in the power circuit. Assume that a transformer is not suitable for its intended function when its output voltage exceeds the tolerance limits of ± 25V. Exceeding the limits results in a loss (denoted by A) of \$300. Before shipping to a customer, the manufacturer can adjust the voltage in the plant by changing a resistor at a cost of \$1. What should the manufacturer's specifications be?

Solution. The loss caused by product variation from the target value, $L(y)$, is

$$L(y) = k(y - m)^2 \tag{2.32}$$

where m is the target value (115 V in this case) and k is the proportionality constant. Therefore,

$$k = \frac{A}{\Delta^2} = \frac{300}{(25)^2} = 0.48$$

The loss function is

$$L(y) = 0.48(y - 115)^2 \tag{2.33}$$

It is assumed that the allowable varying range of the output voltage for

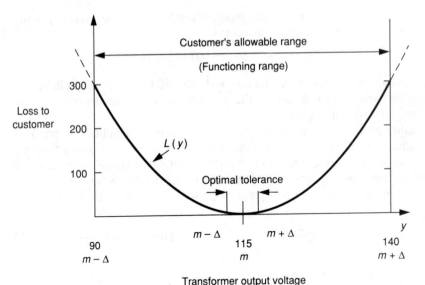

FIGURE 2-7
Tolerance determination for Example 2.12.

the customer is 115 ± 25 V. The allowable varying range in the plant will be different, because it is easy to adjust the voltage to the target value by changing a resistor in the circuit. The loss or cost of adjustment to the manufacturer is \$1. Substitution of this value in Eq. 2.33 yields

$$1.0 = 0.48(y - 115)^2$$

and

$$y = 115 \pm \sqrt{\frac{1}{0.48}}$$

$$y = 115 \pm 1.4 \text{ V}$$

Although the varying range for the customer is 115 ± 25 V, the varying range in production should be 115 ± 1.4 V, and units whose output voltage differs from 115 by more than ± 1.4 V should be considered defective by the manufacturer, as shown in Fig. 2-7. It is beneficial to the customer for a transformer to be adjusted in the plant if its output voltage falls outside the range 115 ± 1.4 V.

As shown above, the manufacturer should adjust (repair) the characteristic y if

$$\frac{A}{\Delta^2}(y - m)^2 \le \frac{A_0}{\Delta_0^2}(y - m)^2 \tag{2.34}$$

and the manufacturer's allowance is

$$\Delta = \sqrt{\frac{A}{A_0}}\Delta_0 \tag{2.35}$$

where 2Δ = manufacturer tolerance limit
$2\Delta_0$ = customer tolerance limit or functional limit
A = manufacturer loss caused by a defective product
A_0 = customer loss caused by a defective product

2.4 SUMMARY

This chapter discussed the use of the loss function concept for evaluating the quality level of a product or process by quantifying the deviations from the target value. The loss function was used to evaluate the effect of process improvement, the impact of tightening tolerances, and the effect of 100-percent inspection.

The chapter also covered the use of the loss function in the quality evaluations of three types of tolerances: The-Nominal-The-Best, The-Smaller-The-Better, and The-Larger-The-Better. An application of the loss function in the determination of tolerances was also explored.

PROBLEMS

2.1. A manufacturer of enhanced graphics adapters (EGAs) for personal computers requires that the distance between any two adjacent pins of a memory chip be 1.5 ± 0.001 mm. The loss due to a defective chip is $3.

The manufacturer measured the distance between two randomly selected adjacent pins on 20 chips and recorded the following observations:

1.500	1.501	1.499	1.501	1.500
1.500	1.500	1.499	1.500	1.501
1.501	1.500	1.499	1.499	1.500
1.501	1.499	1.501	1.501	1.500

What is the quality loss? If the mean is adjusted on target, how much quality improvement can be expected? Develop a system for inspecting the distance between pins.

2.2. A prototype of a robot monitoring system is built to evaluate the performance of the system before the beginning of the high-volume production. The purpose of the monitoring system is to increase productivity by tracking a robot's repeatability, trajectory, and accuracy. Measurements are compared to user-specified target values. The system consists of LEDs (light-emitting diodes) attached to selected points on the robot, two cameras to detect light emitted from the LEDs, a microprocessor, and a central processing unit. The robot should reach the target value (coordinates of a specified point) within a tolerance range of $+0.0005$ and -0.0003 in. The following deviations were recorded:

0.0001	0.0003	0.0002	-0.0002	-0.0001
0.0003	0.0004	-0.0003	-0.0002	0.0002
0.0001	-0.0003	-0.0002	0.0003	0.0004
0.0005	0.0004	-0.0003	0.0001	-0.0002

0.0004	−0.0001	−0.0002	0.0003	0.0001
−0.0003	0.0002	0.0004	0.0005	0.0001
0.0003	0.0003	−0.0002	−0.0003	−0.0001

When the loss per failure is $30, what is the quality loss? If the process engineer replaced the current tolerance range by +0.0004 and −0.0004, what would the quality loss be? Perform sensitivity analyses to find the effect of a change in tolerance range on the quality loss.

2.3. A robot is used in a seam welding process. The robot is programmed so that it tracks the product on an overhead conveyor and welds the seam. The tolerance of the deviations of the weld from the center of the seam is ±0.005 in. The following observations of deviations were taken:

0.003	0.002	0.005	−0.004	−0.003
−0.002	0.003	0.004	−0.003	−0.005
−0.004	0.003	0.005	−0.004	0.003
0.004	0.005	−0.003	−0.003	0.004
−0.003	−0.002	0.005	0.004	0.005

A robot guidance system is introduced to increase the quality of the welded seams. The guidance system, essentially a machine vision system, guides the robot along the seam rather than using previously defined programmed points along the seam. The following deviations were observed after the introduction of the guidance system:

0.001	0.002	−0.001	−0.002	0.003
−0.002	0.003	−0.001	−0.003	0.002
−0.004	−0.002	0.001	0.002	0.001
0.003	0.002	0.001	−0.003	−0.001
0.000	−0.002	−0.003	0.002	0.001

(a) What is the effect of the introduction of the robot guidance?
(b) If the cost of a defective welded product is $150, what would the savings be (if any) after the introduction of the guidance system?

2.4. A manufacturer of heat exchangers requires the plate spacing to be 0.25 ± 0.01 in. The quality control engineer sampled 25 heat exchangers and randomly measured the spacing between two plates on each exchanger. The following are the recorded measurements:

0.251	0.248	0.241	0.251	0.249
0.248	0.249	0.243	0.240	0.245
0.244	0.250	0.251	0.249	0.253
0.246	0.254	0.256	0.258	0.251
0.249	0.253	0.257	0.259	0.250

The loss due to a defective exchanger is $50 (cost of adjusting the spacing). What is the expected loss when 200 units per day are produced?

A new method for plate insertion is introduced that has a C_p index of 1.5. What is the quality loss after introduction of the new method? Relate the C_p index to the quality loss per unit.

2.5. The quality of a product is defined by two characteristics: Brinell hardness number (BHN) and circular diameter. The specifications of these characteristics are:

Hardness in BHN 250 ± 5
Diameter 1.0000 ± 0.002 in

The following BHN measurements were taken:

248	250	249	252	253
249	247	249	250	251
250	249	248	250	251
249	245	246	249	254

The following measurements of the diameter were also taken:

1.0010	1.0020	1.0015	1.0009	1.0019
0.9998	0.9999	1.0020	1.0011	0.9997
0.9980	1.0010	1.0009	0.9996	0.9990
1.0000	1.0013	1.0009	1.0009	1.0009

The loss caused by unacceptable BHN is $20, and the loss caused by unacceptable diameter size is $30. What is the total expected loss caused by deviations from target values?

2.6. A manufacturer of tungsten carbide rollers uses a microabrasive superfinish to obtain a surface finish of 2 μin (micro-inches). The specification for the diameter of the roller is 10 ± 0.0010 in. Measurements are taken on every roller after the finishing process to check for the quality of the process. The cost of a defective roller less than 9.9990 inches in diameter is $100, and the cost of a defective roller greater than 10.0010 inches in diameter is $30. The following measurements were taken in inches:

9.9991	9.9990	9.9995	9.9996
10.0010	10.0008	10.0009	9.9990
9.9995	10.0000	9.9998	10.0007
10.0010	9.9990	9.9999	10.0010
10.0010	9.9996	9.9991	10.0010

What is the quality loss per roller? Assuming that the lower limit of roller diameter is 9.9999 in, what is the quality loss per roller? Assume that there is a measurement error that has a uniform distribution with $\sigma = 0.001$. What is the true loss?

2.7. A producer of steel plug gauges requires the tolerances of the plug diameter to be $\pm^{0.0010}_{0.0000}$mm. The loss due to a defective plug is $25 (a plug is considered defective if its diameter is larger than the target diameter by more than 0.0010 mm). A random sample of 20 units was taken and the following deviations (in millimeters) were recorded:

0.0010	0.0001	0.0002	0.0008	0.0010
0.0010	0.0000	0.0007	0.0008	0.0010
0.0000	0.0003	0.0004	0.0000	0.0010
0.0009	0.0000	0.0000	0.0001	0.0010

(a) What is the quality level of the manufacturing process?
(b) What is the effect of correcting the upper tolerance limit to 0.0009 on the quality level of the process?

2.8. A supplier of automotive electronics uses a laser interferometric transducer whose signals are processed by a microcomputer to ensure that a critical fuel injector's sphere-headed needle will perform through one billion cycles—or for 400,000 miles of driving. The upper tolerance limit on roundness between sphere and injector seat is 1 μm, while the lower limit is 0.5 μm. The target value of the roundness is 0.8 μm. The cost of a defective injector when the roundness exceeds 1 μm is $107, while the cost of a defective injector when the roundness is less than 0.5 μm is $160. The following tolerances (in microns) were recorded.

0.60	0.70	0.55	0.59	0.81
0.90	0.91	0.86	0.57	0.86
0.78	0.98	0.76	0.50	0.50
0.87	0.90	0.86	0.87	0.85
0.78	0.68	0.91	0.92	0.69

What is the quality level of the production process?

2.9. A producer of high-strength wire cables that are used in lifting spreaders and containers in a shipyard requires that the strength of the cable be more than 40,000 lb/in^2. The cost of a defective cable (200 ft in length) is $900. The annual production rate is 6000 cables. The following data (in pounds per square inch) were obtained from destructive tests performed on 15 cables:

41,000	42,000	50,000	46,000	70,000
42,096	41,250	51,000	60,000	49,000
46,000	41,039	40,085	70,000	65,000

What is the quality level of the production process? What is the total quality loss per year?

2.10. Burrs represent a common problem for all machining, punching, or casting processes. The method of removing burrs has a direct effect on the quality of the deburring operation. Manual deburring is a boring, tiring, and monotonous operation, and the quality of deburring varies from one workpiece to another.
     In order to achieve uniformity among the workpieces, a manufacturer

installed an automatic system consisting of a robot equipped with fixtures, deburring tools, and quick-change device. The robot uses the deburring tool and follows the contour of the workpiece with high accuracy to obtain the desired quality. A measure of burring operation quality is the absence of burrs and sharp edges, that is, that material fragments are not visible and sharpness cannot be felt. This can be achieved when the method used to remove the burrs or sharpness produces a chamfer radius of 0.02 in (0.51 mm) maximum. Clearly this is an S-type tolerance. The cost of deburring the workpiece is $3.00. The unit cost of the workpiece before the deburring operation is $15.00, and the operating cost of the robot is $10 per hour. Assuming that there is a production rate of 100 workpieces per hour and that the following measurements of the chamfer radius of 20 workpieces are obtained:

0.015	0.017	0.020	0.021	0.010
0.013	0.022	0.015	0.009	0.015
0.019	0.020	0.012	0.003	0.001
0.020	0.010	0.007	0.013	0.018

what is the quality loss per unit? Assuming that the manufacturer specified that the radius of the chamfer must not be less than 0.002, what would the quality loss be? What should the tolerance be if the manufacturer wishes not to incur quality loss greater than $0.50 per workpiece?

2.11. Most early bearing and seal failures and excessive operating temperatures result from misalignment in coupled equipment. A manufacturer introduced a laser alignment system to align shafts of coupled motors. In this system, the laser is aimed directly at the target where both angular and parallel shaft/coupling displacement measurements are taken. Each measurement includes periodic sampling of the position of the beam from the target. The accuracy of the parallel displacement measurement is 0.001 in; and the accuracy for angular displacement is 0.0001 in/in.

Assume that the manufacturer intends to use this system to detect and measure misalignment between the headstock and tailstock of a lathe. The distance between the headstock and tailstock is 60 in. The quality of the workpieces produced on this lathe is affected by the amount of misalignment of the workpiece. The relationship between cost of quality and amount of misalignment is

$$c(y) = ay^2 + by$$

where c = quality cost per unit
 y = amount of misalignment in inches
 a, b are constants having values of 40 and 70, respectively

The following measurements of misalignments are taken at the beginning of a production period:

0.0020	0.0030	0.0010	0.0009
0.0001	0.0021	0.0012	0.0013
0.0022	0.0031	0.0009	0.0009
0.0025	0.0023	0.0017	0.0013
0.0019	0.0008	0.0040	0.0033

The optimal value of misalignment is zero, resulting in zero loss. Assume that there is a production rate of 800 units during the production period. What is the total quality loss per unit? What do you recommend to reduce this loss to a minimum?

2.12. One objective of the finishing operations on gears is to eliminate slight inaccuracies in the tooth profile, spacing, and concentricity. These inaccuracies are very small dimensionally (< 0.0005 in) and may increase wear of the gears and cause undesirable noises at high speeds. In order to eliminate the inaccuracies in gears that are not heat treated, such operations as shaving are used. Shaving is a machining process (cutting) that removes only a few thousandths of an inch of metal.

A manufacturer uses a shaving operation to eliminate the inaccuracies in the teeth of gears produced by a hobbing operation. The quality of the gear is measured by the maximum inaccuracy in any of its teeth. After the shaving operation, the gear is inspected for the inaccuracies. If any of the gear parameters (tooth profile, spacing, and concentricity) have an inaccuracy greater than 0.0003 in, the gear is reworked through the shaving process until the inaccuracies are eliminated. On the other hand, if the inaccuracies cannot be removed through reworking, the gear is discarded at a cost of $100. The cost of reworking a gear is $10. Assume that the manufacturer produces 300 gears per hour, the probability of the gear being reworked is 0.10, and the probability of the gear being discarded is 0.02. A sample of 30 gears is taken to check the quality after the shaving process. The following measurements represent the maximum inaccuracy of each gear in the sample:

0.0001	0.0002	0.0004	0.0002	0.0003
0.0002	0.0004	0.0006	0.0001	0.0000
0.0001	0.0005	0.0003	0.0002	0.0003
0.0002	0.0000	0.0004	0.0007	0.0003
0.0002	0.0005	0.0006	0.0001	0.0004
0.0003	0.0001	0.0002	0.0003	0.0006

What is the quality loss per gear? How do you propose to improve the quality of the gears?

REFERENCES

Athan, M., and P. Falb. *Optimal Control*. New York: McGraw-Hill, 1966.

Box, G. E. P., and G. M. Jenkins. *Time Series Analysis, Forecasting, and Control*. San Francisco: Holden-Day, 1976.

Feigenbaum, A. V. *Total Quality Control*. New York: McGraw-Hill, 1983.

Jessup, P. "The Value of Continuing Improvement." *IEEE Conference on Communications*, vol. 1 (1985), pp. 89–94.

Sullivan, L. P. "Reducing Variability: A New Approach to Quality." *Quality Progress*, vol. 17, no. 7 (1984), pp. 15–21.

Taguchi, G. *Introduction to Quality Evaluation and Quality Control*. Tokyo: Japanese Standards Association, 1978.

Taguchi, G. *On-line Quality Control during Production*. Tokyo: Japanese Standards Association, 1981.

Taguchi, G., and Y. Wu. *Introduction to Off-line Quality Control*. Tokyo: Central Japan Quality Control Association, 1979.

CHAPTER
3

TOLERANCE
DESIGN
AND
TOLERANCING

Designers often believe that their job is to design a product emphasizing performance, appearance, and perhaps reliability, and that the production and manufacturing engineer's job is to produce whatever has been designed. Design engineers expect that their specifications will be accepted by the production engineers. They do not give serious consideration to production costs and feasibility. Often, there is a natural reluctance to change a proven design for the sake of a reduction in manufacturing cost (Boothroyd, 1982). Therefore, it is important to determine the optimal values of a product's parameters and their tolerances. The parameter design of products, an activity we refer to as off-line quality control, is beyond the scope of this text; however, the tolerance design of the parameters will be treated in detail in this chapter.

Tolerance design and parameter tolerancing are important tasks of design engineers. In fact, the methods stated in this chapter are important to design engineers as well as to production engineers. The objective of this chapter is to examine the effect of tolerance design on the quality evaluation of a product and to introduce methods for economical design of product tolerance and tolerancing.

3.1 FUNCTIONAL LIMITS AND THE SOCIETAL LOSS

The characteristics of a product are usually defined by nominal values and functional limits. Consider, for example, the door-fitting problem for an automobile. Assume that the nominal length of the door (using off-line quality control methods or methods for robust designs) and the nominal length for a window in the door are m_1 and m_2, respectively (measured from the center of the door) and that the clearance Δ_0 of each is 3 mm. In other words, if the door size were 3 mm larger than the nominal size (m_1), the door would fail to close. On the other hand, if the door size were 3 mm smaller than the nominal size, the door would not be tightly closed, causing rainwater leakage. This clearance of 3 mm is defined as the functional limit Δ_0 of door size. The functional limit of a product characteristic is determined from the engineering knowledge of the product or through experimentation.

Consider also the case of the ignition voltage of an automobile engine. Assume that the nominal voltage needed for ignition is 20 kV (determined in the parameter design phase). The functional limit of the ignition voltage is obtained by conducting experiments to find the threshold value of the voltage at which the ignition fails. Suppose it is found that the ignition fails when the voltage drops below 8 kV or when it exceeds 35 kV. Thus, the lower and upper limits of the ignition voltage are 8 kV and 35 kV, respectively. This is expressed in the following way:

$$20^{-12}_{+15} \text{ kV}$$

However, in many applications it is more appropriate to use the smaller limit to give both limits equal values from the nominal. Under this practice, the ignition voltage and its limits become

$$20 \pm 12 \text{ kV}$$

When the ignition voltage exceeds its functional limits, the spark plugs will fail to ignite, causing the engine to stall. In turn, the customer will incur repair costs and other inconveniences. These losses (tangible and intangible) to the customer are referred to as societal loss.

Let $L(y)$ be the quality loss of a product having a characteristic value y. It is defined as follows:

$$L(y) = \frac{1}{n} \sum_{i=1}^{n} \int_{0}^{T} L_i(t,y)\,dt \qquad (3.1)$$

where
T = design life of the product
n = size of the market
$L_i(t,y)$ = actual financial loss to customer i at year t due to a product having an initial characteristic value y.
Note that $L_i(t,y)$ is not a continuous function of time.

The quality loss $L(y)$ of Eq. 3.1 can be approximated by a continuous function for large values of n. As shown in Chap. 2, $L(y)$ can be expanded using the Taylor series and the nominal value m:

$$L(y) = L(m + y - m) \tag{3.2}$$

$$= L(m) + \frac{L'(m)}{1!}(y - m) + \frac{L''(m)}{2!}(y - m)^2 + \cdots$$

Assume that $L(m) = 0$ and $L'(m) = 0$. Disregarding the higher orders $L(y)$ can be approximated by the third term in the above equation:

$$L(y) = k(y - m)^2 \tag{3.3}$$

The constant k is determined by estimating the loss A_0 when y deviates from m by Δ_0. Thus,

$$A_0 = k\Delta_0^2$$

or
$$k = \frac{A_0}{\Delta_0^2}$$

Substituting the above value of k into Eq. 3.3 results in the following loss function expression:

$$L(y) = \frac{A_0}{\Delta_0^2}(y - m)^2 \tag{3.4}$$

Assume that the loss A_0 caused by the failure of the ignition system is $200. Assume also that the failure of the ignition system is caused by the deviation of the ignition voltage from its nominal value by 12 kV; then

$$L(y) = \frac{200}{(12)^2}(y - 20)^2$$

or
$$L(y) = 1.39(y - 20)^2 \tag{3.5}$$

When the ignition voltage is 18 kV, the quality loss becomes

$$L(18) = 1.39(18 - 20)^2 \tag{3.6}$$

$$= \$5.56$$

This is the predicted loss of each customer when the ignition voltage during the design life of the ignition system is 18 kV.

It is clear that the tolerances of the product characteristics significantly affect the total quality loss. The optimal tolerances are those that minimize the total quality loss.

There are three sources of variation of product characteristics from their nominal values. They are environmental factors, deterioration factors, and imperfections in manufacturing processes. The product designer must deal with the first two causes of variation. In fact, an important function of the product designer is to find countermeasures for all sources of variation by using the parameter design approach. After the parameter design step is completed, the product designer should perform tolerance design, that is, trade-off analysis between cost of tight tolerance and product quality. The production and manufacturing engineers focus on the variations caused by manufacturing process imperfections.

In the following sections, we present approaches for determining the optimal tolerances for the three types of cases:

1. The-Nominal-The-Best (N type)
2. The-Larger-The-Better (L type)
3. The-Smaller-The-Better (S type)

3.2 TOLERANCE DESIGN FOR THE-NOMINAL-THE-BEST (N TYPE)

This type of tolerance is required for many products, parts, and components when the nominal size of the characteristic is preferred; dimensions, clearance, and viscosity are typical examples. Under this type of tolerance, the product designer and the manufacturer should aim for the nominal measurement of product characteristics, and the variation should be reduced to a minimum. The following example illustrates the tolerance design for such product characteristics.

Example 3.1. Consider a product whose principal dimension is denoted by y. A deviation of 500 μm in the principal dimension from its nominal value causes product failure and a loss A_0 of \$300. The dimension is affected by the environmental temperature x and the wear of the product. Assume that the standard deviation of temperature is 5°F and the design life T is 10 years. Assume also that the dimension y at year t is given by

$$y = y_0 + b(x - x_0) + \beta t \qquad (3.7)$$

where y_0 = initial dimension
b = coefficient of thermal expansion
β = wear rate per unit of time

The initial dimension y_0 is the nominal dimension (preferred dimension) at normal temperature x_0. The mean squared deviation ν^2 of the dimension y is

$$\nu^2 = E[y_0 + b(x - x_0) + \beta t - m]^2$$

$$= \nu_0^2 + b^2 \nu_x^2 + \frac{T^2}{3} \times \beta^2 \qquad (3.8)$$

Determine the quality loss at the end of the product design life.

Solution. The quality loss L is obtained as follows:

$$L = \frac{A_0}{\Delta_0^2} \nu^2$$

Substituting Eq. 3.8 into the above equation, we obtain

$$L = \frac{A_0}{\Delta_0^2}\left(v_0^2 + b^2 v_x^2 + \frac{T^2}{3} \times \beta^2\right)$$

$$= \frac{300}{(500)^2}\left(v_0^2 + b^2 \times 25 + \frac{10^2}{3} \times \beta^2\right) \tag{3.9}$$

Consider four grades of materials M_1, M_2, M_3, and M_4 that can be used for manufacturing the product. The prices, heat expansion coefficients, wear rates, quality losses, and total costs $(P + L)$ are shown in Table 3.1. Since v_0 is the same for all materials, it is not included in the quality loss calculations shown in the table.

The optimal grade of material is M_3, since it has the lowest total cost ($13.88) of the material grade. Grade M_1, the least expensive grade caused by poor quality, typifies Japanese-made products of the 50s and 60s. On the other hand, when a designer chooses grade M_4 (the most expensive grade), the quality loss decreases significantly. However, the price is too expensive, resulting in a higher value of the total cost than the product made of grade M_3. Thus, choosing M_1 or M_4 will have a negative effect on the product market share.

Usually the price and the quality loss should be about equal, but a difference factor of two or three times is acceptable. A difference factor of more than several times is not acceptable and is a clear sign of poor tolerance design.

As shown in Table 3.1, the optimal grade for tolerance design in this case is M_3. Tolerances for the initial value of the principal dimension need to be determined. The following example shows the estimation of these tolerances.

Example 3.2. Determine the tolerance of the principal dimension y for the product given in Example 3.1.

Solution. The tolerance can be obtained by using the following equation:

$$\Delta = \frac{\Delta_0 \text{ (functional limit)}}{\phi \text{ (factor of safety)}} \tag{3.10}$$

where $\phi = \sqrt{\dfrac{A_0}{A}}$ $\tag{3.11}$

A_0 = loss to the customer caused by the failure of the product

TABLE 3.1
Parameters of the tolerance design

Material grade	Price P ($)	Expansion rate b $\mu m/°F$	Wear rate β $\mu m/year$	Mean squared deviation v^2	Quality loss L	Total $P + L$
M_1	2.00	5	28	26758	32.11	34.11
M_2	4.50	4	20	13733	16.48	20.98
M_3	8.00	2	12	4900	5.88	13.88
M_4	18.00	1	5	858	1.03	19.03

A = manufacturer's loss when the product does not conform to the specification limits

The product in Example 3.1 has the following parameters:

$$\Delta_0 = 500 \ \mu m$$

$$A_0 = \$300$$

$$A = \$8$$

The factor of safety ϕ is

$$\phi = \sqrt{\frac{A_0}{A}} = \sqrt{\frac{300}{8}}$$

$$\phi = 6.124$$

and

$$\Delta = \frac{\Delta_0}{\phi}$$

$$= \frac{500}{6.124}$$

$$= 82 \ \mu m \tag{3.12}$$

3.3 TOLERANCE DESIGN FOR THE-LARGER-THE-BETTER CHARACTERISTICS (L TYPE)

The-Larger-The-Better is applicable to characteristics such as the strength of materials and fuel efficiency. In these cases, the larger the value of the characteristic, the better it is. Tolerance design for The-Larger-The-Better characteristics is explained by the example given below.

Example 3.3. Consider two types of cables, T_1 and T_2. The price and strength for either type are proportional to the cable's cross-sectional area. The prices are $P_1 = \$1750/mm^2$ and $P_2 = \$2250/mm^2$, and the strengths are $S_1 = 220$ kgf/mm^2 and $S_2 = 265$ kgf/mm^2 for types T_1 and T_2, respectively. The lower tolerance limit of the cable's breaking strength is 20000 kgf, and the loss caused by falling below the lower tolerance limit is \$58 million. Perform tolerance design and determine the tolerance limits for the better cable.

Solution. Following the same steps as in Example 3.1, we first calculate the total cost for each cable (price + quality loss). Let x be the cross-sectional area of the cable, which is the parameter being sought.

Cable type T_1. The total cost C is obtained as the sum of the price and the quality loss.

$$C = P_1 x + \frac{A_0 \Delta_0^2}{(S_1 x)^2}$$

$$= 1750x + \frac{58,000,000 \times (20,000)^2}{(220x)^2} \tag{3.13}$$

The total cost is minimized by taking the derivative of Eq. 3.13 with respect to x and equating it to zero.

$$\frac{dC}{dx} = P_1 - \frac{2A_0\Delta_0^2}{S_1^2 x^3} = 0$$

or

$$x = \left(\frac{2A_0\Delta_0^2}{P_1 S_1^2}\right)^{1/3}$$

$$= 818 \text{ mm}^2 \qquad (3.14)$$

The price of this cable is

$$1750 \times 818 = \$1.43 \text{ million} \qquad (3.15)$$

Cable type T_2. The cross-sectional area is

$$x = \left(\frac{2 \times 58,000,000 \times (20,000)^2}{2250 \times (265)^2}\right)^{1/3}$$

$$= 665 \text{ mm}^2 \qquad (3.16)$$

The price of cable T_2 is

$$2250 \times 665 = \$1.50 \text{ million} \qquad (3.17)$$

Cable type T_1 is selected, since the price of T_1 is less than T_2. The tolerance of this cable is obtained using Eq. 2.29, Eq. 3.11, and the concept of section 2.3.

$$\Delta = \phi\Delta_0$$

$$= \sqrt{\frac{A_0}{A}} \times \Delta_0$$

$$= \sqrt{\frac{58,000,000}{1,430,000}} \times 20 \text{ metric tons force}$$

$$\Delta = 127.4 \text{ metric tons force} \qquad (3.18)$$

3.4 TOLERANCE DESIGN FOR THE-SMALLER-THE-BETTER CHARACTERISTICS (S TYPE)

A typical example of a Smaller-The-Better characteristic is the residual dynamic unbalance of a rotor. Wear, machine accuracy, deterioration, and noise level are also examples of this type. Tolerance design for The-Smaller-The-Better characteristics is illustrated by the following examples.

Example 3.4. A new machine, M_1, is being considered for the replacement of an existing machine, M_2. The processing speed of M_1 is twice that of M_2, reducing the manufacturing cost by \$1.20 per unit of production. The tolerance on the roundness of the production unit produced by machine M_1 is 20 μm (or less). Defective products are scrapped at a loss of \$6.00 per defective unit.

Compare the quality levels of the two machines, based on 20 units produced by each machine under the same conditions of control, with the roundness measured in μm. The measurements are given in Table 3.2.

Solution. Assuming that the tolerance limit of the current machine (M_2) is acceptable, the quality losses for M_1 and M_2 are calculated as follows:

Machine M_1:

$$v_1^2 = \frac{1}{20}(3^2 + 5^2 + 0^2 + \cdots + 10^2)$$

$$= 72.35$$

$$L_1 = \frac{A}{\Delta^2} \times v_1^2$$

$$= \frac{6.00}{20^2} \times 72.35$$

$$= \$1.09$$

Machine M_2:

$$v_2^2 = \frac{1}{20}(7^2 + 14^2 + 15^2 + \cdots + 14^2)$$

$$= 95.10$$

$$L_2 = \frac{6.00}{20^2} \times 95.10$$

$$= \$1,43$$

Comparing L_1 and L_2, the quality loss of M_2 exceeds that of M_1 by \$0.34. The manufacturing cost per unit produced on M_1 is \$1.20 less than the manufacturing cost of M_2. The net result is an improvement of \$1.54 per unit of production when M_1 replaces M_2.

If the annual production is 200,000 units, the annual gain becomes \$308,000. When M_1 replaces M_2, a new tolerance limit for the roundness of the products must be determined. The upper tolerance limit of products produced by the existing machine is related to the factor of safety ϕ_0.

TABLE 3.2
Measurements of roundness

Machine	Roundness (μm)									
M_1	3	5	0	14	12	5	10	7	4	8
	8	15	6	7	4	17	6	2	0	10
M_2	7	14	15	3	0	5	7	9	13	2
	16	2	6	13	7	4	14	13	2	14

$$\phi_0 = \sqrt{\frac{A_0}{6.00}}$$

The new machine, M_1, should have the following factor of safety:

$$\phi = \sqrt{\frac{A_0}{4.80}}$$

The new tolerance limit for the roundness is

$$\text{New tolerance limit} = \text{current tolerance limit} \times \frac{\phi_0}{\phi}$$

$$= 20 \times \frac{\sqrt{A_0/6.00}}{\sqrt{A_0/4.80}}$$

$$= 20 \times \sqrt{\frac{4.80}{6.00}}$$

$$\approx 18 \ \mu m$$

Example 3.5. The nominal thickness of the plastic coating on an electrical wire is an important variable in determining the wear characteristics of the wire. The smaller the wear, the better the wire. The loss caused by the wear of the coating is $20.00, when the coating thickness is ± 1 (in thousandths of an inch) from its nominal value. Ten measurements of the wire coating taken from selected points along a wire gave the following deviations from the nominal thickness:

$$1, 0, 0.5, 2, 1.5, 1, 2, 0.25, 0.5, 1.3$$

A new coating process will be introduced to reduce the loss by 50 percent. The following measurements of deviations are taken along a wire coated by the new process:

$$1.0, 1.0, 0.3, 0.5, 0.9, 1.0, 1.1, 0.8, 0.75, 0.9$$

Determine the tolerance of the coating thickness for the new process and the loss for each unit for the current and new processes.

Solution. The mean squared deviations of the current and new process, v_1 and v_2, are estimated as

$$v_1^2 = \frac{1}{10}(1^2 + 0^2 + 0.5^2 + 2^2 + 1.5^2 + 1^2 + 2^2 + 0.25^2 + 0.5^2 + 1.3^2)$$

$$= 1.45$$

$$v_2^2 = \frac{1}{10}(1^2 + 1^2 + 0.3^2 + 0.5^2 + 0.9^2 + 1^2 + 1.1^2 + 0.8^2 + 0.75^2 + 0.9^2)$$

$$= 0.74$$

The tolerance of the coating thickness for the new process is

$$\Delta_2 = \sqrt{\frac{A_2}{A_1}} \times \Delta_1$$

where Δ_1 = tolerance limit of the current process
A_1 = loss due to the wear of a wire produced by the current process
Δ_2 = tolerance limit of the new process
A_2 = loss due to the wear of a wire produced by the new process

Thus
$$\Delta_2 = \sqrt{\frac{10}{20}} \times \Delta_1$$

$$\Delta_2 = \pm 0.71$$

The losses per unit are

$$L_1 = \frac{A_1}{\Delta_1^2} \nu_1^2$$

$$= \frac{20}{1} \times 1.45$$

$$= \$29$$

$$L_2 = \frac{A_2}{\Delta_2^2} \nu_2^2$$

$$= \frac{10}{(0.71)^2} \times 0.74$$

$$= \$14.8$$

3.5 TOLERANCE ALLOCATION FOR MULTIPLE COMPONENTS

In the foregoing sections, methods of tolerance design for three types of product characteristics were presented. They placed emphasis on determining the tolerance for the product characteristics so that the total cost (price and quality loss) is minimized. This section is intended to determine the optimal tolerance allocation for all components that constitute the final product. In other words, when a product consists of k components, the characteristics of the product are affected by the tolerances of these components, and tolerance design for each component is needed so that the output characteristic of the product conforms to the functional limit.

Suppose that x is the characteristic of a component that affects an output y (the desired characteristic of the product) having functional limit Δ_0. Assume that y is linearly affected by x, and that β is the linear constant; that is,

$$y = m_0 + \beta(x - m) \tag{3.19}$$

where m_0 is the nominal value of y (the target value) and m is the nominal value of x. Let A_0 be the loss when the value of the output characteristic y does not conform to the functional limits, $m_0 \pm \Delta_0$. The loss function is

$$L = \frac{A_0}{\Delta_0^2}(y - m_0)^2 \tag{3.20}$$

Substituting Eq. 3.19 into Eq. 3.20, the loss becomes

$$L = \frac{A_0}{\Delta_0^2}[\beta(x - m)]^2 \tag{3.21}$$

Replacing L by A, which is the price of the component with the characteristic x (or the loss when x deviates from its functional limits),

$$A = \frac{A_0}{\Delta_0^2}[\beta(x - m)]^2 \tag{3.22}$$

Solving Eq. 3.22 for x, we obtain

$$x = m \pm \sqrt{\frac{A}{A_0}} \times \frac{\Delta_0}{\beta} \tag{3.23}$$

which is the optimal tolerance specification for the component characteristic x.

Suppose a product has k components which have characteristics x_i nominal values m_i, and prices A_i ($i = 1, \ldots, k$). In addition, the linear constant for component i, which affects the characteristic of the product, is β_i ($i = 1, \ldots, k$). The tolerances $\Delta_1, \Delta_2, \ldots, \Delta_k$ for each component are given as follows:

$$\Delta_1 = \sqrt{\frac{A_1}{A_0}} \times \frac{\Delta_0}{\beta_1}$$

$$\Delta_2 = \sqrt{\frac{A_2}{A_0}} \times \frac{\Delta_0}{\beta_2}$$

$$\vdots$$

$$\Delta_k = \sqrt{\frac{A_k}{A_0}} \times \frac{\Delta_0}{\beta_k}$$

Note that $\beta_i \Delta_i$ is the contribution to the displacement of y caused by characteristic x_i when $x_i = m_i + \Delta_i$. Thus the square of the tolerance of the output y caused by the variation of components' characteristics $x_1, x_2, \ldots, x_k$, is

$$\Delta^2 = (\beta_1 \Delta_1)^2 + (\beta_2 \Delta_2)^2 + \cdots + (\beta_k \Delta_k)^2$$

$$= \left(\sqrt{\frac{A_1}{A_0}} \times \Delta_0\right)^2 + \left(\sqrt{\frac{A_2}{A_0}} \times \Delta_0\right)^2 + \cdots + \left(\sqrt{\frac{A_k}{A_0}} \times \Delta_0\right)^2$$

thus
$$= \frac{A_1 + A_2 + \cdots + A_k}{A_0} \Delta_0^2 \qquad (3.24)$$

or
$$\Delta = \sqrt{\frac{\sum_{i=1}^{k} A_i}{A_0}} \Delta_0$$

Consider the following three cases:

(a) If $\sum_{i=1}^{k} A_i \ll A_0$, then $\Delta \ll \Delta_0$

This situation occurs when the final assembled product must be scrapped, because the cost of repair is greater than $\sum_{i=1}^{k} A_i$ and the loss A_0 is several times the total price of all parts ($\sum_{i=1}^{k} A_i$). If, for example, A_0 is 5 times the sum of the total price for all components, then

$$\Delta = \frac{1}{\sqrt{5}} \Delta_0 = 0.447\Delta_0$$

This means that even when all components' characteristics have the same uniform distribution within the range of their respective tolerances (i.e., process capability index is 0.577), the output characteristic (characteristic of the assembled product) would have a distribution with standard deviation of $2 \times 0.447\Delta_0/\sqrt{12} = 0.258\Delta_0$, and a C_p of

$$\frac{2\Delta_0}{6 \times (0.447\Delta_0/\sqrt{3})} \approx 1.3$$

If $\sum_{i=1}^{k} A_i \ll A_0$ and since $\Delta < \Delta_0$, then the final assembly should be discarded.

(b) If $\sum_{i=1}^{k} A_i \gg A_0$ then possibly $\Delta \gg \Delta_0$

This situation often occurs when an assembled product can be adjusted after observing that the output y does not conform to the specification $m_0 \pm \Delta_0$. Naturally, it is expected that the adjustment cost A_0 is less than the total price of the product's components. The actual distribution of the output characteristic may satisfy its tolerance, $m_0 \pm \Delta_0$, because the control limits of components are usually smaller than $m_i \pm \Delta_i$. However, there is a high probability that the output y does not conform to its tolerance or adjustment limits even though all components conform to their tolerances, $m_i \pm \Delta_i$.

(c) If $\displaystyle\sum_{i=1}^{k} A_i \approx A_0$ then $\Delta \approx \Delta_0$

Situations (a) and (b) are much more likely to occur than situation (c). In the last case, output tolerances are allocated among component characteristics that affect the output characteristic y. The tolerance for each component can be estimated using Eq. 3.23.

Example 3.6. A product consists of three components: C_1, C_2, and C_3. The nominal values of their characteristics are m_1, m_2, and m_3, and their prices are $p_1 = \$20$, $p_2 = \$60$, and $p_3 = \$130$, respectively. Each component characteristic has an approximately linear effect on a product's characteristics around nominal values m_1, m_2, and m_3, with linear constants 2, 3, and 1.5 for C_1, C_2, and C_3, respectively. The quality loss when the product's characteristic does not conform to the specification is \$500, and the functional tolerance of the product characteristic is 3 (i.e., $\Delta_0 = 3$). Assuming that losses caused by component failures are equal to component prices, what is the tolerance for each component?

Solution. Let y be the characteristic of the product. Then the relationships between the product's characteristics and the components' are (see Eq. 3.19):

For component C_1, $\qquad y = m_0 + \beta_1(x_1 - m_1)$

For component C_2, $\qquad y = m_0 + \beta_2(x_2 - m_2)$

For component C_3, $\qquad y = m_0 + \beta_3(x_3 - m_3)$

The total quality loss for the product is

$$L = \frac{A_0}{\Delta_0^2}\left[\sum_{i=1}^{3} \beta_i(x_i - m_i)\right]^2$$

The above equation is solved to obtain

$$x_i = m_i \pm \sqrt{\frac{A_i}{A_0}} \times \frac{\Delta_0}{\beta_i} \qquad i = 1, 2, 3$$

or

$$\Delta_i = \sqrt{\frac{A_i}{A_0}} \times \frac{\Delta_0}{\beta_i} \qquad i = 1, 2, 3$$

Thus, the tolerance limits for the three components are

$$\Delta_1 = \sqrt{\frac{A_1}{A_0}} \times \frac{\Delta_0}{\beta_1} = \sqrt{\frac{20}{500}} \times \frac{3}{2} = 0.30$$

$$\Delta_2 = \sqrt{\frac{A_2}{A_0}} \times \frac{\Delta_0}{\beta_2} = \sqrt{\frac{60}{500}} \times \frac{3}{3} = 0.34$$

$$\Delta_3 = \sqrt{\frac{A_3}{A_0}} \times \frac{\Delta_0}{\beta_3} = \sqrt{\frac{130}{500}} \times \frac{3}{1.5} = 1.02$$

and the tolerance for the product characteristic, Δ, is obtained using Eq. 3.24 as follows:

$$\Delta^2 = \frac{\displaystyle\sum_{i=1}^{3} A_i}{A_0} \times \Delta_0^2 = \frac{20 + 60 + 130}{500} \times (3)^2$$

$$\Delta^2 = 3.78$$

or $\qquad \Delta = 1.94$

3.6 NONLINEAR TOLERANCING

In the previous section, we discussed an approach for tolerance design when the characteristics of each component have an approximately linear effect on the product's characteristics. We now introduce a methodology for tolerance design when the component characteristic x has a nonlinear effect on characteristic y (functional limits $m_0 \pm \Delta_0$). In such a case, a graphical methodology as shown in Fig. 3-1 is recommended.

In order to determine the tolerance limits for x, we first obtain the functional limits $m - \Delta_1$ and $m + \Delta_2$, which are the projections of $m_0 - \Delta_0$ and $m_0 +$

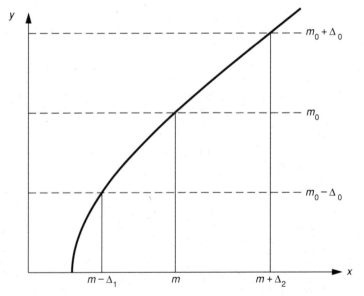

FIGURE 3-1
Nonlinear tolerancing.

Δ_0, respectively. Let A_1 and A_2 be the losses when the characteristic of the component does not meet the lower specification and the upper specification limits, respectively. Then

$$\Delta_1 = \sqrt{\frac{A_1}{A_0}} \times \Delta_0$$

and
$$\Delta_2 = \sqrt{\frac{A_2}{A_0}} \times \Delta_0$$

To simplify the tolerancing, we choose the smaller tolerance limit as the tolerance limit for both sides of m. That is,

$$\Delta = \min(\Delta_1, \Delta_2)$$

is the tolerance limit for the characteristic x.

3.7 SUMMARY

This chapter introduced the concept of tolerance design and the methods of tolerancing. It discussed the effect of tolerance on the quality loss of a product.

Tolerance designs for The-Nominal-The-Best, The-Larger-The-Better and The-Smaller-The-Better characteristics were illustrated with examples. Finally, the chapter explained tolerance allocation for component characteristics having linear or nonlinear effects on a product's characteristics.

PROBLEMS

3.1 A manufacturer of tungsten carbide rollers requires that a critical dimension of the roller be 1 ± 0.1 in. The societal loss A_0 is \$100. The particular dimension is affected by environmental temperature x and rate of wear. The standard deviation of temperature x is $15°F$. Design life T is 4 years, and $v = 0.03$ in.

There are four grades of material, S_1, S_2, S_3, and S_4, that may be used for the roller. These materials have different prices, heat expansion coefficients, and wear-out rates as shown below.

	Price $p(\$)$	Expansion rate (in/°F)	Wear-out rate (in/yr)
S_1	14.00	0.01	0.03
S_2	20.00	0.005	0.02
S_3	25.00	0.003	0.01
S_4	42.00	0.001	0.006

Choose a material from S_1, S_2, S_3, and S_4 that minimizes the overall cost. If $A = \$0.40$, calculate the manufacturing tolerance Δ for the best material. If a new heat treatment method is used to improve the wear-out rate of the S_1 grade material to 0.009 in/yr, what is the effect of the new method on the quality loss? Calculate the tolerance for S_1.

3.2   The existing tolerance on a certain clearance of a product is 15 μm or less. Products not conforming to certain specifications are scrapped at a loss of $24.00. There are two types of machines, A_1 and A_2, that may be used to produce the product. The manufacturing cost using A_2 is $2 less than that of A_1 for each piece. The following list contains data on 15 pieces of product produced by the two types of machines.

Clearance (μm)				
A_1	3	7	4	13	8
	4	7	3	6	7
	5	9	4	4	3
A_2	8	9	11	9	7
	9	11	6	7	14
	14	11	11	9	7

Which machine should be chosen? What should be the tolerance on clearance?

3.3   Consider the power circuit of a television set that includes several resistors. The output voltage of the power circuit is 115 V with a functional limit of ± 25 V. The in-factory loss caused by a defective power circuit is 94¢. The resistance x of the power circuit affects its output voltage. An increase of the resistance by 1% results in an output-voltage decrease in the power circuit by 0.4 V. Consider three grades of resistors having the following mse (mean squared errors) from the nominal resistance. What is the best choice?

Grade	Price (¢)	mse
3rd	5	$(10\%)^2$
2nd	15	$(5\%)^2$
1st	40	$(2\%)^2$

3.4   Consider a manufacturer of automobile brake systems. A brake system is considered defective when the brake shoes wear by more than 3 mm, at which time the shoes are replaced at a cost of $70 to the customer. The in-factory cost of replacing the brake shoes, if it is found that they do not meet the manufacturer's specifications, is $20. The brake shoes currently used have a standard deviation of manufacture variation of 0.2 mm and a wear rate β of 0.5 mm/year, assuming preventive maintenance is done every 2 years. Estimate the quality loss.

3.5   A supplier of bumper bars (nickel plated) uses the electroplating process to improve appearance, protect base metal from corrosive attack, and to provide a wear-resistant surface. The thickness of the plated deposit depends upon the plating time and the amount of current passed. The specification of the thickness for the nickel plating ranges from 0.0002 to 0.0008 in, with a nominal value of 0.0005. If the plating is less than 0.0002 in thick, the supplier reworks the product at a cost of $5. The following measurements of electric current are recorded below, in amperes (A):

16	15	12	13	14	13	14	14	16	14
14	16	15	14	13	14	13	15	15	13

The nominal value of electric current is 14 A. Find the quality level of the process, assuming the thickness is 0.0005 in at 14 amperes.

3.6 Assume that the supplier in Prob. 3.5 uses a more accurate electric power control system to ensure that the plating thickness is within the specified range. The cost of the new system is \$4000 each year. Consider that the annual production of bumpers is 50,000, and that the system improves the root mean squared deviation by a factor of 3.0. What is the total quality cost for the supplier?

3.7 Cemented carbide cutting tools used in a certain plant must be ground on their rake faces to resharpen them. This process can be completed in two minutes for each tool by an electrochemical grinding machine. The machine and equipment cost is \$6000. Depreciation for 10 years, interest, and taxes amount to \$1000 each year. The tolerance on the rake angle of the tool is $\pm 2°$. If the resharpened rake angle does not conform to the specified tolerance, it is discarded at a loss of \$150. Resharpening the tool can also be done in 4 minutes per tool using a diamond wheel on a conventional grinder, costing about \$1800 each year with an overhead cost of \$7.00 for each hour of operation. Twenty tools were resharpened, 10 using the electrochemical grinding and 10 using the conventional grinding. The following deviations of the rake angle from its nominal are obtained:

Electrochemical grinding: $1.5°$, $1.2°$, $1.3°$, $1.0°$, $1.0°$, $0.9°$, $0.8°$, $0.9°$, $0.7°$, $0.9°$

Conventional grinding: $1.5°$, $1.3°$, $1.4°$, $1.6°$, $1.4°$, $1.3°$, $1.0°$, $1.0°$, $0.9°$, $0.9°$

Which grinding method should be used so that the total cost is minimized? What is the annual loss if the number of tools to be resharpened annually is 3000?

3.8 A lamination consists of five layers, with the average dimensions shown below.

Layer	1	2	3	4	5
Dimension (0.001 in)	3	4	2	1	5

After the deposition of each layer, the mean squared deviations are found to be 0.0002, 0.0003, 0.0004, 0.0002, 0.0001, respectively. What are the optimal tolerances of each layer, if the overall tolerance is to be ± 0.0006 in?

3.9 A glass manufacturer uses ultrasonic machining where material is removed from the glass surface by microchipping or erosion with abrasive particles. The tip of the tool vibrates at low amplitude and high frequency. This, in turn, transmits a high velocity to the fine abrasive grains between the tool and the surface of the workpiece. With fine abrasives, tolerances of 0.0005 in or better can be achieved in the process. The manufacturer uses the ultrasonic machining to cut square glass plates with a principal dimension of 20 ± 0.0003 in. Glass plates having dimensions less than 19.9997 in are scrapped at a cost of \$60 per plate. On the other hand, glass plates with dimensions greater than 20.0003 in are recut with a 0.70-percent probability that the recut glass will meet the specifications of 20 ± 0.0003 in. The cost of recutting is \$10. A sample of 30 plates is taken, the principal dimension is measured, and the measurements are recorded as follows:

19.9990	19.9991	19.9998	19.9999	20.0000
19.9998	20.0001	20.0002	20.0001	19.9998
20.0006	19.9991	20.0005	20.0003	19.9999
19.9997	19.9998	20.0004	20.0002	20.0006
20.0000	19.9990	20.0003	19.9997	20.0000
19.9899	19.9998	19.9999	20.0000	20.0001

Assuming that the measurements follow a normal distribution, what is the quality loss per plate? What should the tolerance be so that the total quality loss per plate is minimized? What is the effect of recutting on the quality loss? Which of the following has greater effect on the quality loss:

(a) changing the tolerance of the principal dimension to 20 ± 0.0005 in; or

(b) reducing the cost of recutting to $5 per plate?

3.10 An assembly having four components has a total tolerance on the assembly of 0.30 mm. A design engineer redesigned the assembly to have seven components, but for functional reasons the assembly must maintain the same tolerance of 0.30 mm. Assuming that the components have equal tolerances and that the loss of scrapping the assembly is $25, what is the tolerance of each component? Suppose the cost of producing a component is directly related to its tolerance by the following equation:

$$C(\Delta) = a\Delta^2 + b\Delta^3$$

where Δ = tolerance of the component
a = a constant, 20
b = a constant, 100
$C(\Delta)$ = cost of producing the product with tolerance Δ

Which design for the assembly results in lower cost?

3.11 Single coatings of titanium carbide and titanium nitride, 5–10 μm thick, have improved the wear resistance factor of conventional cemented carbide tools. A manufacturer wishes to improve the wear resistance factor by layered coatings. However, the transition from substrate to coating, as well as between coating materials, usually involves abrupt changes in hardness and thermal expansion properties. During operation and during the cool-down period of manufacture, the difference in these properties produces stresses that often lead to cracking. Thick coatings of brittle refactory compounds also promote cracking when subjected to the heat caused by high speed and feed rates. The manufacturer devised a method that uses a microprocessor control on chemical vapor deposition furnaces to significantly improve the bonding processes. In addition, the microprocessor provides control of layer thickness to within a micron, resulting in uniform coatings.

It is extremely important that the coating thicknesses are within tolerance limits. The manufacturer intends to produce tools having eight layers—four layers of titanium nitride and titanium carbides separated by four layers of the bonding compound. The tolerance for thickness of the titanium layers is ± 0.001 in, and the tolerance for the bonding layers is ± 0.002 in. The tolerance in the tool should be ± 0.003 in. After using the microprocess for layer applications, 20 layers of the bonding compounds and 20 layers of the titanium were measured, and the tolerances of their thicknesses were as follows:

Titanium layers:

0.001	0.002	0.001	0.003	0.000
0.002	0.000	0.002	0.004	0.001
0.001	0.000	0.001	0.001	0.002
0.002	0.001	0.002	0.003	0.001

Bonding compound layers:

0.002	0.003	0.002	0.003	0.004
0.003	0.005	0.004	0.002	0.002
0.001	0.004	0.001	0.002	0.004
0.005	0.004	0.005	0.001	0.002

The loss caused by scrapping a defective tool (a tool that has tolerance greater than 0.003 in) is $200. What is the quality loss per tool? What are the optimal tolerances for each type of layer that minimize the total quality loss per tool?

REFERENCES

Boothroyd, G., C. Poli, and L. E. Murch. *Automatic Assembly*. New York: Marcell Dekker, 1982.

Dallas, D. B. *Tool and Manufacturing Engineers Handbook*. New York: McGraw-Hill, 1976.

Farago, F. T. *Handbook of Dimensional Measurement*. New York: Industrial Press, 1982.

Kennedy, C. W., and D. E. Andrews. *Inspection and Gauging*. New York: Industrial Press, 1977.

Taguchi, G. "Off-line and On-line Quality Control Systems." *Proceedings of the International Conference on Quality Control*, vol. B4 (1978), pp. 1–5.

Taguchi, G., and Y. Wu. *Introduction to Off-line Quality Control*. Tokyo: Central Japan Quality Control Association, 1979.

CHAPTER

4

ON-LINE FEEDBACK QUALITY CONTROL: VARIABLE CHARACTERISTICS

Chapter 3 discussed the loss function technique for determining the tolerances of product characteristics. Keeping product characteristics close to the target values requires continuous monitoring and adjustments to the manufacturing processes during the production cycle.

There are many methods for controlling product quality during production cycles. Inspection of products during manufacturing, employment of diagnostic and adjustment processes, improvement of production processes, and the use of automatic control systems are some of the methods used. These methods constitute what is referred to as *on-line quality control*. An on-line quality control system that encompasses several of the above methods should be employed so that the desired target values of product characteristics can be controlled economically.

Unlike the traditional procedures for quality control, the methods explained in this chapter and those in Chaps. 5, 6, 7, and 8 determine the optimal control limits for parameters of the production process, and checking intervals that minimize the total loss of production. A principal objective of this chapter is to discuss the concept of on-line feedback quality control and its elements.

Before proceeding, a formal definition of on-line quality control would be useful. On-line quality control can be defined as *a set of quality control activities that are conducted during the production cycle of a product*. One such activity is on-line feedback quality control, wherein measurements of product characteristics are obtained and analyzed, and the results fed back to upstream processes for adjustments. In this way, deviations of the characteristics of subsequent products are reduced.

4.1. FEEDBACK CONTROL WITH MEASUREMENT INTERVAL OF ONE UNIT OF PRODUCTION

In many of the companies belonging to the Toyota Group, the characteristic values of the products are automatically measured immediately after processing. When there is a deviation from the target value it is adjusted for the next piece of production. Moreover, the automatic measurements are often made by comparing every piece of production with an actual standard piece. This automatic control, with a measurement interval of one piece of production, is the unrecognized factor that made such drastic improvements in the quality level of Toyota's products. The reader might wonder: Is it really rational to make an adjustment in the production process even for the slightest deviations from the target values? That question and the basic concept of on-line feedback control systems are discussed in this section.

4.1.1 Mean Squared Drift

The mean squared drift per unit of production is obtained from the difference in measurements of two pieces of production produced in succession. It is denoted by σ_0^2. Assume that the measurements of quality characteristics of n pieces of production in succession are $y_1, y_2, \ldots, y_n$. The mean squared drift per unit of production is

$$\sigma_0^2 = \frac{1}{n-1}\left[(y_2 - y_1)^2 + (y_3 - y_2)^2 + \cdots + (y_n - y_{n-1})^2\right] \qquad (4.1)$$

When measurements are taken at regular intervals on three pieces of production produced in succession, and the measurements of k sets of these pieces are denoted by

$$
\begin{array}{ccc}
y_{11} & y_{12} & y_{13} \\
y_{21} & y_{22} & y_{23} \\
\cdot & \cdot & \cdot \\
\cdot & \cdot & \cdot \\
\cdot & \cdot & \cdot \\
y_{k1} & y_{k2} & y_{k3}
\end{array}
$$

where y_{ij} is the measurement of piece j in set i, then the mean squared drift per unit of production is

$$\sigma_0^2 = \frac{1}{2k}[(y_{12} - y_{11})^2 + (y_{13} - y_{12})^2 + (y_{22} - y_{21})^2 + (y_{23} - y_{22})^2 + \cdots$$
$$+ (y_{k2} - y_{k1})^2 + (y_{k3} - y_{k2})^2] \tag{4.2}$$

It should be noted that an estimation of σ_0^2, as given in Eqs. 4.1 and 4.2, may include measurement errors; that is, the change in the measurement values between successive pieces of production may contain a drift of measurement error. Suppose there is a three-minute interval between the production times of two successive pieces. The difference due to the drift of the measurement error during the three minutes will be included in the measurement values of the pieces.

Let the mean squared drift of the true characteristic value of two pieces of production in succession be denoted by σ_1^2 and the mean squared drift of measurement error be denoted by σ_m^2; then the following relationship holds:

$$\sigma_0^2 = \sigma_1^2 + \sigma_m^2 \tag{4.3}$$

The subject of large mean squared drift of measurement error will be discussed later. At the moment, it is assumed that the measurement error mean squared drift σ_m^2 is sufficiently small when compared with the mean squared drift from one piece to another, σ_1^2. That is, the following assumption is made:

$$\sigma_0^2 \approx \sigma_1^2 \tag{4.4}$$

The following two examples show how the mean squared drift and the mean squared drift of measurement errors are estimated:

Example 4.1. The dimensions of a certain product are measured immediately after its final manufacturing process. Measurements are taken twice daily on four work-pieces processed in succession for a period of 10 days. Measurement data (deviation from target) are shown in Table 4.1. What is the mean squared drift per unit of production?

TABLE 4.1
Measurement data of dimension (μm)

Day	A.M.				P.M.			
1	0	−1	1	0	2	2	2	1
2	0	1	1	2	−1	0	1	1
3	−1	1	2	3	−1	−1	−2	−1
4	−1	−2	−3	−3	1	1	1	2
5	6	5	5	5	−3	−2	−2	−2
6	0	1	1	2	3	4	4	2
7	0	0	1	1	−3	−4	−5	−6
8	1	2	2	1	0	2	1	2
9	7	6	6	6	−5	−6	−7	−7
10	0	0	0	0	2	0	0	0

Solution. Using Eq. 4.1, the mean squared drift per unit of production, σ_0^2, is

$$\sigma_0^2 = \frac{1}{20 \times 3}[(0 + 1)^2 + (-1 - 1)^2 + (1 - 0)^2 + \cdots$$
$$+ (2 - 0)^2 + (0 - 0)^2 + (0 - 0)^2]$$

$$= \frac{1}{60} \times 50$$

$$= 0.833 \ \mu\text{m}^2$$

Example 4.2. In order to eliminate the impact of measurement error, the manufacturer in Example 4.1 randomly selects one unit of production and repeats the measurements on the same dimension of the product several times. Assume that the manufacturer performs four consecutive measurements of the dimension of one unit of production and that the measurements are made for six days, once in the morning and once in the afternoon. The results of these measurements are shown in Table 4.2. Find the true mean squared drift of the dimension.

Solution. Using Eq. 4.1 and the data of Table 4.2, the mean squared drift caused by measurement error, σ_m^2, is obtained as

$$\sigma_m^2 = \frac{1}{12 \times 3}[(5 - 5)^2 + (5 - 4)^2 + (4 - 4)^2 + \cdots$$
$$+ (0 - 0)^2 + (0 - 0)^2 + (0 - 1)^2]$$

$$= \frac{1}{36} \times 11$$

$$= 0.306 \ \mu\text{m}^2$$

The mean squared drift per unit of production as it relates to the product characteristic value, σ_1^2, is

$$\sigma_1^2 = \sigma_0^2 - \sigma_m^2$$

$$= 0.833 - 0.306$$

$$= 0.527 \ \mu\text{m}^2$$

TABLE 4.2
Measurement data for Example 4.2

Day	Morning				Afternoon			
1	5	5	4	4	3	3	3	2
2	0	0	0	0	1	1	1	1
3	-2	-2	-1	-1	-5	-4	-4	-3
4	0	1	1	1	-1	-1	0	0
5	4	4	3	3	2	2	1	0
6	-3	-3	-3	-3	0	0	0	1

4.2 THE LOSS FUNCTION

The concept of the loss function, as discussed in Chap. 2, can be applied to estimate the losses due to the inclusion of both the mean squared drift of the product characteristic and the mean squared drift of measurement error. Let the annual cost of an automatic control system be Q, and the annual production be N units. The tolerance limit of the product characteristic value is $\pm\Delta$, and the loss due to a defective item is A. When the automatic control system operates properly without failure, its loss function is given by Eq. 4.5, provided that adjustments are made when there is a difference between the value of the measured characteristic and its target value.

$$L = \frac{Q}{N} + \frac{A}{\Delta^2}\sigma_0^2 \tag{4.5}$$

Example 4.3. The annual cost of the control system in Examples 4.1 and 4.2 is $15,000, and the annual production is 800,000 units. The characteristic value to be controlled is the dimension of the product, which has a tolerance of $\pm 10\ \mu m$. The loss caused by a defective piece (rework cost) is $6. What is the quality cost per unit of production?

Solution. The mean squared drift per unit of production, σ_0^2, which includes both the mean squared error among the manufactured units and the mean squared error caused by measurement, is 0.833.

Using Eq. 4.5, the quality cost per unit of production is obtained as

$$Q = \$15,000$$

$$N = 800,000$$

$$A = \$6$$

$$\Delta = \pm 10$$

$$L = \frac{15,000}{800,000} + \frac{6}{10^2} \times 0.833$$

$$= 0.01875 + 0.045$$

$$= \$0.064$$

4.3 FEEDBACK CONTROL WITH MEASUREMENT INTERVALS GREATER THAN ONE UNIT OF PRODUCTION

Automatic control systems for which every piece of production is measured immediately after processing, using a standard piece for comparison, were discussed in a previous section. In many situations, it is difficult (if not impossible) to have an automatic control system capable of such measurements and controlling the production system. In these cases, operators usually undertake the measurements and the checking of the product. The cost of measurements, when made by operators, is usually higher than when automatic control systems are used. Moreover, the operator may not be able to measure every piece of production, resulting in a higher loss of quality per unit of production.

Decreasing the measurement interval to one piece of production is recommended when operators are performing the measurements, provided it is economically feasible. Obviously, if the operator is capable of measuring every piece, the loss function will be identical to that of an automatic control system, given by Eq. 4.5. This section is intended to determine, using the loss function, the optimal measurement interval when operators are performing the measurements so that the quality cost per unit is minimized. The following parameters are defined:

m = target value of the product characteristics

Δ = tolerance of the product characteristics

A = in-plant cost of reworking or scrapping a unit that falls outside of tolerance interval

B = cost per measurement of the product characteristics

C = cost per adjustment

n_0 = current measurement interval (units)

n = measurement interval

D_0 = current adjustment or control limit

D = adjustment or control limit

l = time lag of measurement

u_0 = current average number of products (units) between successive adjustments

$\bar{u}$ = predicted average number of products between successive adjustments

L = total cost of measurement and adjustment per unit: the sum of diagnosis cost, measurement cost, adjustment cost, and cost of time lag

σ_m^2 = measurement error

The diagnosis cost per product is given by

$$\text{Diagnosis cost per product} = \frac{B}{n} \qquad (4.6)$$

The adjustment cost per product is

$$\text{Adjustment cost per product} = \frac{C}{\bar{u}} \qquad (4.7)$$

The loss per product and the cost of time lag per product are obtained as follows. From Chap. 2, the loss caused by a product variation from nominal is

$$L_1 = kv^2 = \frac{A}{\Delta^2} v^2 \qquad (4.8)$$

Assume that the control limits for production process adjustment are set at $\pm D$, and the product characteristics being measured follow a uniform distribution within this range ($\pm D$).

If the production process is found to be under control during diagnosis (the product characteristics are within the control limits), then the mean squared deviation from the target value is approximated by $D^2/3$ (the variance of the uniform distribution $= [(m + D) - (m - D)]^2/12$). The loss per unit is related only to the amount of deviation from the target value (no units are outside the control limits). Loss caused by deviation when the production process is under control is obtained by substituting $v^2 = D^2/3$ in Eq. 4.8.

$$L_1 = \frac{A}{\Delta^2} \times \frac{D^2}{3} \qquad (4.9)$$

If the production process is found to be out of control during diagnosis, then the mean squared deviation is

$$v^2 = \left(\frac{n+1}{2} + l \right) \frac{D^2}{\bar{u}} \qquad (4.10)$$

Equation 4.10 establishes that the variance of deviation is proportional to the number of defective products between successive diagnoses. Note that $(n + 1)/2$ is the average number of defective units between successive diagnoses and l is time lag (in units). (Figure 6-1 in Chap. 6 illustrates this in more detail.) By substituting Eq. 4.10 in Eq. 4.8, the following result is obtained:

$$L_2 = \frac{A}{\Delta^2} \left(\frac{n+1}{2} + l \right) \frac{D^2}{\bar{u}} \qquad (4.11)$$

Measurement error is an independent source of variation, causing an increase of quality loss by

$$L_3 = \frac{A}{\Delta^2} \times \sigma_m^2$$

The total quality cost per product is obtained by adding Eqs. 4.6, 4.7, 4.9, and 4.11, and L_3.

$$L = \frac{B}{n} + \frac{C}{\bar{u}} + \frac{A}{\Delta^2} \left[\frac{D^2}{3} + \frac{D^2}{\bar{u}} \left(\frac{n+1}{2} + l \right) + \sigma_m^2 \right] \qquad (4.12)$$

The predicted average number of products between successive adjustments, $\bar{u}$, is

$$\bar{u} = \frac{D^2}{D_0^2} \times u_0 \tag{4.13}$$

This proportion is based on the Brownian motion principle, which is derived from the assumption that the average time for a randomly-moving particle to go a certain distance is proportional to the distance squared. When the current average adjustment interval u_0 and the current control limit D_0 are not available, the average adjustment interval can be estimated using the following equation (Taguchi, 1984)

$$u = \frac{(\text{distance})^2}{\text{variance of drift per unit product}} \tag{4.14}$$

The optimal diagnosis interval is obtained by substituting Eq. 4.13 into Eq. 4.12 and taking the derivative of Eq. 4.12 with respect to n and setting it to zero. This results in

$$n* = \sqrt{\frac{2u_0 B}{A}} \times \frac{\Delta}{D_0} \tag{4.15}$$

The optimal control limit is derived by differentiating Eq. 4.12 with respect to D (assuming Eq. 4.13) and setting the derivative to zero:

$$D* = \left(\frac{3C}{A} \times \frac{D_0^2}{u_0} \times \Delta^2 \right)^{1/4} \tag{4.16}$$

The predicted process capability index C_p, as defined in Eq. 2.1, of the production process is obtained by adding the deviation when the production process is under control ($D^2/3$) and the deviation given by Eq. 4.10:

$$C_p = \frac{2\Delta}{6\sqrt{\dfrac{D*^2}{3} + \left(\dfrac{n*+1}{2} + l \right) \dfrac{D*^2}{\bar{u}}}} \tag{4.17}$$

Example 4.4. The manufacturer of integrated circuits for computers wishes to install an automatic measurement control system that has the same parameters as those given in Example 4.3. Presently, the measurements are taken by an operator, and the system has the following parameters:

Tolerance Δ:	10 μm
Loss due to a defective piece, A:	$6.00
Measurement cost B:	$1.50
Adjustment cost C:	$12.00
Time lag l:	3 units
Current control limit D_0:	3 μm
Observed average adjustment interval u_0:	180 units

What are the quality losses per unit of production for both the automatic and the present measurement control systems?

Solution. Substitute the above information in Eqs. 4.15 and 4.16 to obtain the optimal measurement interval n^* and the optimal control limit D^*, respectively, for the present control system:

$$n^* = \sqrt{\frac{2u_0 B}{A}} \times \frac{\Delta}{D_0}$$

$$= \sqrt{\frac{2 \times 180 \times 1.50}{6}} \times \frac{10}{3}$$

$$\approx 30 \text{ units} \tag{4.18}$$

$$D^* = \left(\frac{3C}{A} \times \frac{D_0^2}{u_0} \times \Delta^2 \right)^{1/4}$$

$$= \left(\frac{3 \times 12}{6} \times \frac{3^2}{180} \times 10^2 \right)^{1/4}$$

$$\approx 2.3 \tag{4.19}$$

The predicted average number of products between successive adjustments is

$$\bar{u} = u_0 \times \frac{D^{*2}}{D_0^2}$$

$$= 180 \times \frac{2.3^2}{3^2}$$

$$= 106 \tag{4.20}$$

The quality cost per unit of production under the present measurement system with optimized measurement interval n^* and optimal control limit D^* is

$$L = \frac{B}{n^*} + \frac{C}{\bar{u}} + \frac{A}{\Delta^2} \left[\frac{D^{*2}}{3} + \left(\frac{n^* + 1}{2} + l \right) \frac{D^{*2}}{\bar{u}} \right]$$

$$= \frac{1.50}{30} + \frac{12.00}{106} + \frac{6}{10^2} \left[\frac{2.3^2}{3} + \left(\frac{31}{2} + 3 \right) \times \frac{2.3^2}{106} \right]$$

$$= 0.050 + 0.113 + 0.106 + 0.055$$

$$= \$0.324 \tag{4.21}$$

In Eq. 4.21, the first term ($0.05) is the cost of measurement per unit, the second term ($0.113) is the cost of adjustment, the third term ($0.106) is the loss associated with deviation within the control limits, and the fourth term is the loss caused by drift from target between diagnoses. The quality loss caused by the measurement error has been ignored.

Comparison between quality cost of the automated measurement control system, as given in Example 4.3, and the cost of the present measurement system shows that the quality cost of the present system is 5.1 times the cost of the automated system. Consequently, we recommend that the present measurement system be replaced by the automatic measurement system, resulting in annual savings of

$$(0.324 - 0.064) \times 800,000 = \$208,000$$

4.3.1 Control Systems for Lot or Batch Types of Production

Example 4.5. Lot type production. An injection molding process produces 12 pieces at a time (12 pieces per "shot"). The average value of the width of each piece is checked once every 2 hours at a cost of $2. The checking process involves the immersion of the piece in ice water and then measurement of its width with error variance $(2.5 \ \mu m)^2$. The tolerance of the width is $m \pm 15 \ \mu m$, where m is the target value of the width. The loss for each defective piece is $0.16, but if one piece in a shot of 12 measured is out of specification, all 12 pieces in the shot are discarded. The current control limit for the mean width is $m \pm 5 \ \mu m$, and the average adjustment interval is 8 hours.

The adjustment cost is $15 and time lag l is 10 shots. Assuming there is an hourly production rate of 120 shots, 2000 working hours per year, and that one shot is the basic unit of production, find the parameters of the optimal control system and estimate the yearly savings.

Solution. The parameters of the injection molding process are:

$$\Delta = 15 \ \mu m$$

$$A = \$0.16 \times 12 = \$1.92$$

$$B = \$2.00$$

$$C = \$15.00$$

$$n_0 = 2 \times 120 = 240 \text{ shots (current checking interval)}$$

$$D_0 = 5 \ \mu m$$

$$u_0 = 8 \times 120 = 960 \text{ shots}$$

$$l = 10 \text{ shots}$$

$$\sigma_m^2 = (2.5 \ \mu m)^2$$

The quality cost per shot of the current control system, L_0, is

$$L_0 = \frac{B}{n_0} + \frac{C}{u_0} + \frac{A}{\Delta^2} \left[\frac{D_0^2}{3} + \left(\frac{n + 1}{2} + l \right) \frac{D_0^2}{u_0} + \sigma_m^2 \right]$$

$$= \frac{2.00}{240} + \frac{15.00}{960} + \frac{1.92}{15^2} \left[\frac{5^2}{3} + \left(\frac{241}{2} + 10 \right) \times \frac{5^2}{960} + 2.5^2 \right]$$

$$= 0.008 + 0.016 + 0.071 + 0.029 + 0.053$$

$$= \$0.179$$

The optimal checking interval n^* is

$$n^* = \sqrt{\frac{2 u_0 B}{A}} \times \frac{\Delta}{D_0}$$

$$= \sqrt{\frac{2 \times 960 \times 2.00}{1.92}} \times \frac{15}{5}$$

$$= 134 \rightarrow 120 \text{ (once per hour)}$$

The optimal control limit is

$$D^* = \left(\frac{3C}{A} \times \frac{D_0^2}{u_0} \times \Delta^2 \right)^{1/4}$$

$$= \left(\frac{3 \times 15}{1.92} \times \frac{5^2}{960} \times 15^2 \right)^{1/4}$$

$$= 3.4 \rightarrow 3.5$$

The average number of units between adjustments is

$$\bar{u} = u_0 \times \frac{D^{*2}}{D_0^2}$$

$$= 960 \times \frac{3.5^2}{5^2}$$

$$= 470$$

Quality cost per shot after the implementation of the optimal parameters of the control system, L, becomes

$$L = \frac{B}{n^*} + \frac{C}{\bar{u}} + \frac{A}{\Delta^2} \left[\frac{D^{*2}}{3} + \left(\frac{n^* + 1}{2} + l \right) \frac{D^{*2}}{\bar{u}} + \sigma_m^2 \right]$$

$$= \frac{2}{120} + \frac{15}{470} + \frac{1.92}{15^2} \left[\frac{3.5^2}{3} + \left(\frac{121}{2} + 10 \right) \frac{3.5^2}{470} + 2.5^2 \right]$$

$$= 0.017 + 0.032 + 0.034 + 0.016 + 0.053$$

$$= \$0.152$$

The yearly savings are

$$(0.177 - 0.152) \times 120 \times 2000 = \$6,000$$

Example 4.6.   Batch type production. In a typical batch type production system, 500 photo receptors are coated at a time. The critical characteristic of the coating is its thickness, which is specified to be 100 ± 30 μm. The loss of a defective unit is $25. The quality of the process is checked by comparing the average thickness of the coating against the target value m at a cost of $20. The difference from target m is adjusted when the amount of deviation is more than 2 percent of nominal value. The cost of adjustment is $12 and the average adjustment interval is 2.5 batches with a time lag of zero. The annual production is 1200 batches. Assuming the estimated measurement error variance is $\sigma_m^2 = (1.2 \ \mu\text{m})^2$, (1) find the optimal parameters of the control system and the annual savings (if any) when such a system is employed; and (2) find the annual savings if the control system obtained in (1) is improved by introducing a new device, so that the measurement cost is $45, and the estimated measurement error variance is $(0.3 \ \mu\text{m})^2$.

Solution. (1) The parameters of the present control system are

$$\Delta = 30 \ \mu m$$

$$A = 500 \times 25 = \$12,500 \text{ per batch}$$

$$B = \$20$$

$$C = \$12$$

$$D_0 = 2 \ \mu m$$

$$n = 1 \text{ batch}$$

$$u_0 = 2.5 \text{ batches}$$

$$l = 0$$

$$\sigma_m^2 = (1.2 \ \mu m)^2$$

The quality cost per batch for the present system is obtained by using Eq. 4.12:

$$
L = \frac{B}{n} + \frac{C}{u_0} + \frac{A}{\Delta^2} \left[\frac{D_0^2}{3} + \left(\frac{n+1}{2} + l \right) \frac{D_0^2}{u_0} + \sigma_m^2 \right]
$$

$$
= \frac{20}{1} + \frac{12}{2.5} + \frac{12500}{30^2} \left[\frac{2^2}{3} + \left(\frac{2}{2} + 0 \right) \frac{2^2}{2.5} + 1.2^2 \right]
$$

$$
= 20.00 + 4.80 + 18.50 + 22.20 + 20.00
$$

$$
= \$85.50
$$

The optimal parameters of the control system are

$$
n^* = \sqrt{\frac{2 u_0 B}{A}} \times \frac{\Delta}{D_0}
$$

$$
= \sqrt{\frac{2 \times 2.5 \times 20}{12500}} \times \frac{30}{2}
$$

$$
= 1.3 \rightarrow 1 \text{ batch}
$$

$$
D^* = \left(\frac{3C}{A} \times \frac{D_0^2}{u_o} \times \Delta^2 \right)^{1/4}
$$

$$
= \left(\frac{3 \times 12}{12500} \times \frac{2^2}{2.5} \times 30^2 \right)^{1/4}
$$

$$
= 1.4 \rightarrow 1.5 \ \mu m
$$

and $\bar{u}$ is

$$
\bar{u} = u_0 \times \frac{D^{*2}}{D_0^2}
$$

$$= 2.5 \times \frac{1.5^2}{2^2}$$

$$= 1.4$$

The quality cost of the control system when operating at optimal parameters is

$$L = \frac{B}{n^*} + \frac{C}{\bar{u}} + \frac{A}{\Delta^2}\left[\frac{D^{*2}}{3} + \left(\frac{n^*+1}{2} + l\right)\frac{D^{*2}}{\bar{u}} + \sigma_m^2\right]$$

$$= \frac{20}{1} + \frac{12}{1.4} + \frac{12500}{30^2}\left[\frac{1.5^2}{3} + \left(\frac{2}{2} + 0\right)\frac{1.5^2}{1.4} + 1.2^2\right]$$

$$= 20.00 + 8.60 + 10.40 + 22.30 + 20.00$$

$$= \$81.30$$

The annual savings are only

$$(85.50 - 81.30) \times 1200 = \$5040$$

(2) The parameters of the new system are

$$A = \$12500$$

$$B = \$45$$

$$C = \$12$$

$$D^* = 1.5 \ \mu m$$

$$n = 1 \ \text{batch}$$

$$\bar{u} = 1.4 \ \text{batches}$$

$$l = 0$$

$$\sigma_m^2 = (0.3 \ \mu m)^2$$

From Eq. 4.14, we obtain

$$n^* = \sqrt{\frac{2\bar{u}B}{A}} \times \frac{\Delta}{D_0}$$

$$= \sqrt{\frac{2 \times 1.4 \times 45}{12500}} \times \frac{30}{1.5}$$

$$= 2 \ \text{batches}$$

$$D^* = 1.5 \ \mu m \ \text{(unchanged)}$$

$$\bar{u} = 1.4 \ \text{(unchanged)}$$

$$L = \frac{B}{n^*} + \frac{C}{\bar{u}} + \frac{A}{\Delta^2}\left[\frac{D^{*2}}{3} + \left(\frac{n^*+1}{2} + l\right)\frac{D^{*2}}{\bar{u}} + \sigma_m^2\right]$$

$$= \frac{45}{2} + \frac{12}{1.4} + \frac{12500}{30^2}\left[\frac{1.5^2}{3} + \left(\frac{3}{2} + 0\right) \times \frac{1.5^2}{1.4} + 0.3^2\right]$$

$$= 22.50 + 8.57 + 10.42 + 33.48 + 1.25$$
$$= \$76.22 < \$81.30$$

The new device lowers the quality cost of the control system obtained in (1) by $5.08.

4.4 SUMMARY

This chapter introduced the concept of on-line feedback quality control systems and discussed the effect of mean squared drift of measurements on the parameters of the feedback quality control systems. Two types of feedback control systems were also discussed: (1) feedback control systems that require measurements on every piece of production; and (2) feedback control systems that require measurements after the production of a number of products. In all cases, total quality cost, including the loss function, is used as a criterion for design and evaluation.

PROBLEMS

4.1. A feedback control system is used in measuring the surface roughness of gauge blocks. The following successive measurements (in microns) are taken:

10	11	7	9	11	10	8	7	6	12
10	7	4	9	8	8	7	6	10	11
11	14	3	7	9	8	8	6	10	12
11	14	7	11	9	10	8	9	4	7

The specification for the surface roughness is that it not be more than 15 μm, and the loss caused by a defective gauge block is $30. What is the quality loss per block?

4.2. A quality characteristic for the diameter of steel shafts is defined by the specification 0.750 ± 0.002 in, and defective shafts are scrapped at a cost of $0.8. The production processes for producing such shafts involve sawing them to their required lengths, and then turning them to their specified diameters. The shafts are then inspected to ensure that their diameters meet the defined specifications.

The turning operation is diagnosed once every 50 shafts. The direct cost of a measurement is $1.5, and the time lag of the adjustment procedure is represented by 5 shafts.

The adjustment cost of the turning operation is $30, and the average number of shafts produced between successive adjustments (with adjustment limit of 0.75 $\pm$ 0.001 in) is 800. Find the optimal parameters of the control system, and compare the total cost per unit.

4.3. The paint department of an automobile manufacturer uses 20 robots for spraying paint on the metal frames of automobiles. The robot requires operator service to unclog the spray nozzle or to replace the nozzle when necessary. The quality characteristic of the painting process is thickness uniformity of the applied paint within the specification limits of ± 30 μm. A robot takes 2 minutes to complete the painting process needed per frame. The spraying process is evaluated by measuring the paint thickness at intervals of 50 automobiles at a cost of $4 per measurement.

A frame that has a thicker or thinner layer of paint than required is repainted (after preparation) at a cost of $70, and the time lag of diagnosis is 2 frames. The average number of automobiles painted between successive adjustments is 1000, and the average adjustment time is 1 hr, at a cost of $20 per adjustment. Find the optimal diagnosis interval and the optimal number of operators to be assigned for robot diagnosis and robot adjustment.

4.4. Consider an EMD (electro-machining discharge) method for razor-blade production. The quality characteristic of the process is measured by the length of a slot to be made in the blade with a tolerance of ±0.01 in. The cost of a defective unit is $1, and the cost of measuring is $0.50. The time lag is 20 units, and the direct cost of adjustment is $10. The current control limit is ±0.005 in, and the current average adjustment interval is 2000 units. The process is diagnosed once every 500 units of production. Find the total loss per unit under the current operating conditions. What are the optimal $n*$ and $D*$ that minimize quality cost per unit?

4.5. Assume that there is a measurement error in Prob. 4.1. The measurement error has been checked once a week with calibration limit $D = 0.5$ μm. The average calibration interval is 7 days. Assuming the rms (root mean square error) of the gauge block used as the standard is 0.1 μm, and using the following formula:

$$\sigma_m^2 = \frac{D^2}{3} + \left(\frac{n+1}{2}\right) \times \frac{D^2}{u} + \sigma_s^2$$

where σ_s^2 is the rms of the standard block, obtain the error variance of the measuring device.

4.6. An industrial engineer wishes to determine whether a fully automated feedback control system or a semiautomated system should be used in the control of a manufacturing process. The following are the parameters of the two systems:

Parameter	Fully automated system	Semiautomated system
B	$2.50	$1.00
C	$12.00	$10.00
σ_0^2	1.5 μm^2	2.5 μm^2
u_0	300 units	220 units
l	0 units	2 units

The tolerance of the dimension to be measured, Δ, is ±10 μm, and the loss due to a defective unit, A, is $6. The annual operating costs of the fully automated and semiautomated systems are $100,000 and $75,000, respectively. The production rate is 200,000 units per year. Which system should be used?

4.7. Assume that the semiautomated feedback control system described in Prob. 4.6 can be improved by introducing a personal computer and additional sensors. The cost of such improvement is $7000. This results in a mean squared drift per unit production of 1.85 and reduces the time lag l to 1 unit of production. What is the effect of the improvement on the decision making of the engineer?

4.8. In electrostatic powder spraying, dry powder is pneumatically fed from a supply reservoir to a spray gun, where a low-amperage, high-voltage charge is imparted to the powder particles. The part to be coated is electrically grounded so that the projected charged particles are firmly attracted to the part's surface and held there until melted and fused into a smooth finish in a baking oven.

An automobile manufacturer uses the electrostatic powder spraying operation to deposit a polishing layer of paint on car door handles. One of the major factors that affect the quality of the paint finish is the powder flow rate. Low flow rate will result in the application of a nonuniform layer of paint powder. On the other hand, excessive flow rate will result in a thicker layer than desired. Therefore, the manufacturer installed a microcomputer system to monitor the powder flow rate and to ensure that it is within a range of 25–28 lb/hr. The thickness of the paint layer on one door handle is measured at different locations, and the following measurements are recorded over the course of five days.

Day	Measurements (mm)				
1	0.5	0.3	0.2	0.1	0.4
2	0.3	0.3	0.2	0.2	0.1
3	0.1	0.2	0.1	0.2	0.3
4	0.2	0.4	0.5	0.4	0.5
5	0.3	0.4	0.2	0.6	0.1

The mean squared drift per unit of production is found to be 0.120. When the thickness of the paint layer falls outside the tolerance limits of 0.1 and 0.3, the door handle is scrapped at a cost of $8.00. What is the quality loss per unit of production?

Assume that the manufacturer installed a microprocessor with high-accuracy sensors to detect any deviations in the powder flow rate. The cost of the system is $7000, and its annual operating cost is $3000. Measurements of paint layers after the installation of the new system are as follows:

Day	Measurements (mm)				
1	0.10	0.05	0.20	0.30	0.40
2	0.10	0.20	0.10	0.30	0.20
3	0.12	0.32	0.05	0.20	0.10
4	0.13	0.40	0.31	0.30	0.28

What is the quality loss per unit of production?

4.9. Optical fiber cables are replacing copper cables in the modern telecommunication systems. In order to protect the optical fiber as much as possible from external influences and to keep it functioning within mechanically permissible limits, it is protected by a loose buffer that is actually a small plastic tube. Each optical fiber is placed in one tube to ensure that it is protected against deformation and friction. To manufacture the loose buffers, two extruders are put together, so that the production of the single-fiber loose buffer's inner and outer tube is achieved in one continuous process. For this purpose, a control system is needed that functions very precisely and guarantees a constant extrusion rate of the buffer tube materials at about 250° C. This will also ensure maintenance of the wall thickness of the tubes, measuring only a few tenths of a millimeter. Assume that the control system has the following parameters:

Tolerance of the wall thickness	5 μm
Loss due to a defective tube	$20.00
Measurement cost per tube	$5.00
Cost of the system adjustment	$17.00
Current control limits of the process	4 μm
Time lag for system adjustment	7 tubes
Observed average adjustment interval	200 tubes

Find the quality loss per tube. What is the optimal adjustment interval of the control system? After the implementation of the optimal adjustment interval, the following measurements of the wall thickness are taken for 20 tubes (in mm):

0.008	0.009	0.007	0.005	0.003
0.006	0.007	0.009	0.008	0.006
0.004	0.006	0.004	0.009	0.006
0.005	0.007	0.008	0.008	0.004

What is the effect of the new adjustment interval on the quality loss per tube?

4.10. A workpiece 10 inches in diameter is to be faced down to a 4 inch diameter on the end. This can be performed by using a lathe equipped with an electronic device that controls the spindle speed and maintains the cutting speed at 200 ft/min (for the diameter being cut at any instant). Deviations in the cutting speed result in a final diameter different from the required 4 inches. The tolerance of the cutting speed is 10 ft/min. A workpiece that has a final diameter greater than 4 inches is reworked at a cost of $25. A workpiece with a diameter less than 4 inches is discarded at a cost of $70.00. The cost of adjusting the control system is $5, and the average adjustment interval is 25 workpieces. The following measurements are recorded for the cutting speeds and the final diameters of workpieces produced during the measurement period.

Cutting speeds (ft/m):

210	211	200	215	199	190	198	190
200	220	210	215	199	210	205	200
210	230	205	200	195	196	200	197
200	200	210	195	199	200	196	215

Final diameter (in):

4.001	4.002	4.001	4.005	4.001
4.000	3.996	3.999	4.000	3.998

3.997	3.999	4.000	4.003	4.006
3.990	4.005	4.007	4.001	3.998
3.993	4.000	4.002	4.006	4.000

The tolerance for the workpiece diameter is ± 0.002 in. The time lag for the control system is one workpiece. What are the parameters of the optimal control system?

REFERENCES

Bodenstab, J. "Machine Vision for Electronics Manufacturing." *Robotics*, vol. 8, Sept. 1986, p. 21.

Devore, J. L. *Probability and Statistics for Engineering and the Sciences*. Pacific Grove, CA: Brooks/Cole Publishing Company, 1982.

Eliason, L., and J. West. "Vision-Based Robotics for Process Management." *Robotics*, vol. 8, Sept. 1986, p. 12.

Elsayed, E. A., and T. O. Boucher. *Analysis and Control of Production Systems*. Englewood Cliffs, NJ: Prentice-Hall, 1985.

Hunter, R. P. *Automated Process Control Systems: Concepts and Hardware*. Englewood Cliffs, NJ: Prentice-Hall, 1978.

Taguchi, G. "The Role of Metrological Control for Quality Control." *Proceedings of the International Symposium on Metrology for Quality Control in Production,* 1984, pp. 1–7.

CHAPTER

5

ON-LINE
PROCESS
PARAMETER
CONTROL:
VARIABLE
CHARACTERISTICS

Chapter 4 introduced the use of on-line feedback systems to ensure the quality of manufactured products during production. The quality characteristics of the product are measured, and the results of the measurements are fed back to upstream manufacturing processes of the production line. Appropriate adjustment decisions are made based on the amount of deviations (as shown by the measurements) from the target characteristics. The concept of controlling the parameters of production processes in order to control the quality of the product characteristics during production is common knowledge among Japanese industries and has been gaining wider recognition among American industries. This recognition is reflected by the widespread use of SPC (statistical process control) in many industries.

It is important to determine the parameters of the production process to be controlled and the optimal control system for each parameter. With the exception of the traditional literature on automatic control engineering, there is, unfortunately, only limited material available on parameter control of the production process. In addition, the literature on automatic control engineering lacks the evaluation of product (or process) quality as it relates to the parameters of the automatic control systems.

The objective of this chapter is to address different methods of controlling process parameters and to discuss the relationships between process parameters and quality characteristics of the product.

5.1 PROCESS PARAMETER TOLERANCE

In this section, the effect of variations in process parameters on the quality characteristics of a product is discussed. Consider a case where the process parameter x affects the quality characteristic y of a product. Assume that the specification of the product characteristic y is given by

$$m_o \pm \Delta_0 \qquad (5.1)$$

where m_0 is the target value of the product characteristic y, and Δ_0 is the tolerance of y.

The defective loss per unit of production found to be out-of-specification is A. When the process parameter x changes by one unit, it changes the product characteristic y by b units. Thus, the process produces defective units when the process parameter x deviates from its nominal value m by

$$m \pm \Delta \qquad \Delta = \frac{\Delta_0}{b} \qquad (5.2)$$

We refer to Δ in Eq. 5.2 as the tolerance of the production process parameter. In other words, when process parameter x deviates by Δ from its nominal value m, the product characteristic reaches its specification limit, resulting in a loss of A per unit.

Obviously, there are other forms of relationships between the value of the product characteristic and the value of the process parameter. In the case where the effect on the characteristic value is nonlinear, the relationship is approximated by a quadratic polynomial, and the tolerance limits of the process parameter are obtained graphically as shown in Fig. 5-1.

Figure 5-1 shows the relationship between the process parameter x and the product characteristic y. In order to determine the tolerance limit of the process parameter, the target value of the product characteristic, m_0, and its tolerance limits $m_0 - \Delta_0$ and $m_0 + \Delta_0$ are placed on the vertical axis. Horizontal lines are then drawn through these values to the points where they intersect the x-y curve. Vertical lines are drawn at the points of intersection to meet the horizontal (x) axis at values $m - \Delta_1$, m, and $m + \Delta_2$, which represent lower tolerance limit, nominal value, and upper tolerance limit of the process parameter, respectively. Then,

$$m \begin{array}{c} -\Delta_1 \\ +\Delta_2 \end{array} \qquad (5.3)$$

is the tolerance for the process parameter x. However, the actual control limit for x is usually very small, and the following symmetrical tolerance is often recommended:

$$m \pm \Delta \qquad \text{where} \qquad \Delta = \min(\Delta_1, \Delta_2) \qquad (5.4)$$

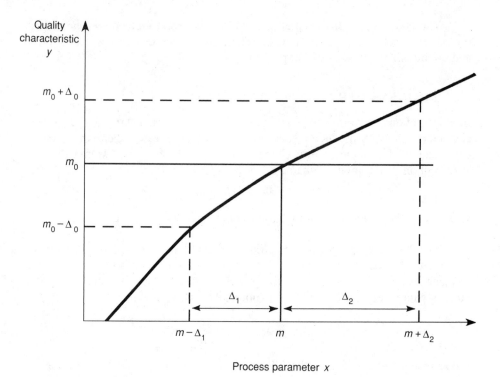

FIGURE 5-1
Estimation of the process parameter when the tolerance of the quality characteristic is given.

5.2 PROCESS PARAMETER FEEDBACK CONTROL SYSTEMS

In the previous section, the tolerance limit of a process parameter was estimated based on m_0 and Δ_0 of the product characteristic. In this section, the design of production process parameter control is presented in the same way the quality control system was discussed in Chap. 4. Parameters to be used for the present discussion are:

A = loss due to product characteristic being out-of-specification

B = measurement cost of production process parameter x

C = adjustment cost of production process parameter x

Δ = tolerance of production process parameter x

n_0 = current measurement interval of production process parameter x

D_0 = current control limit of production process parameter x

u_0 = current average adjustment interval of production process parameter x

The parameters of the optimal control system for production process parameter x are obtained by using the following steps:

1. Determine the tolerance (Δ) of the production process parameter, and the target value m, as discussed earlier in this chapter.

2. Obtain the optimal measurement interval n^* and the optimal control limit D^*:

$$n^* = \sqrt{\frac{2\,u_0\,B}{A}} \times \frac{\Delta}{D_0} \tag{5.5}$$

$$D^* = \left(\frac{3C}{A} \times \frac{D_0^2}{u_0} \times \Delta^2 \right)^{1/4} \tag{5.6}$$

If n^* and D^* are found to be significantly different from the current n_0 and D_0, then obtain new values of n and D as follows:

$$n = (n_0 + n^*)/2$$

$$D = (D_0 + D^*)/2$$

These values are then used as the optimal parameters of the system.

3. Compare the loss of the current control system and that of the optimal control system using Eqs. 5.7 and 5.8, respectively:

$$L_0 = \frac{B}{n_0} + \frac{C}{u_0} + \frac{A}{\Delta^2}\left[\frac{D_0^2}{3} + \left(\frac{n_0 + 1}{2} + l \right) \frac{D_0^2}{u_0} \right] \tag{5.7}$$

$$L = \frac{B}{n^*} + \frac{C}{\bar{u}} + \frac{A}{\Delta^2}\left[\frac{D^{*2}}{3} + \left(\frac{n^* + 1}{2} + l \right) \frac{D^{*2}}{\bar{u}} \right] \tag{5.8}$$

where

$$\bar{u} = u_0 \times \frac{D^{*2}}{D_0^2} \tag{5.9}$$

These equations are the same as those given in Chap. 4, with the exceptions of Δ being the tolerance of the production process parameter and A being the loss due to the product characteristic being out-of-specification. The following examples illustrate these steps:

Example 5.1. Consider a product that is produced by a single-shot injection-molding process. The tolerance limit of the critical dimension of the product is

$$m_0 \pm 30 \ \mu m$$

where m_0 is the target value of the dimension. The loss caused by out-of-specification is $0.20, and the number of shots per hour is 250. The temperature of the molding pattern is checked every 2 hours and is controlled within a control limit of

$$m_t \pm 2°C$$

where m_t is the target value of the temperature.

The temperature measuring cost B is $2.50. The temperature adjustment cost C is $1.50, and the average adjustment interval is approximately once per day (i.e., 8 working hours). A change in the temperature by 1°C results in a change of 6 μm in the dimension of the product. Since this is a single-shot injection molding operation, the time lag is zero.

Obtain the optimal measurement interval n^* for the temperature and the optimal control limit D^*. Assuming 40 operating hours per week, what are the weekly savings?

Solution.

Step 1. Obtain temperature tolerance Δ as

$$\Delta = \frac{\text{tolerance of dimension}}{\text{effect of temperature change by 1°C}}$$

$$= \frac{30}{6} = 5.0$$

The parameters of the molding process are

$$\Delta = 5.0°C$$

$$A = \$0.20$$

$$B = \$2.50$$

$$l = 0$$

$$C = \$1.50$$

$$n_0 = 2 \text{ hr} \times 250 \text{ shots/hr} = 500 \text{ shots}$$

$$u_0 = 8 \times 250 \text{ shots} = 2000 \text{ shots}$$

$$D_0 = 2°C$$

Step 2. Obtain the optimal measurement interval n^* and the optimal control limit D^* using Eqs. 5.5 and 5.6, respectively.

$$n^* = \sqrt{\frac{2 u_0 B}{A}} \times \frac{\Delta}{D_0}$$

$$= \sqrt{\frac{2 \times 2000 \times 2.5}{0.2}} \times \frac{5}{2}$$

$$= 559 \approx 500 \text{ shots}$$

$$D^* = \left(\frac{3C}{A} \times \frac{D_0^2}{u_0} \times \Delta^2 \right)^{1/4}$$

$$= \left(\frac{3 \times 1.5}{0.2} \times \frac{2^2}{2000} \times 5.0^2 \right)^{1/4}$$

$$= 1.03 \approx 1.0°C$$

Consequently, the optimal measurement interval is once every 2 hours, and the optimal control limit is $\pm 1.0°C$.

Step 3. The loss in the current process is

$$L_0 = \frac{B}{n_0} + \frac{C}{u_0} + \frac{A}{\Delta^2}\left[\frac{D_0^2}{3} + \left(\frac{n_0 + 1}{2} + l \right) \frac{D_0^2}{u_0} \right]$$

$$= \frac{2.5}{500} + \frac{1.5}{2000} + \frac{0.20}{5^2}\left(\frac{2^2}{3} + \frac{501}{2} \times \frac{2^2}{2000} \right)$$

$$= 0.005 + 0.000075 + 0.0146$$

$$= \$0.020$$

The loss when the process operates under optimal conditions is

$$L = \frac{B}{n^*} + \frac{C}{\bar{u}} + \frac{A}{\Delta^2}\left[\frac{D^{*2}}{3} + \left(\frac{n^* + 1}{2} + l \right) \frac{D^{*2}}{\bar{u}} \right]$$

where
$$\bar{u} = u_0 \times \frac{D^{*2}}{D_0^2}$$

$$= 2000 \times \frac{1^2}{2^2}$$

$$= 500$$

and therefore
$$L = \frac{2.5}{500} + \frac{1.5}{500} + \frac{0.20}{5^2}\left(\frac{1^2}{3} + \frac{501}{2} \times \frac{1^2}{500} \right)$$

$$= 0.005 + 0.003 + 0.006$$

$$= \$0.014$$

This results in an improvement of

$$L_0 - L = 0.020 - 0.014$$

$$= \$0.006 \text{ per unit of production}$$

The weekly savings are

$$0.006 \times 250 \times 40 = \$60$$

Example 5.2. In a welding process wherein 8000 spots are welded hourly by several robots, the electric power, which affects the quality of the welds, is controlled by checking its value once during an 8-hour workday. The adjustment limit is ± 8 percent of the nominal power, and the average adjustment interval is approximately one week, that is, 40 hours.

Given the following parameters, find the optimal values of the parameters for an on-line process control system, and estimate the annual gain.

Functional limit Δ	50% of nominal power
Cost of rewelding A	$0.20
Checking cost B	$2.40
Adjustment cost C	$20.00
Current control limit D_0	8% of nominal power
Current checking interval n_0	$8000 \times 8 = 64000$
Observed average adjustment interval u_0	$8000 \times 40 = 320,000$
Time lag l	150 spots

Solution.

$$L_0 = \frac{B}{n_0} + \frac{C}{u_0} + \frac{A}{\Delta^2}\left[\frac{D_0^2}{3} + \left(\frac{n_0 + 1}{2} + l\right) \times \frac{D_0^2}{u_0}\right]$$

$$= \frac{2.40}{64,000} + \frac{20.00}{320,000} + \frac{0.2}{50^2}\left[\frac{8^2}{3} + \left(\frac{64,001}{2} + 150\right) \times \frac{8^2}{320,000}\right]$$

$$= 0.000038 + 0.000062 + 0.001707 + 0.000514$$

$$= 0.002231$$

for a yearly loss of

$$0.002231 \times 8000 \times 8 \times 250 = \$35,696 \text{ per year}$$

The optimal parameters are

$$n^* = \sqrt{\frac{2\,u_0\,B}{A}} \times \frac{\Delta}{D_0}$$

$$= \sqrt{\frac{2 \times 320,000 \times 2.40}{0.20}} \times \frac{50}{8}$$

$$= 17,320 \approx 16,000 \text{ (once every 2 hours)}$$

$$D^* = \left(\frac{3C}{A} \times \frac{D_0^2}{u_0} \times \Delta^2\right)^{1/4}$$

$$= \left(\frac{3 \times 20.00}{0.20} \times \frac{8^2}{320,000} \times 50^2\right)^{1/4}$$

$$= 3.5 \approx 4\%$$

$$\bar{u} = u_0 \times \frac{D^2}{u_0^2} = 320,000 \times \frac{4^2}{8^2}$$

$$= 80,000 \text{ (once every 10 hours)}$$

The loss when the welding process operates at optimal conditions is

$$L = \frac{2.40}{16,000} + \frac{20.00}{80,000} + \frac{0.2}{50^2}\left[\frac{4^2}{3} + \left(\frac{16,001}{2} + 150\right) \times \frac{4^2}{80,000}\right]$$

$$= 0.000150 + 0.000250 + 0.000427 + 0.000130$$

$$= 0.000957$$

or $\qquad 0.000957 \times 8000 \times 8 \times 250 = \$15,312$ per year

The annual savings derived from the improvement in the process are

$$35,696 - 15,312 = \$20,384$$

Example 5.3. The viscosity of the emulsion in a continuous emulsion-coating process is carefully controlled in order to maintain the coating thickness at the desired level. The specification of the coating thickness is $m \pm 12$ μm, and the loss incurred when the thickness exceeds the product specification is $3 per squared meter. Current control limits are set at ± 5.0 poise (a measure of viscosity). A change in the viscosity of the emulsion by one poise affects the coating thickness by 0.6 μm. The average adjusting interval is 12,000 m^2, with a direct adjustment cost of $10 and a time lag l of 30 m^2. The coating thickness is checked every 6000 m^2 (once during an 8-hour workday) at a direct cost of $5. Determine the optimal diagnosis interval of the process, n^*, and the optimal control limit D^*.

Solution. The tolerance of the emulsion process, Δ, is

$$\Delta = \frac{12.0}{0.6} = 20 \text{ poise}$$

and the other parameters are

$$A = \$3$$

$$B = \$5$$

$$C = \$10$$

$$n_0 = 6000 \text{ m}^2$$

$$D_0 = 5.0 \text{ poise}$$

$$u_0 = 12,000 \text{ m}^2$$

$$l = 30 \text{ m}^2$$

The loss for the current checking system is

$$L_0 = \frac{B}{n_0} + \frac{C}{u_0} + \frac{A}{\Delta^2}\left[\frac{D_0^2}{3} + \left(\frac{n_0 + 1}{2} + l\right)\frac{D_0^2}{u_0}\right]$$

$$= \frac{5}{6000} + \frac{10}{12,000} + \frac{3}{20^2}\left[\frac{5^2}{3} + \left(\frac{6001}{2} + 30\right)\frac{5^2}{12,000}\right]$$

$$= 0.0008 + 0.0008 + 0.0625 + 0.0474$$

$$= \$0.1115 \text{ per m}^2$$

The optimal checking interval is

$$n^* = \sqrt{\frac{2\,u_0\,B}{A}} \times \frac{\Delta}{D_0}$$

$$= \sqrt{\frac{2 \times 12,000 \times 5}{3}} \times \frac{20}{5}$$

$$= 800 \approx 750 \text{ (once per hour)}$$

The optimal control limit is

$$D^* = \left(\frac{3C}{A} \times \frac{D_0^2}{u_0} \times \Delta^2 \right)^{1/4}$$

$$= \left(\frac{3 \times 10}{3} \times \frac{5^2}{12,000} \times 20^2 \right)^{1/4}$$

$$= 1.7 \approx 2.0$$

and the predicted interval between adjustments becomes

$$\bar{u} = u_0 \times \frac{D^{*2}}{D_0^2}$$

$$= 12,000 \times \frac{2^2}{5^2}$$

$$= 1920$$

The loss after the implementation of the optimal parameters is

$$L = \frac{B}{n^*} + \frac{C}{\bar{u}} + \frac{A}{\Delta^2} \left[\frac{D^{*2}}{3} + \left(\frac{n^* + 1}{2} + l \right) \frac{D^{*2}}{\bar{u}} \right]$$

$$= \frac{5}{750} + \frac{10}{1920} + \frac{3}{20^2} \left[\frac{2^2}{3} + \left(\frac{751}{2} + 30 \right) \frac{2^2}{1920} \right]$$

$$= 0.0067 + 0.0052 + 0.0100 + 0.0063$$

$$= \$0.0282$$

This results in an annual savings of

$$(0.1115 - 0.0282) \times 6000 \times 250 = \$124,950$$

5.3 MEASUREMENT (PREDICTION) ERROR AND PROCESS CONTROL PARAMETERS

The objective of this section is to discuss the effect of measurement errors on parameter control, as they were not fully covered in earlier sections.

The larger measurement errors are, the larger the variations in the quality of the products manufactured. For example, if there is a measurement error of $+3\ \mu m$, the adjustment of the process parameters is in error by the same degree. Suppose that the characteristic value of a product deviates from the target value by 7 μm, which includes 3 μm as a measurement error. The adjustment of the production process will experience a corresponding error if its calibration is made at 7 μm instead of the true deviation of 4 μm. Consequently, after adjustment the process parameter will be set at a value 3 μm from the target value. This will contribute to deviations of subsequent pieces of production from the target value before the process reaches the next measurement point. Thus, the amount of time that the process takes to go beyond the control limits is shortened.

Measurement error can be taken into account when the optimal values of the parameters of the quality control system are obtained by the method explained earlier in this chapter. We define the following:

u_0 = observed average adjustment interval of the current process

σ_m^2 = mean squared error of the measurement

D_0 = current control limit of the production process

Denoting the measurement cost of the current measurement method by B, adjustment cost of the process by C, and the time lag of adjustment by l, the loss function is

$$L = \frac{B}{n_0} + \frac{C}{u_0} + \frac{A}{\Delta^2}\left[\frac{D_0^2}{3} + \left(\frac{n_0+1}{2} + l\right)\frac{D_0^2}{u_0} + \sigma_m^2\right] \qquad (5.10)$$

where Δ = tolerance of the process parameter
  A = loss due to out-of-specification product
  n_0 = current measurement interval

The optimal measurement interval n^* and the optimal control limit D^* are

$$n^* = \sqrt{\frac{2u_0 B}{A}} \times \frac{\Delta}{D_0} \qquad (5.11)$$

$$D^* = \left(\frac{3C}{A} \times \frac{D_0^2}{u_0} \times \Delta^2\right)^{1/4} \qquad (5.12)$$

The predicted average adjustment interval $\bar{u}$, can be approximated by

$$\bar{u} = u_0 \times \frac{D^{*2}}{D_0^2} \qquad (5.13)$$

The following examples illustrate the above procedure:

Example 5.4. Assume that the dimensions of certain parts are measured once every two hours, and that the production process has the following parameters:

Control limit	± 8 μm
Loss due to a defective product, A	$3
Measurement cost B	$2
Time lag l	10 parts
Variance of measurement error, σ_m^2	3 μm^2
Tolerance of dimension, Δ	± 25 μm
Hourly production	800 parts
Adjustment cost C	$12
Average adjustment interval u_0	1.5 times per day

(a) Find the parameters of the optimal control system, and calculate its annual savings in comparison with the current system. (Assume 2000 production hours per year.)

(b) An engineer proposed a new measurement method that reduces the measurement error variance to one-fifth of its current value while it increases the time lag to 1.5 times the current value. The measurement cost is $3. Calculate the loss per unit of production for the proposed method.

Solution.

(a) The parameters of the current process are

$$\Delta = 25 \ \mu\text{m}$$

$$A = 300\text{¢}$$

$$B = 200\text{¢}$$

$$C = 1,200\text{¢}$$

$$n_0 = 1,600 \text{ parts}$$

$$D_0 = 8 \ \mu\text{m}$$

$$u_0 = \frac{800 \times 8}{1.5} = 4300 \text{ parts}$$

$$l = 10 \text{ parts}$$

$$\sigma_m^2 = 3 \ \mu\text{m}^2$$

The loss function of the current process is obtained by substituting the above parameters in Eq. 5.10:

$$L = \frac{B}{n_0} + \frac{C}{u_0} + \frac{A}{\Delta^2}\left[\frac{D_0^2}{3} + \left(\frac{n_0 + 1}{2} + l\right)\frac{D_0^2}{u_0} + \sigma_m^2\right]$$

$$= \frac{200}{1600} + \frac{1200}{4300} + \frac{300}{25^2}\left[\frac{8^2}{3} + \left(\frac{1601}{2} + 10\right)\frac{8^2}{4300} + 3\right]$$

$$= 0.12 + 0.28 + 10.24 + 5.72 + 0.07 + 1.44$$

$$= 17.87\text{¢}$$

The optimal measurement interval n^* and the optimal control limit D^* are

$$n^* = \sqrt{\frac{2\,u_0\,B}{A}} \times \frac{\Delta}{D_0}$$

$$= \sqrt{\frac{2 \times 4300 \times 200}{300}} \times \frac{25}{8}$$

$$= 240$$

$$D^* = \left(\frac{3C}{A} \times \frac{D_0^2}{u_0} \times \Delta^2\right)^{1/4}$$

$$= \left(\frac{3 \times 1200}{300} \times \frac{8^2}{4300} \times 25^2\right)^{1/4}$$

$$= 3.3 \ \mu m$$

A predicted average adjustment interval $\bar{u}$ is calculated by using Eq. 5.13:

$$\bar{u} = u_0 \times \frac{D^{*2}}{D_0^2}$$

$$= 4300 \times \frac{3.3^2}{8^2}$$

$$= 740$$

The loss function is

$$L = \frac{200}{240} + \frac{1200}{740} + \frac{300}{25^2}\left[\frac{3.3^2}{3} + \left(\frac{241}{2} + 10\right) \times \frac{3.3^2}{740} + 3\right]$$

$$= 0.83 + 1.62 + 4.10$$

$$= 6.55¢$$

The annual savings are

$$\frac{1}{100} \times (17.78 - 6.55) \times 800 \times 2000 = \$179,680$$

(b) The loss function L for the new system is

$$L = \frac{B}{n^*} + \frac{C}{\bar{u}} + \frac{A}{\Delta^2}\left[\frac{D^{*2}}{3} + \left(\frac{n^* + 1}{2} + l\right)\frac{D^{*2}}{\bar{u}} + \sigma_m^2\right]$$

$$= \frac{200}{240} + \frac{1200}{740} + \frac{300}{25^2}\left[\frac{3.3^2}{3} + \left(\frac{241}{2} + 15\right)\frac{3.3^2}{740} + 0.6\right]$$

$$= 0.83 + 1.62 + 2.99$$

$$= 5.44¢$$

The proposed control system is preferred to the current system, since a saving of 1.11¢ per piece is realized.

Thus far, we have used the loss function approach to determine the optimal parameters for both quality control systems and production processes. This approach can also be applied to determine the optimal calibration interval of measurement systems, as illustrated by the following example.

Example 5.5. An air gauge is used for the measurement of the principal dimension of a multiturn encoder. The specification of the dimension is $m \pm 10 \ \mu m$, where m is the target value of the dimension, and the loss for a defective part is $3.50. The air gauge is checked once each day, using a standard gauge having mean squared error $\sigma_s^2 = (0.5 \ \mu m)^2$, to determine whether it needs calibration or not. The checking cost is $1.80, and the calibration limits are $\pm 2.0 \ \mu m$. The average calibration interval is 3 days, and the calibration cost is $0.20. The time lag of calibration is 0 units and the daily production is 5000 units. Given 250 working days per year, find the optimal parameters of the calibration system and the annual savings (if any) when the optimal parameters are used in the system.

Solution. The parameters of the current checking and calibration system are

$$\Delta = 10 \ \mu m$$

$$A = \$3.50$$

$$B = \$1.80$$

$$C = \$0.20$$

$$n = 5000 \ \text{units}$$

$$D_0 = 2.0 \ \mu m$$

$$u_0 = 15,000 \ \text{units}$$

$$l = 0$$

$$\sigma_s^2 = (0.5 \ \mu m)^2$$

The loss per unit of the current system is

$$L = \frac{B}{n} + \frac{C}{u_0} + \frac{A}{\Delta^2} \left[\frac{D_0^2}{3} + \left(\frac{n_0 + 1}{2} + l \right) \frac{D_0^2}{u_0} + \sigma_s^2 \right]$$

$$= \frac{1.80}{5000} + \frac{0.20}{15,000} + \frac{3.50}{10^2} \left[\frac{2^2}{3} + \left(\frac{5001}{2} + 0 \right) \times \frac{2^2}{15,000} + 0.5^2 \right]$$

$$= 0.0004 + 0.0000 + 0.0467 + 0.0233 + 0.0088$$

$$= \$0.0792$$

The optimal checking interval of the air gauge is

$$n^* = \sqrt{\frac{2 u_0 B}{A}} \times \frac{\Delta}{D_0}$$

$$= \sqrt{\frac{2 \times 15000 \times 1.80}{3.50}} \times \frac{10}{2}$$

$$\approx 625 \text{ or once each hour}$$

The optimal control limit $D*$ is

$$D* = \left(\frac{3C}{A} \times \frac{D_0^2}{u_0} \times \Delta^2 \right)^{1/4}$$

$$= \left(\frac{3 \times 0.20}{3.50} \times \frac{2^2}{15000} \times 10^2 \right)^{1/4}$$

$$= 0.3 \approx 0.5 \ \mu m$$

and

$$\bar{u} = u_0 \times \frac{D*^2}{D_0^2}$$

$$= 15,000 \times \frac{0.5^2}{2^2}$$

$$= 938$$

The measurement error σ_m^2 is given by

$$\sigma_m^2 = \frac{D*^2}{3} + \left(\frac{n*+1}{2} + 1 \right) \frac{D*^2}{\bar{u}} + \sigma_s^2 = \frac{0.5^2}{3} + \left(\frac{626}{2} + 0 \right) \times \frac{0.5^2}{938} + 0.5^2$$

$$= 0.417$$

The loss per unit of production for the optimal control system is

$$L = \frac{B}{n*} + \frac{C}{\bar{u}} + \frac{A}{\Delta^2} \left[\frac{D*^2}{3} + \left(\frac{n*+1}{2} + l \right) \frac{D*^2}{\bar{u}} + \sigma_s^2 \right]$$

$$= \frac{1.80}{625} + \frac{0.20}{938} + \frac{3.5}{10^2} \left[\frac{0.5^2}{3} + \left(\frac{626}{2} + 0 \right) \times \frac{0.5^2}{938} + 0.5^2 \right]$$

$$= 0.0029 + 0.0002 + 0.0146$$

$$= \$0.0177$$

The yearly savings are

$$(0.0792 - 0.0177) \times 5000 \times 250 = \$76,875$$

5.4 SUMMARY

This chapter discussed the effect of variations in process parameters on the quality characteristics of the product, and reviewed the methods for determining the optimal values of those process parameters. These methods were also used to determine the optimal parameters of measurement systems in order to minimize the effects of measurement error and the calibration cost of measurement systems.

Two types of on-line feedback quality control were discussed, namely:

1. Repairing or discarding of defective products found by an inspection
2. Adjusting or recovering processes found out-of-control by checking either quality characteristics or process conditions

There is a third type of action for controlling product quality; it is used on processes in which predicted quality differs from the target or targets. This method, called feed-forward control, is introduced briefly in Appendix B.

PROBLEMS

5.1 The specification for the dimension of an injection molding product is $m \pm 50$ μm. The parameters of the process are as follows:

Loss caused by out-of-specification	30¢
Current measurement method	Measurement is taken after every 10 pieces of production
Measurement cost B	50¢
Time lag l	300 pieces
Control limit	± 20 μm
Adjustment cost C	$90
Measurement error variance	18 μm
Average adjustment interval	One adjustment every 2 days
Daily production	2400 pieces (8 hours daily production)

(a) Determine the optimal measurement interval n^*, the optimal control limit D^*, and the annual savings.
(b) A new measurement method is to be used immediately after processing is devised: measurement cost is $5 per measurement, measurement error standard deviation is 3.3 μm, and time lag is 1. Compute savings for each piece and annual savings, respectively. Annual production hours are 2000.

5.2 A hot-dip plating process requires putting a protective coating on a cast-iron casing by dipping the casing into molten zinc. This process requires that the thickness of the coating be 150 ± 10 μm. The temperature of the molten zinc is measured once a day. A $1°$ change in the temperature of the molten zinc results in a 2-μm decrease in the thickness of the coating. The cost to measure the temperature is $3, and the cost of an adjustment is $30. The average daily production is 800 casings. Assume that the control limit on the temperature is currently set at $m \pm 5°C$, with no time lag. The cost of a defective unit is $10, and the variance of the temperature measurement error is 3 μm^2. What are the optimal control limit, the measurement interval, and the gain per unit of production against the current control system?

5.3 Seamless steel tubes are made by a hot extrusion process. The specification of the inner diameter of the tube is 20.000 ± 0.001 in. The control limits of the pressure required for the extrusion are $100,000 \pm 5,000$ lb/in^2. The pressure is currently checked twice a day. Pressure in the extrusion process is adjusted once every 5 days at an average cost of $100. The cost of checking pressure is $2, the time lag is 5 tubes, and the loss caused by a defective tube is $200. The daily production is 300 tubes. What are the annual savings if a quality control system with optimal parameters is implemented?

5.4 A manufacturer uses cylindrical center type grinders for grinding the surface of a workpiece. The amount of grinding is specified to be ± 0.002 in from the target dimension of the workpiece. The control limits are set at ± 0.001 in, and the loss caused by a defective product is $20. Measurements of the surface of the workpiece are made at a cost of $10. If the process is found to be out-of-control, it is adjusted at a cost of $30 and a time lag of 3 workpieces. The measurement error is checked once a day with a standard mean squared error $v_s^2 = (0.0002 \text{ in})^2$ at a cost of $3.00. The calibration limit is currently 0.0005 in, and average calibration interval is 3.5 working days. Find the optimal control system, including the calibration of the measurement system, and estimate annual earnings.

5.5 Assume that the manufacturer in Prob. 5.4 uses an automatic measurement system with an error variance of $(0.0003 \text{ in})^2$ at an annual cost of $8000. The new system measures each item. What is the effect of the automatic measurement on the quality loss of the process?

5.6 Waterjet cutting involves the removal of material by the cutting action of high-velocity (sometimes two to three times the speed of sound), extremely high pressure water or water-based fluid with abrasive additives. The clean edge cuts produced through waterjet cutting lend themselves to improved product characteristics. Two critical factors affect the accuracy of the waterjet cutting process: (1) the velocity of the abrasive additives, and (2) the pressure of the waterjet.

A numerical control waterjet system is developed to accurately control the contour of the cut, the velocity of the abrasive additives, and the pressure of the waterjet. Cavities shaped as equilateral triangles are to be made in a sheet of 6-in-thick mild steel. The lengths of each side of the triangle equal 4.5200 in. The velocity of the abrasive additives is fixed at 150 ft/s, and the pressure of the waterjet is 55,000 lb/in^2. A change of the velocity by 10 percent will result in a 2-percent change in the length of the triangle sides. Also, a change of the waterjet pressure by 10 percent will result in a change of the final dimension of the triangle by 5 percent.

Observations of the current setup are given below:

Waterjet pressure in thousandths of a pound per square inch:

54	55	53	55	56	60	52	50
61	55	61	62	55	57	53	55
50	51	52	53	55	54	56	59

Velocity of the abrasive additives in feet per second:

120	130	132	135	125	140	145	150
150	152	150	141	148	139	142	155
156	150	149	146	145	150	143	150

Length of the triangle sides in inches:

4.5000	4.5100	4.4901	4.4530	4.5301
4.6120	4.5320	4.5321	4.5000	4.5120
4.5210	4.5301	4.5325	4.4981	4.5000
4.6000	4.5301	4.5212	4.5100	4.6102

The loss caused by a defective sheet is $360, the average adjustment intervals for the water pressure and velocity are 300 and 250, and the time lags are 5 and 7, respectively. The cost of inspection is $20. Determine the optimal parameters of the waterjet system.

5.7 A producer of screws and bolts uses a flat-die machine to roll the screws and bolts. The flat-die machines operate by rolling a blank across the face of a stationary die with a traversing stroke of a reciprocating die. A pneumatically operated starting finger positions the blank in the dies. The blank then rolls between the die faces and is penetrated progressively, so that the final size is reached before the blank rolls off the finish end of the dies. The quality of the final thread is affected by the number of revolutions of the blank between the dies and the pressure applied on the dies. The quality of the thread is measured by the depth of the crest seam produced as a result of the metal displacement. The tolerance of the crest depth is ± 0.1 mm.

The production rate of the machine is 5000 bolts per hour. The machine's pressure is adjusted every 20,000 bolts at a cost of $27.00. Bolts are then inspected. If found defective, they are discarded at a cost of $0.50 per bolt. The checking cost is $0.10 per bolt. The time lag of the machine is 300 bolts. Assume that the measurement errors for the depth of the crest follow a normal distribution with mean 0.02 mm and standard deviation of 0.01 mm. A 200-bolt sample is taken, and the mean depth of the crest is found to be 0.103 mm with a standard deviation of 0.05 mm. Find

(*a*) the quality loss per bolt, and

(*b*) the optimal adjustment interval of the machine's pressure.

5.8 The producer mentioned in Prob. 5.7 wishes to replace the flat-die system with a cylindrical-die machine capable of accomplishing the same operation. The advantages of the cylinder-die machine are versatility in producing a wide array of bolts with different lengths, and the ability to produce bolts with crest seam tolerances ± 0.05 mm. In order to determine the optimal pressure for the process, the production engineer set the pressure at P_1 and measured the crest depths of 20 consecutive bolts. The pressure was changed to P_2 and 20 other measurements are taken. The measurements are given below:

Pressure	Depth of crest				
P_1	0.03	0.02	0.01	0.00	0.01
	0.02	0.01	0.03	0.04	0.01
	0.05	0.04	0.03	0.05	0.02
	0.06	0.05	0.02	0.01	0.03
P_2	0.01	0.02	0.03	0.02	0.01
	0.00	0.03	0.02	0.01	0.00
	0.04	0.03	0.01	0.02	0.01
	0.00	0.05	0.06	0.06	0.01

Using the same cost values and assuming the same measurement errors as given in Prob. 5.7, what is the quality loss per bolt for pressures P_1 and P_2?

Assuming that the manufacturer uses the pressure determined above, what is the corresponding optimal adjustment interval?

5.9 Commonly, in the boring process, a workpiece is mounted on a lathe and rotated. During this time, a boring bar, mounted rigidly on the carriage, is fed into the workpiece. When an initially round workpiece is clamped in a chuck with a given amount of force, the workpiece will be elastically deformed. As the workpiece is bored, the initial surface produced will be a true circle; that is, it will have zero roundness error. Upon releasing the chucking force, the workpiece, as a result of its elastic nature, will tend to return to its initial shape. Thus, permanent roundness error is unavoidable. The roundness error is perhaps the most important geometrical error because it affects dimensional accuracy and other important factors, such as fitting machine parts and wear in rotating elements.

A machining center is used for boring the inner diameter of tubes 2.5 inches in length. The tolerance of the inner diameter ± 0.0001 in. The workpiece is held in position by an automatic chuck whose clamping force is adjustable. The inner diameters of the tubes are measured during manufacturing. The out-of-roundness is measured radially from the center of the circle of minimum radial separation.

It is found that the roundness error increases quadratically with the chucking force as given below:

$$r = aF^2 + bF + c$$

where r = roundness error
$$a = 2 \times 10^{-8}$$
$$b = 3 \times 10^{-5}$$
$$c = 1 \times 10^{-4}$$

F is the force in lbf. Assume that the nominal chucking (clamping) force is 150 lbf, and that the loss caused by a defective tube (roundness error outside the range from 0.0000 to $+0.0001$) is $37.00. The cost of measuring the roundness is $10 per tube, and the clamping force is adjusted at intervals of 200 tubes to ensure that the roundness error is within the specified range.

(*a*) Determine the tolerance of the clamping force.
(*b*) Develop a control system that adjusts the clamping force after the roundness measurement is taken.
(*c*) What are the parameters of the control system?
(*d*) Assume that the process is adjusted every 100 tubes at a cost of $30.00. What should the optimal adjustment interval be?

REFERENCES

Divine, C. A., Jr., and A. R. Walsh. "Forging vs. Machining." *Machine Design,* May 13, 1965, pp. 192–196.

Doyle, L. E. *Manufacturing Processes and Materials for Engineers*. Englewood Cliffs, NJ: Prentice-Hall, 1985.

Hunter, R. P. *Automated Process Control System: Concepts and Hardware*. Englewood Cliffs, NJ: Prentice-Hall, 1978.

Jamieson, J. L., and L. A. Holmes. "Electrogel Machining of Honeycomb Core." *The Tool and Manufacturing Engineer,* vol. 51, no. 5 (November 1963), pp. 105–106.

CHAPTER
6

ON-LINE
QUALITY
CONTROL:
ATTRIBUTE
CHARACTERISTICS

Chapters 4 and 5 discussed on-line quality control for variable characteristics. They also emphasized the relationship between product tolerance and the optimal process diagnosis and process adjustment intervals of the production process. To determine those relationships, one must make measurements of product characteristics and calculate deviations of those measurements from their target values. Some of the product characteristics that can be measured are dimensions, hardness, operating temperature in degrees, tensile strength in pounds per unit area, percentage of a particular impurity in a chemical compound, weights, and mean time to adjustment of items.

Specifications for most variable characteristics are given with upper and lower limits for the measured value of the characteristic. Other variable characteristics may only have an upper or a lower limit, such as strength (lower limit only), or impurity in a chemical compound (upper limit only). Because of time, cost, or availability of technology, measurements of some product characteristics are not possible, or are not made even though they could be. These characteristics are referred to as attribute characteristics. Some of these characteristics may be judged by visual inspection. Typical examples of these may be whether a plastic cover of a stereo system is scratched, joints of integrated circuits have been soldered properly, lithographed labels have certain desired colors, or soft-drink bottles have labels.

As in the case of variable characteristics, an attribute characteristic may have upper and lower limits; it may have one of the limits or none. The presence of a label on a bottle has no limits; however, the diameter of a bored hole can have upper and lower limits. For example, consider a plug gauge used to inspect a 1.000/1.002-in diameter specification: the *go* gauge member inspects the lower limit of 1.000 in, and the *no-go* gauge member inspects the upper limit of 1.002 in.

This chapter examines methods for on-line quality control of attribute characteristics. These methods focus on the determination of checking intervals and preventive maintenance controls. The chapter also reviews feedback control systems with periodic checking, using one sample.

6.1 CHECKING INTERVAL FOR ATTRIBUTE CHARACTERISTICS

Attribute characteristics are verified in a manner similar to the variable control systems introduced in Chaps. 4 and 5. The production process is diagnosed at fixed intervals (usually expressed as a number of products). When a defective product is found, the process is adjusted so that the characteristics of the subsequent products (excluding those produced during time lag) are brought within the product specifications. This section presents a method for estimating the optimal checking interval for products with attribute characteristics.

Because of the lack of information for the attribute characteristic case compared to the variable characteristic case, it is difficult to consider the loss for nondefective products in the quality loss formula. However, if the loss caused by nondefective products is taken into account, it would be $A/3$ as predicted in Chap. 4, calculated as follows:

$$\frac{A}{\Delta^2} \times \frac{\Delta^2}{3} = \frac{A}{3}$$

The methods described in Chaps. 6 and 7 should be used only in cases where there is no way to measure the variable characteristics of the product, or no knowledge of the parameters of characteristics that should be checked, aside from whether the product works or not. We define:

A = loss caused by producing one unit of a defective product

B = cost of checking a product

C = recovery cost for abnormality in the production process.
This cost consists of both the recovery cost and the cost
of stopping the production process in order to recover it.
C is expressed as

$$C = C_1 t + C_2$$

where C_1 is the cost of stopping the process for one unit of time, t is the
average recovery time, and C_2 is the direct recovery cost including labor,
material, and equipment.

$\bar{u}$ = average predicted time between recoveries (expressed in production units)

l = number of products produced from the time an out-of-control product is
found during the checking process until the time the production process
is stopped for recovery (time lag)

n = diagnosis interval; number of products produced between two successive
diagnoses

L = total cost of process checking and recovery per unit; this is the sum of
checking cost, cost of defective products, recovery cost, and loss caused
by time lag.

DIAGNOSIS COST PER PRODUCT. Diagnosis cost per product is the cost of
checking a product divided by the number of products produced between two
successive diagnoses.

$$\text{Diagnosis cost per product} = \frac{B}{n} \qquad (6.1)$$

COST OF DEFECTIVE PRODUCTS. This cost is obtained by multiplying the
average number of defective products by the cost of a defective product. The
result is then divided by the total number of products produced between successive
recovery actions.

The average number of defective units between successive diagnoses is
approximately $(n + 1)/2$. This is explained as follows: After the ith process
diagnosis is performed, the process may follow any of the patterns shown in Fig.
6-1. (It is assumed that once a process begins to produce defective units, every
unit produced will be defective, until the problem is corrected.) For example,
Pattern 1 represents the case wherein nondefective products are produced until the
$(i + 1)^{th}$ process diagnosis, where the first defective unit is produced. In Pattern n
the process begins to produce defective products immediately after the ith process
diagnosis is performed. The total number of defective units for all n patterns is
$\frac{1}{2}n(n + 1)$, and so the average number of defective products is $\frac{1}{2}n(n + 1)/n$
or $\frac{1}{2}(n + 1)$, as mentioned earlier.

$$\text{Cost per product because of defective products} = \frac{n + 1}{2} \times \frac{A}{\bar{u}} \qquad (6.2)$$

n products

Pattern	Diagnosis i				Diagnosis $(i + 1)$	
1	o o	o	....	o	o	x
2	o o	o	....	o	x	x
.	.					
.	.					
$n-1$	o o	x	....	x	x	x
n	o x	x	....	x	x	x

| Defective products | (1) | (2) | | $(n-2)$ | $(n-1)$ | (n) |

o   Nondefective product

x   Defective product

FIGURE 6-1
Distribution of defective products.

RECOVERY COST.   This cost represents the direct cost of recovering the process to normal operations:

$$\text{Recovery cost per product} = \frac{C}{\bar{u}} \tag{6.3}$$

COST OF TIME LAG.   This cost is a delay cost caused by the number of defective units produced from the time a sample is taken for checking its characteristics until the production process is stopped for recovery:

$$\text{Cost of time lag per product} = \frac{lA}{\bar{u}} \tag{6.4}$$

The total cost of diagnosis and recovery per unit of production, L, is obtained by adding Eqs. 6.1 through 6.4.

$$L = \frac{B}{n} + \frac{n+1}{2} \times \frac{A}{\bar{u}} + \frac{C}{\bar{u}} + \frac{lA}{\bar{u}} \tag{6.5}$$

Example 6.1.   An automatic spot-welding machine is diagnosed by sampling one of every 100 products. The diagnosis involves checking the welded parts of the product. If a product is found to be defective because parts are not welded, or the welding is incomplete, the welding machine is stopped to permit adjustments, and all defective parts found are scrapped at a cost of $0.50 per defective product. Direct cost of a diagnosis is $1.60, and it consumes 8 minutes, during which 30 units of production could have been produced. Therefore, the time lag is $l = 30$

products. Once the machine is found to be abnormal, it must be stopped for 20 minutes. The loss of stopping the welding machine is $12.00 per hour. An inspection of 5 products is required in order to detect and scrap all defective products from the 100 products produced between successive diagnoses. The inspection cost equals $8.00 ($1.60 × 5 = $8.00). The direct cost of recovery of the welding process is, C_2, $8.00. Therefore, the total recovery cost C is

$$12.00 \times \frac{20}{60} + 1.60 \times 5 + 8.00 = \$20.00$$

Assume that 16 adjustments to the welding machine have been performed during the last two months, and the total number of products produced during the same period was 84,000 units. What is the total cost (per product) of process diagnosis and recovery of the welding process?

Solution.

A = loss caused by production of a defective product = $0.50

B = diagnosis cost = $1.60

C = recovery cost = $20.00

$\bar{u}$ = average number of units produced between adjustments

$$= \frac{84,000}{16} = 5250$$

l = 30 units (products)

n = 100 units (products)

The total cost per unit of production is obtained by substituting the above values in Eq. 6.5:

$$L = \frac{B}{n} + \frac{n+1}{2} \times \frac{A}{\bar{u}} + \frac{C}{\bar{u}} + \frac{lA}{\bar{u}}$$

$$= \frac{1.60}{100} + \frac{101}{2} \times \frac{0.50}{5250} + \frac{20.00}{5250} + \frac{30 \times 0.50}{5250} = \$0.0275 \text{ per unit}$$

If a new automatic welding machine exists that does not require adjustments, then the total cost per product would be zero. Though such a machine does not exist, let us assume that the interest and the capital recovery cost of such a machine is $0.10 per product. Then the cost per product of the new machine would be $0.0725 higher than that for the present machine.

One parameter that affects the total cost per product in Eq. 6.5 is the number of products produced between successive diagnoses. Example 6.2 illustrates the effect of the length of the diagnosis interval on the quality loss per unit of production.

Example 6.2. Consider the same automatic welding machine described in Example 6.1. Assume that the parameters of the production process are the same except that the number of products between successive diagnoses is (*a*) increased to 1500 units from its present value of 100 units; or (*b*) decreased to 50 units from its present value of 100 units. Determine the costs per product for (*a*) and (*b*).

Solution. (*a*) Consider the case when n is increased to 1500 units. The total cost per product is obtained by using Eq. 6.5:

$$L = \frac{1.60}{1500} + \frac{1501}{2} \times \frac{0.50}{5250} + \frac{20.00}{5250} + \frac{30 \times 0.50}{5250} = \$0.0792$$

The cost increase caused by increasing the time between diagnoses is

$$0.0792 - 0.0275 = \$0.0517 \text{ per unit}$$

(*b*) Consider now decreasing the time between successive diagnoses to 50 units. The cost per product is

$$L = \frac{1.60}{50} + \frac{51}{2} \times \frac{0.50}{5250} + \frac{20.00}{5250} + \frac{30 \times 0.50}{5250} = \$0.0411$$

Again, the cost per product is higher (by \$0.0136) than that for the original diagnosis interval (100 units).

From this example, one can conclude that there is an optimal diagnosis interval n that minimizes the cost of diagnosis and adjustments per product. How the optimal interval is determined is explained next.

6.1.1 Optimal Interval between Successive Diagnoses

Equation 6.5 relates the total cost per product to the interval between successive diagnosis, time lag, time between recovery actions, and to the cost values A, B, and C. The optimal interval between diagnoses can be determined by setting the derivative of Eq. 6.5, with respect to n, to zero:

$$\frac{dL}{dn} = -\frac{B}{n^2} + \frac{A}{2\bar{u}} = 0$$

$$n^* = \sqrt{2\bar{u}\frac{B}{A}} \tag{6.6}$$

The total cost per product for the optimal n^* is obtained by substituting Eq. 6.6 into Eq. 6.5.

$$L = \sqrt{\frac{AB}{2\bar{u}}} + \frac{1}{2}\sqrt{\frac{2\bar{u}B}{A}}\frac{A}{\bar{u}} + \frac{A/2 + C + lA}{\bar{u}}$$

$$= \sqrt{\frac{2AB}{\bar{u}}} + \frac{A/2 + C + lA}{\bar{u}} \tag{6.7}$$

Example 6.3. Determine the optimal diagnosis interval for the automatic spot-welding machine of Example 6.1. What is the cost per product corresponding to the optimal diagnosis interval?

Solution. The optimal diagnosis interval is determined by substituting the values of $\bar{u}$, B, and A in Eq. 6.6:

$$n^* = \sqrt{2\bar{u}\frac{B}{A}} = \sqrt{\frac{2 \times 5250 \times 1.60}{0.50}} = 183 \text{ units}$$

and the cost per product is obtained by using Eq. 6.7:

$$L = \sqrt{\frac{2 \times 50 \times 1.60}{5250}} + \frac{0.50/2 + 20.00 + 30 \times 0.50}{5250} = \$0.0242$$

Since Eq. 6.6 ignores the effect of l, C, and $\bar{u}$, the value of n^* will not be accurately estimated unless the following conditions are satisfied. First, the time lag l should be much smaller than the average time between adjustments. Second, the loss caused by a defective product, A, should be much greater than $C/\bar{u}$, the adjustment cost per product. What happens if either of these conditions or both of them are not satisfied? Another expression is developed for n so that these conditions need not be satisfied. The alternative expression for the optimal diagnosis interval is obtained by setting the diagnosis cost per product approximately equal to the loss caused by producing defective products in Eq. 6.5. This equalization results in

$$n^* = \sqrt{\frac{2(\bar{u} + l)B}{A - C/\bar{u}}} \tag{6.8}$$

Solutions to Eq. 6.8 exist when $A \gg C/\bar{u}$; otherwise one should use Eq. 6.6 instead. The derivation of Eq. 6.8 is as follows:

Let P_i ($i = 1, 2, \ldots$) be the probability that the first defective unit is the ith unit of production. The interval between two successive diagnoses is n units of production, as depicted in Fig. 6-2. The probability of observing a defective unit for the first time after the kth diagnosis is:

$$P_{n(k-1)+1} + P_{n(k-1)+2} + \cdots + P_{n(k-1)+n} \tag{6.9}$$

The average number of defective units produced between the $(k - 1)^{th}$ and k^{th} diagnoses is .

$$\frac{nP_{n(k-1)+1} + (n - 1)P_{n(k-1)+2} + \cdots + P_{n(k-1)+n}}{P_{n(k-1)+1} + P_{n(k-1)+2} + \cdots + P_{n(k-1)+n}} \tag{6.10}$$

Assume that the probabilities of the first, second, third, $\ldots$, n^{th} product being the first defective are equal. In other words,

$$P_{n(k-1)+1} = P_{n(k-1)+2} = \cdots = P_{n(k-1)+n} \tag{6.11}$$

The average number of defective units in this case is $(n + 1)/2$. This

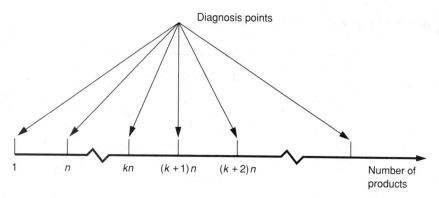

FIGURE 6-2
Diagnosis points.

explains the second term in Eq. 6.5. We now calculate the average number of units produced between two successive adjustments.

As mentioned above, we assume that the probabilities of the first, second, third, . . . , n^{th} product being the first defective are equal. When a defective unit is found at the kth diagnosis, then the cause of defect (trouble) must have occurred between the $(k-1)^{th}$ and the kth diagnoses, and the average number of defective units after the trouble has occurred is $n/2$. Thus, the actual number of products between two successive adjustments should be $\bar{u}+n/2$, instead of $\bar{u}$ as given in Eq. 6.5.

Replacing $\bar{u}$ by $\bar{u}+n/2$ in Eq. 6.5 results in

$$L = \frac{B}{n} + \frac{n+1}{2} \times \frac{A}{\bar{u}+n/2} + \frac{C}{\bar{u}+n/2} + \frac{lA}{\bar{u}+n/2} \qquad (6.12)$$

By using the following approximation in Eq. 6.12:

$$\frac{1}{\bar{u}+n/2} \approx \frac{1}{\bar{u}}\left(1 - \frac{n}{2\bar{u}}\right) \qquad (6.13)$$

and by taking the derivative of resulting equation with respect to n, the following is obtained:

$$\frac{dL}{dn} = \frac{B}{n^2} + \frac{A}{2\bar{u}} - \frac{2n+1}{2} \times \frac{A}{u^2} - \frac{C}{2\bar{u}^2} - \frac{lA}{2\bar{u}^2} \qquad (6.14)$$

Since the third term, on the right-hand side of Eq. 6.14 is much smaller than the second term, the third term is neglected. The equation is then set to zero, giving

$$-\frac{B}{n^2} + \frac{A}{2\bar{u}} - \frac{C}{2\bar{u}^2} - \frac{lA}{2\bar{u}^2} = 0$$

or

$$n^* = \sqrt{\frac{2\bar{u}B}{A - C/\bar{u} - lA/\bar{u}}} \qquad (6.15)$$

Because $A \gg C/\bar{u}$ and $A \gg lA/\bar{u}$,

$$\frac{1}{A - C/\bar{u} - lA/\bar{u}} = \frac{1}{(A - C/\bar{u})\left(1 - \dfrac{lA/\bar{u}}{A - C/\bar{u}}\right)}$$

$$\approx \frac{1}{A - C/\bar{u}}\left(1 + \frac{lA/\bar{u}}{A - C/\bar{u}}\right)$$

$$\approx \frac{1}{A - C/\bar{u}}\left(1 + \frac{l}{\bar{u}}\right) \qquad (6.16)$$

Substituting Eq. 6.16 into Eq. 6.15, the following is obtained:

$$n^* = \sqrt{\frac{2(\bar{u} + l)B}{A - C/\bar{u}}} \qquad (6.17)$$

This completes the derivation of Eq. 6.8.

Example 6.4. Use Eq. 6.8 to obtain the optimal diagnosis interval for the automatic welding machine in Example 6.1. Determine the total cost per product.

Solution. By Eq. 6.8, n^* is

$$n^* = \sqrt{\frac{2(5250 + 30) \times 1.60}{0.50 - 20.00/5250}} = 185$$

and the cost per product is

$$L = \frac{1.60}{185} + \frac{186}{2} \times \frac{0.50}{5250} + \frac{20.00}{5250} + \frac{30 \times 0.50}{5250} = \$0.0242$$

By changing the diagnosis interval from 100 products to 185 products, the total cost per product is reduced from \$0.0275 to \$0.0242 — a cost reduction of \$0.0033 per product. The expected cost reduction per month is 0.0033 multiplied by 42,000 products per month, or \$138.60.

A significant difference in results between the use of Eq. 6.6 and Eq. 6.8 to determine the optimal diagnosis interval is shown in Example 6.5.

Example 6.5. Berry (1974) reports the results of production monitoring of a large number of machine tools. A computerized monitoring system was installed to minimize loss for a total of 160 automatic screw machines in a single plant. The diagnosis procedure for the production process was similar to the procedure given in Example 6.1. The following are the parameters of the production process:

$$A = \$5$$

$$B = \$150$$

$$C = \$4000$$

$$l = 1000 \text{ units}$$

$$\bar{u} = 4000$$

Determine the optimal n by using Eqs. 6.6 and 6.8. What are the corresponding costs per product?

Solution. By using Eq. 6.6, the following is obtained:

$$n^* = \sqrt{2\bar{u}\frac{B}{A}} = \sqrt{\frac{2 \times 4000 \times 150}{5}} = 490 \text{ units}$$

$$L = \frac{B}{n} + \frac{n+1}{2} \times \frac{A}{\bar{u}} + \frac{C}{\bar{u}} + \frac{lA}{\bar{u}}$$

$$= \frac{150}{490} + \frac{491}{2} \times \frac{5}{4000} + \frac{4000}{4000} + \frac{1000 \times 5}{4000} = \$2.86$$

Substitution of the parameters of the production process in Eq. 6.8 results in

$$n^* = \sqrt{\frac{2(\bar{u} + l)B}{A - C/\bar{u}}} = \sqrt{\frac{2 \times 5000 \times 150}{5 - 4000/4000}} = 612 \text{ units}$$

$$L = \frac{150}{612} + \frac{613}{2} \times \frac{5}{4000} + \frac{4000}{4000} + \frac{1000 \times 5}{4000} = \$2.88$$

Although the difference in cost per product appears to be insignificant, the difference between the two diagnosis-interval values is significant. The difference between the results of Eqs. 6.6 and 6.8 diminishes when $A \gg C/\bar{u}$ and $l \ll \bar{u}$. It is better to use Eq. 6.8 than Eq. 6.6, when either or both of these conditions are not satisfied.

6.1.2 Optimal Interval between Successive Diagnoses for Processes with Small Numbers of Defects

When a process operates under abnormal conditions and consistently produces a relatively large number of defective units, as has been assumed so far, Eq. 6.8 can be effectively used in determining the optimal diagnosis interval. However, when a process produces only a small fraction of defective units, Eq. 6.8 may lead to an overestimation of the optimal diagnosis interval. Therefore, in this section, new expressions are derived to determine the optimal diagnosis intervals under these conditions.

Assume that the fraction of defective products is p. Also, assume that the loss D incurred when a defective unit of production is not disposed of at the diagnosis point, but is sent on to the next production process, is much larger than A. The probability of detecting the deviation of the production process from the normal condition at the diagnosis point is p, and the probability of failure to detect such deviation is $1 - p$.

The average number of defective units produced from the moment the process begins to operate improperly until the first diagnosis point thereafter is $(n + 1)p/2$. The probability of detecting the trouble at the second diagnosis point after failing to detect it at the first is $(1 - p)p$. If the problem is detected at this point, the average number of defective units that have gone undetected is $(n + 1)p/2$, while the number detected is np. Table 6.1 carries this analysis forward to further diagnosis points.

From Table 6.1, the average loss due to defective units when the production process deviates from normal conditions is

$$\left\{ \frac{(n + 1)p^2}{2} + np\left[(1 - p)p + (1 - p)^2 p + \cdots\right] \right\} A$$

$$+ \left\{ \frac{(n + 1)p}{2}\left[(1 - p)p + (1 - p)^2 p + \cdots\right] \right.$$

$$\left. + np\left[(1 - p)^2 p + 2(1 - p)^3 p + \cdots + (i - 2)(1 - p)^{i-1}p\right] \right\} D$$

$$= \left[\frac{n + 1}{2}p^2 + np(1 - p)\right] A + \left[\frac{n + 1}{2}p(1 - p) + n(1 - p)^2\right] D \quad (6.18)$$

Substituting $p = 0$ in Eq. 6.18, the loss becomes nD. Assuming p is near zero, then, the loss for each abnormal condition is nD, which corresponds to the loss $\frac{1}{2}(n + 1)A$ for $p = 1$ as was seen in the preceding section.

Substitution of the loss $2D$ for A in Eq. 6.5 and 6.8 results in the following respective equations:

TABLE 6.1
Number of undetected defective units at diagnosis points

Diagnosis point	Probability of detecting deviation in the process	Number of defective units found	Number of undetected defective units
1	p	$(n + 1)p/2$	0
2	$(1 - p)p$	np	$(n + 1)p/2$
3	$(1 - p)^2 p$	np	$(n + 1)p/2 + np$
4	$(1 - p)^3 p$	np	$(n + 1)p/2 + 2np$
.	.	.	.
.	.	.	.
.	.	.	.
i	$(1 - p)^{i-1}p$	np	$(n + 1)p/2 + (i - 2)np$
.	.	.	.
.	.	.	.
.	.	.	.

$$L = \frac{B}{n} + \frac{n+1}{2} \times \frac{2D}{\bar{u}} + \frac{C}{\bar{u}} + \frac{lA}{\bar{u}} \qquad (6.19)$$

and

$$n = \sqrt{\frac{2(\bar{u}+l)B}{2D - C/\bar{u}}} \qquad (6.20)$$

When $p \neq 1$ (the number of defective units during deviation of the production process is less than 100-percent), it is possible to detect all defective units by tracing back to the point when the production process begins to deviate from normal conditions. If this is done, there are no undetected defective units, and $D = A$. Therefore, Eq. 6.18 reduces to

$$\left[\left(\frac{n+1}{2}\right)p^2 + np(1-p) + \left(\frac{n+1}{2}\right)p(1-p) + n(1-p)^2\right]A \qquad (6.21)$$

Using the approximation $n + 1 \approx n$ in Eq. 6.21 results in

$$\left[\frac{n}{2}p^2 + \frac{3}{2}np(1-p) + n(1-p)^2\right]A = n\left(1 - \frac{p}{2}\right)A \qquad (6.22)$$

Therefore, the loss after tracing the defective units is nA (maximum) when $p = 0$ and $\frac{1}{2}nA$ (minimum) when $p = 1$. The corresponding losses per defective unit are $2A$ and A, respectively. When the loss per defective unit is A, the loss per unit and the optimal diagnosis period are given by Eqs. 6.5 and 6.8, respectively. The corresponding equations, when the loss per defective unit is $2A$, are

$$L = \frac{B}{n} + \frac{n+1}{2}\frac{2A}{\bar{u}} + \frac{C}{\bar{u}} + \frac{lA}{\bar{u}} \qquad (6.23)$$

and

$$n^* = \sqrt{\frac{2(\bar{u}+l)B}{2A - C/\bar{u}}} \qquad (6.24)$$

Equation 6.24 results in an overdiagnosis of the production process. Practically, it is appropriate to use Eqs. 6.5 and 6.8 when p is about 0.5, since these equations are not significantly affected by the error estimation of A, as shown in the following section.

Example 6.6. In a production process, the surface-mounted devices are held in place on the circuit board by their solder connections. However, with surface mounting, there is no solder plug surrounding a pin in a hole of the PCB (printed circuit board) to give the connection added strength. Instead, the solder alone bonds the device to the circuit board. Thus, the electrical integrity of the PCB depends on the structural integrity of the solder connection. Therefore, the soldered connections of each board are inspected to detect missing devices, bridges outside the devices, and the absence of solder fillets. Inspection is made at different diagnosis points along the production line. The loss caused by producing a defective circuit board is $30, and the cost of checking a board is $10. The process is adjusted with an average interval of 500 circuit boards, at a cost of $25. The time lag of the adjustment process, as expressed in units of production, is 5. When a defective board is detected, a tracing-back screening is performed. What is the optimal diagnosis interval and the corresponding loss per unit of production?

Solution. We first determine the diagnosis interval while disregarding the effect of the probability of detecting abnormality. The optimal diagnosis interval and corresponding loss per unit of production are obtained using Eq. 6.8 and 6.5, respectively:

$$n = \sqrt{\frac{2(\bar{u} + l)B}{A - C/\bar{u}}}$$

$$n = \sqrt{\frac{2(500 + 5)10}{30 - 25/500}} \approx 18$$

and

$$L = \frac{10}{18} + \frac{19}{2} \times \frac{30}{500} + \frac{25}{500} + \frac{5 \times 30}{500} \approx \$1.48$$

When the possibility of the worst-case occurrence at the diagnosis points is taken into account, then the optimal diagnosis interval and the loss per defective unit are obtained by using Eqs. 6.24 and 6.23, respectively.

$$n = \sqrt{\frac{2(\bar{u} + l)B}{2A - C/\bar{u}}}$$

$$= \sqrt{\frac{2(500 + 5)10}{2(30) - 25/500}} = 13$$

and

$$L = \frac{B}{n} + \frac{n + 1}{2} \times \frac{2A}{\bar{u}} + \frac{C}{\bar{u}} + \frac{lA}{\bar{u}}$$

$$= \frac{10}{13} + \frac{14}{2} \times \frac{60}{500} + \frac{25}{500} + \frac{5 \times 30}{500} = \$1.96$$

6.1.3 Sensitivity Analysis

Although errors in estimating parameters A, B, C, $\bar{u}$, and l may affect the optimal diagnosis interval, they may not significantly affect the total cost per product.

Example 6.7. Assume that an error was made in estimating the loss caused by a defective product in the case of Example 6.1, and that the actual loss is $1.00 instead of $0.50. What is the total cost of diagnosis and adjustment per product?

Solution. By using Eq. 6.8 and substituting $A = \$1.00$, the following is obtained:

$$n^* = \sqrt{\frac{2(5250 + 30) \times 1.60}{1.00 - 20.00/5250}} = 130 \text{ units}$$

and the true L is given by

$$L = \frac{1.60}{130} + \frac{131}{2} \times \frac{0.50}{5250} + \frac{20.00}{5250} + \frac{30 \times 0.50}{5250}$$

$$= \$0.0252 \text{ per product}$$

Although there is a 100-percent error in estimating A, the error in quality loss is only $[(0.0252 - 0.0242)/0.0242] \times 100 = 4.1$ percent

Example 6.8. Assume that the direct cost of diagnosis B in Example 6.5 was erroneously underestimated by 100 percent and its actual value is \$300. What is the true quality cost per product?

Solution. By Eq. 6.8,

$$n^* = \sqrt{\frac{2 \times 5000 \times 300}{5 - 4000/4000}} = 866 \text{ units}$$

and $\qquad L = \dfrac{300}{866} + \dfrac{867}{2} \times \dfrac{5}{4000} + \dfrac{4000}{4000} + \dfrac{1000 \times 5}{4000} = \$3.13$

A 100-percent error in estimating the direct cost of diagnosis results in an 8-percent error in the total cost per product.

It is important to perform sensitivity analyses for different cost elements. In Example 6.7, a 100-percent error in estimating A results in a 4.1-percent error in quality cost per unit, whereas in Example 6.8, a 100-percent error in estimating B results in an 8-percent error in quality cost.

Results of sensitivity analyses can be useful in manpower allocation in the quality control area. For example, changing n from 490 to 612 in Example 6.5 increases the total quality cost per product from \$2.86 to \$2.88. Therefore, if there is a shortage in manpower at any time period, the diagnosis interval can be changed from 490 to 612 or higher during that period without significantly affecting the total cost of quality.

6.1.4 Number of Operators Required for Process Diagnosis and Process Recovery

In recent years, there have been several trends in automation—both in the automation of machines and in the automation of their controls and integrations. These trends have altered many of the functions that operators used to perform, such as continuous tending of machines, loading and unloading, and tool changing. Continuous functions such as diagnosis, adjustment, and inspection are difficult, costly, and perhaps even impossible to automate, thus requiring operator attention. The following example illustrates how the number of operators required for such functions is determined.

Example 6.9 A manufacturer of LP (long-playing) records uses 40 press machines. Each machine is capable of producing one record per minute. Defective records may be produced either because of drift of machine condition or because of the existence of foreign particles (such as dust) in the production environment. Therefore, the production process is diagnosed at intervals of 100 records. The loss caused by producing a defective record is \$0.80; the cost of each diagnosis is \$10; the number of records produced during the time lag is 30; the average number of records produced between successive recoveries is 8000; the average recovery time is 2 hours, and the direct recovery cost is $30. Find the optimal diagnosis interval and the optimal number of operators that should be assigned for process diagnosis and process adjustment.

Solution. The parameters of the production process are

$$A = \$0.80$$

$$B = \$10$$

$$C = \$30$$

$$l = 30 \text{ records}$$

$$\bar{u} = 8000 \text{ records}$$

$$n = 100$$

The number of records produced per week (using a 40-hour work week) by the manufacturer is determined as follows: 1 record/min $\times$ 60 min/hr $\times$ 40 hrs/week $\times$ 40 press machines = 96,000 records/week. Because a diagnosis is made every 100 records, the number of records inspected weekly is 960. The total time for the weekly diagnosis is 960 $\times$ 30 min = 28,800 min = 480 hr.

Therefore, the number of operators required for process diagnosis is

$$480 \text{ hrs} \div 40 \text{ hr/operator} = 12 \text{ operators}$$

In addition, the number of adjustments performed per week is 96,000 $\div$ 8000 = 12, and the total hours required for adjustment per week is 12 $\times$ 2 hr = 24 hr which is equivalent to one operator's time per week. Thus, the total number of operators required for both diagnosis and recovery is 13.

The optimal diagnosis interval can be determined by using Eq. 6.8:

$$n^* = \sqrt{\frac{2(\bar{u} + l)B}{A - C/\bar{u}}}$$

$$= \sqrt{\frac{2(8000 + 30)10}{0.8 - 30/8000}} = 450 \text{ records}$$

The above result shows that the diagnosis interval should be increased from the current 100 records to 450 records, thereby reducing the number of diagnoses per week to 213. Consequently, the number of operators required for the weekly diagnosis will be decreased to 2.7 operators or a total of 3 operators for process diagnosis.

The present quality cost per record (diagnosis interval of 100 records), L_0, is

$$L_0 = \frac{B}{n} + \frac{n + 1}{2} \times \frac{A}{\bar{u}} + \frac{C}{\bar{u}} + \frac{lA}{\bar{u}}$$

$$= \frac{10}{100} + \frac{101}{2} \times \frac{0.8}{8000} + \frac{30}{8000} + \frac{30 \times 0.8}{8000} = \$0.112$$

and the quality cost per record when the diagnosis interval is increased to 450 is

$$L_1 = \frac{10}{450} + \frac{451}{2} \times \frac{0.8}{8000} + \frac{30}{8000} + \frac{30 \times 0.8}{8000} = \$0.052$$

Comparison between L_1 and L_0 shows a cost reduction of \$0.060 per record, or a total of \$5760 per week, when the diagnosis interval is increased to 450 units. The average defective rate of this manufacturing facility, P, is

$$P = \frac{\text{expected number of defectives between recovery actions}}{\text{number of products produced between recovery actions}}$$

$$= \frac{(n + 1)/2 + l}{\bar{u}} = \frac{451/2 + 30}{8000} = 0.032$$

$$= 3.2 \text{ percent}$$

The cost of reducing the defective rate is not linearly proportional to the defective rate itself.

Table 6.2 shows some of the relationships between the length of the diagnosis interval, the quality cost per product, and the defective rate corresponding to the diagnosis interval for the cost data given in Example 6.9.

The defective rate, as illustrated in Table 6.2, increases with the length of the diagnosis interval, whereas the quality cost per unit is a convex function of the length of the diagnosis interval. These different relationships between the factors may result in an unacceptable defective rate at the optimal diagnosis interval, and managerial decisions will have to be made regarding the trade-off between quality cost per product and defective rate.

Example 6.10. An electrostatic spray finishing machine uses the particle-attracting method for applying primer and underseal to the chassis of medium-sized cars.

TABLE 6.2
Relationship between the diagnosis interval, quality cost per product, and defective rate

Diagnosis interval n	Quality cost per product L	Defective rate P
100	\$0.112	1.00%
200	\$0.068	1.63%
300	\$0.055	2.25%
400	\$0.051	2.89%
500	\$0.049	3.50%
600	\$0.049	4.13%

The coating of the chassis is continuously monitored by checking for uniformity and consistency. The electrostatic attraction of any coating material is greater on outer edges and hole edges, causing a heavier build-up of coating in these areas. This build-up and the uniformity of coating can be controlled by adjusting the applied charge. The diagnosis cost per unit is $30. If a chassis coating is found defective (nonuniform buildup of coating), the chassis is repaired and recoated at a cost of $250. If the electrostatic spraying process causes nonuniformity or build-up of coating material at edges or holes of the chassis, the process is adjusted to eliminate the causes of these problems. The number of chassis coated between the time of problem diagnosis and the recovery time of the spraying process is 2, and the average number of coated chassis between successive recoveries is 800. The recovery cost is $155. What is the optimal diagnosis interval of the process? What is the quality cost per unit of production?

Solution.

$$A = \$250$$

$$B = \$30$$

$$C = \$155$$

$$\bar{u} = 800$$

$$l = 2$$

Substituting the above values in Eq. 6.8, the optimal diagnosis interval is calculated as:

$$n^* = \sqrt{\frac{2(800 + 2)(30)}{250 - 155/800}}$$

$$n^* \approx 14 \text{ chassis}$$

The quality cost per unit of production is obtained by substituting the above values in Eq. 6.5:

$$L = \frac{B}{n^*} + \frac{n^* + 1}{2} \times \frac{A}{\bar{u}} + \frac{C}{\bar{u}} + \frac{lA}{\bar{u}}$$

$$= \frac{30}{14} + \frac{15}{2} \times \frac{250}{800} + \frac{155}{800} + \frac{2(250)}{800}$$

$$= \$5.30$$

6.2 FREQUENCY OF PROCESS DIAGNOSIS

The previous two sections have presented approaches for estimating the optimal diagnosis intervals and the optimal sampling inspection frequency, based on the loss function. This section presents a different approach for determining the optimal frequency of process sampling for attribute characteristics, as a function of the production rate of the process. This approach is applicable in situations where cost and time constraints dictate the use of sampling inspection instead of 100-percent inspection and where administrative difficulties preclude the use of other traditional process control methods.

The production process is checked for acceptance (of products) or control (of the process) by periodically inspecting a number of products and determining the status of the product and/or process. Clearly, the frequency of diagnosis (inspection) is affected by the cost incurred by defective products and the cost of process control. As the frequency of diagnosis increases, the cost incurred by defective products decreases, whereas the cost of process control increases, as shown in Fig. 6-3.

Process checking intervals (diagnosis intervals) can be established according to the rate of production. When a production process is operating at a high production rate, it requires a greater frequency of diagnosis than when it is operating at medium or lower production rates. Obviously production processes with a high production rate will produce many more units in the time lag period compared to production processes with low production rates. The objective is to find the frequency of diagnosis as a function of production rate so that the total quality cost for each unit of production is minimized. The following examples illustrate this point.

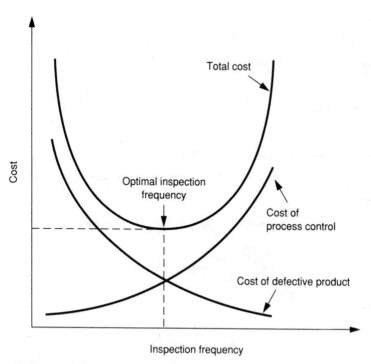

FIGURE 6-3
Optimal diagnosis frequency.

Example 6.11. The plinth of a turntable forms the unit base. It contains the turntable mechanism, electronics, and tone arm, and is molded in polystyrene by using an injection molding machine. It is inspected after molding for defects, such as flow lines (flow lines occur when the plastic "knits" together after it has flowed around either side of a core pin or similar obstruction during the molding process), sink marks (sink marks usually occur whenever there is a change in section thickness: ribs, locating pegs, mounting pillars), and shadow marks (shadow marks are caused by dramatic changes in direction of the plastic flow during injection into the mold; when it strikes a core pin or goes around a sharp corner to fill a recess or changes from one level to another [Shaw, 1985]).

    If a plinth is found to be defective, it is scrapped to be reground and remolded. The loss caused by producing a defective plinth is $50 when remolding is done and $80 when remolding cannot be done. The former case occurs 60 percent of the time, and the latter occurs 40 percent of the time. The diagnosis cost is $25 per diagnosis. The direct cost of process adjustment is $100, and the time lag between the moment a sample is taken (and a defective product detected) and the moment the process is adjusted (so that no further defectives are produced) is 10 minutes. The average trouble occurrence interval of the injector is 400 products. Assuming that the process is in a controlled condition, determine the frequency of sampling inspection when the production rates are 2000, 1000, and 500 products per day.

Solution.

  A = cost of a defective product

     = $50 \times 0.60 + 80 \times 0.40 = \$62$

  B = diagnosis cost (inspection cost)

     = $25

  C = adjustment cost

     = $100

  l = time lag expressed as number of products

  $\bar{u}$ = average number of products produced between two successive adjustments

     = 400

    Consider a production rate of 2000 units/day. Assume that there are 480 working minutes per day; then

$$l = \frac{2000}{480} \times 10 = 41 \text{ units}$$

By Eq. 6.8,

$$n^*_{2000} = \sqrt{\frac{2(400 + 41)(25)}{62 - 100/400}} = 19$$

where n^*_x is the optimal diagnosis period in terms of number of products when the production rate is x. In this case, the frequency of diagnosis is 105 per day.

Consider a production rate of 1000 units per day:

$$l = \frac{1000}{480} \times 10 = 21 \text{ units}$$

$$n^*_{1000} = \sqrt{\frac{2(400 + 21)(25)}{62 - 100/400}} = 18 \text{ units}$$

and the frequency of diagnosis is 56 per day.

Now consider a production rate of 500 units per day:

$$l = \frac{500}{480} \times 10 \approx 10 \text{ units}$$

and

$$n^*_{500} = \sqrt{\frac{2(400 + 10)(25)}{62 - 100/400}} = 18 \text{ units}$$

and the frequency of diagnosis is 28 per day.

The frequencies of process diagnosis at different production rates are

Production rate (per day)	Frequency (per day)
2000	105
1000	56
500	28

6.3 SUMMARY

This chapter discussed on-line quality control for attribute characteristics. It also examined methodologies similar to those used in the on-line quality control procedure for variable characteristics. They permit one to estimate the optimal diagnosis interval and the loss per unit for production processes when operating under normal conditions or when large numbers of defective items are produced. The chapter also discussed the frequency of production process diagnosis as a function of the production rate of a process.

PROBLEMS

6.1 An optical inspection system is used to identify defects in multilayer printed wiring boards (PWB) at a cost of $B = \$3$. The defects include open, short, and nonconductive wiring in the boards. The cost incurred because of a defective printed wiring board is $90. If a defective board is found during diagnosis, the production process is adjusted at a cost of $150, and 10 boards are produced during the time lag. The average number of boards produced between adjustments is 300.

What is the optimal diagnosis interval in terms of the number of boards produced? What is the quality cost per board?

6.2 A manufacturer of electronic assemblies uses a machine vision system to inspect resistor networks with 6, 8, or 10 pins. To determine whether or not a network is within specification, the system does the following:

1. It inspects the pins to determine that the correct number is present and that the pins are properly spaced.
2. It inspects the network's two ceramic standoffs for presence and proper shape.

The loss caused by producing a defective resistor is $25. The direct cost of process adjustment is $150, and the time lag from the diagnosis to the adjustment of the process (if the resistor is found to be defective) is 5 minutes. The average trouble occurrence of the production process is 60 products. Determine the frequency of sampling inspection when the production rates are 5000, 3000, and 1000 resistors per day.

6.3 Consider the manufacturer in Prob. 6.2. The average number of resistors produced between successive adjustments may be 150, 300, or 600. Determine the frequency of diagnosis for each of these process adjustment intervals when the production rates of the process are 10,000, 5000, and 2000 per day.

6.4 A manufacturer of high-volume integrated circuits is experiencing difficulty with the soldering process. Soldered connections may have problems with insufficient or excess solder, lead projection, or incorrect positioning of a device or lead.

Automated X-ray inspection systems are installed at different diagnosis points of the production line to check the solder quality of the product and to provide quantitative data for feedback control of the soldering process. Although defect detection is most often thorough, defective products occasionally go undetected and are sent to the next step in the production process. The loss caused by a defective unit is $20, the cost of the diagnosis is $15. The loss incurred when a defective unit is not disposed of at the diagnosis point is $35. The soldering process is adjusted at intervals of 1000 units of production at a cost of $80 per adjustment. The time lag of adjustment as expressed in terms of production units is 10. What are the optimal diagnosis interval and the loss per unit of production?

6.5 The production engineers of a cold reduction mill produce sheet steel by reducing the thickness of hot rolled steel coils to consumer specifications. The sheets are checked for surface defects. Because of the very high traveling speeds of the cold rolled strips (6000 ft/min), the engineers devised an optical system that checks for the surface defects. The average adjustment interval of the system is 4 hours, and the time lag is 3 minutes. The inspection cost is $20/min, the adjustment cost is $120, and the loss per unit of production (one foot of the sheet steel represents one unit of production) is $0.05. What are the optimal parameters of the on-line control system that minimize the quality loss per unit?

If a new device costing twice as much as the current device reduces the time lag by one-half, and the quality loss per unit is kept the same as that of the current system, what is the adjustment interval of the new system?

6.6 A manufacturer of high-temperature, high-pressure textile dyeing machines uses a high-speed microprocessor to monitor the dyeing process. Change in moisture content, temperature, and textile lint cause quality and maintenance problems. Sensors are connected to measure the change in temperature and moisture content of the dyeing process. Probes are also used to measure the amount of lint in the dyeing solution. The tolerance limits for these parameters are:

Temperature $\pm 3°C$
Moisture content $\pm 5\%$
Amount of lint $+0.1$ oz/cubic foot of solution

The quality of the dyeing process is checked by observing faded or darker-colored patches of the textile material.

The temperature and moisture content are adjusted at intervals of 10,000 and 15,000 feet of textile, respectively. The cost of adjusting the temperature is $5, and the cost of adjusting the moisture content is $20. Once the amount of lint is greater than 0.1 oz/ft^3, the process is stopped for maintenance at a cost of $250. The average time between maintenance (when converted to feet of textiles) is 200,000 feet.

The quality of the dyeing process is checked by using a high-speed vision system which takes continuous snapshots of the textile and compares the color of the material with a preprogrammed color. The cost of inspection is $0.10 per foot. What are the optimal control parameters for both temperature and moisture content? Assume that the loss per defective unit (one foot) of textile is $0.20.

6.7 A manufacturer of light accessories for automobiles checks the quality of taillight bulbs produced in a high-speed production line by testing them for light intensity. A defective bulb is automatically ejected from the line and discarded at a cost of $0.15. The ejection mechanism is monitored for accuracy. The mechanism may fail to eject the defective bulbs, or it may eject acceptable bulbs. The cost of inspecting the mechanism is $0.02, and the current adjustment interval is 20,000 bulbs. The probability that the mechanism ejects a good bulb is 0.01.

Assuming that there is a production rate of 10,000 bulbs per hour, what is the maximum acceptable adjustment cost for the mechanism if the quality loss per unit must not exceed $0.015 per bulb?

6.8 In a sheet metal forming operation, variations in process parameters are known to cause considerable variations in the unloaded shape of the formed part, even if the part is formed to the exact specifications before leaving the forming die. The phenomenon in which a formed part takes an unloaded shape different from the loaded shape is called "springback." This phenomenon may cause significant misalignment problems during the assembly of the affected part with other parts.

In order to reduce the "springback" effect, a producer developed an on-line quality control system for the sheet metal forming operation. Depending on variations in the sheet metal material, and on-line measurements of the friction coefficients at the punch (tool) and die interfaces, the control system adjusts the applied force at the punch interface and the speed of the rolling die. Assume that the tolerance of the applied force is ±10 lbf, and the forming process produces sheets with thickness specifications of ±0.002 in. The sheet is continuously monitored to ensure its quality. A change in the applied force by 10% will result in a 20% change in thickness of the formed sheet. The process is adjusted once every 1000 feet of sheet production at a cost of $25.00. The cost of measuring sheet thickness is $0.05 per foot. The time lag of the process expressed in sheet production is 26 feet of sheet metal, and the maximum quality loss allowed by the producer is $0.10 per foot. Assuming there is a defective loss of $2.00 per foot, determine the optimal tolerance of the sheet thickness.

REFERENCES

Berry, S.A. "Techniques in the Application of Computers to Industrial Monitoring." In *CAD/CAM and the Computer Revolution,* Society of Manufacturing Engineers, 1974, pp. 221–239.

Durrant, N.F. "Some Case Studies in Acceptance Sampling by Attributes." *Quality Assurance,* vol. 7, June 1981, pp. 21–22.

Kirkpatrick, E.G. *Quality Control for Managers and Engineers*. New York: John Wiley and Sons, 1970.

Shaw, M.B. "Process Study for an Injection-Moulded and Painted Hi-Fi Turntable Deck." *Quality Assurance,* vol. 11, December 1985, pp. 98–102.

Wadsworth, H.M., K.S. Stephens, and A.B. Godfrey. *Modern Methods for Quality Control and Improvement*. New York: John Wiley and Sons, 1986.

CHAPTER

7

ON-LINE QUALITY CONTROL: METHODS FOR PROCESS IMPROVEMENTS

The effects of production process parameters on product quality for variable and attribute characteristics were discussed in previous chapters. The total quality cost of a product is a function of many parameters, such as $\bar{u}, A, B, C$, and l. These can be classified according to the processes of the on-line quality control of the product. For example, A and $\bar{u}$ are parameters associated with the production process. B and l are parameters associated with the checking (diagnosis) process, and C is associated with the adjustment and recovery processes. These parameters have a direct effect on the estimation of the optimal checking interval and the optimal control limits of the production process. Table 7.1 lists the parameters and their associated processes.

The objective of this chapter is to present methods to improve the parameters of the production, diagnosis, and adjustment processes so that the total quality loss is minimized. We first introduce methods for improving the parameters of the production process.

7.1 PRODUCTION PROCESS IMPROVEMENT METHODS

As shown in Table 7.1, the parameters of the production process that affect the total quality cost per product are $\bar{u}$ and A. These parameters can be improved by

TABLE 7.1
Processes and parameters
of the total quality cost

Process	Parameters
Production process	$A, \bar{u}$
Diagnosis process	B, l
Adjustment process	C

using any of the following methods individually or in combination:

1. Introduction of preventive maintenance measures such as tool changes (increases $\bar{u}$)
2. Use of tools with long lives (increases $\bar{u}$)
3. Improvement in the production process itself to achieve longer time between successive adjustments
4. Improvement of scrap and disposition methods for defective products (decreases A)

7.1.1 Preventive Tool Change

Preventive maintenance methods can be classified as either deterministic or probabilistic. Deterministic problems are those in which the timing and the outcome of the replacement (or maintenance) action are assumed to be known with certainty. For example, a cutting tool may not break down, but the loss caused by producing defective products increases with use. To reduce this loss, a replacement (or preventive maintenance) can be implemented.

Probabilistic problems are those where the timing and outcome of the replacement action depend on probability. In the simplest situation, the tool may be good or bad. The probability describing the state of the tool may be obtained by using a random variable whose distribution may be termed the tool's failure distribution.

Though failure distributions of tools play a major role in deciding on their optimal preventive maintenance schedules, this section will emphasize the preventive maintenance methods for deterministic problems. Throughout the chapter, there are references made to the cost caused by tool change, C', and the corresponding adjustment interval u'.

The effect of periodic tool changes as an approach to preventive maintenance is illustrated by the following example:

Example 7.1. A supplier of blocks for truck engines produces 3000 units per month. The production of the cylinder blocks requires a reaming operation. Defective products are produced when one of the reamers makes a defective hole. Process diagnosis is performed at constant intervals at a cost of $4 per diagnosis. All defective products found are scrapped at a loss of $60 per defective product.

The adjustment cost is $150, and the average number of products produced between successive adjustments (failures of the process) is 2500 units. Assuming that the time lag is 1 cylinder block, what is the total quality control cost per product?

Solution. The parameters of the reaming process are

$$A = \$60$$

$$B = \$4$$

$$C = \$150$$

$$l = 1 \text{ unit}$$

$$\bar{u} = 2500 \text{ units}$$

By using Eqs. 6.8 and 6.5 the following results are obtained:

$$n^* = \sqrt{\frac{2(\bar{u} + l)B}{A - C/\bar{u}}}$$

$$= \sqrt{\frac{2(2500 + 1) \times 4}{60 - 150/2500}} \approx 18 \text{ units}$$

$$L = \frac{B}{n^*} + \frac{n^* + 1}{2} \times \frac{A}{\bar{u}} + \frac{C}{\bar{u}} + \frac{lA}{\bar{u}}$$

$$= \frac{4}{18} + \frac{19}{2} \times \frac{60}{2500} + \frac{150}{2500} + \frac{1 \times 60}{2500}$$

$$= 0.222 + 0.228 + 0.060 + 0.024$$

$$= \$0.534$$

The total quality cost of the reaming process per month is $0.534 \times 3000 = \$1602$.

As mentioned previously, the wearing of the reamers causes the production of defective products. Therefore, changing all reamers after the production of 1500 cylinder blocks instead of the current average failure interval of 2500 products will reduce the number of failures. In other words, the reamers are replaced by a new set, whether or not they are capable of producing nondefective products. This replacement procedure (a preventive maintenance measure) is called a periodic tool change. Of course, periodic changes of the reamers at smaller intervals of production u' will increase the cost per product. Let C' be the cost incurred by the change of the reamers. (This cost includes tool cost, labor cost, and the loss incurred by stopping the production process; usually $C' = C$.) It is estimated that if all reamers are replaced at every 1500th product, the probability of tool failure is 0.02.

The average interval between failures (after introducing the periodic tool change) is now expected to be

$$\bar{u} = \frac{1500}{0.02} = 75,000 \text{ units}$$

and the corresponding optimal diagnosis interval is

$$n^* = \sqrt{\frac{2 \times 75,000 \times 4}{60 - 150/75,000}} \approx 100 \text{ units}$$

Using Eq. 6.5 and adding the cost of tool change per unit, the total quality loss L is

$$L = \frac{C'}{u'} + \left(\frac{B}{n^*} + \frac{n^* + 1}{2} \times \frac{A}{u} + \frac{C}{u} + \frac{lA}{u} \right) \quad (7.1)$$

$$= \frac{150}{1500} + \left(\frac{4}{100} + \frac{101}{2} \times \frac{60}{75,000} + \frac{150}{75,000} + \frac{1 \times 60}{75,000} \right)$$

$$= 0.100 + 0.083 = \$0.183$$

Introduction of periodic tool changes results in a reduction of total quality cost per unit by \$0.36. The reduction in the annual cost is

$$0.36 \times 3000 \times 12 = \$12,636$$

In Example 7.1, the introduction of a preventive tool change at every 1500 units resulted in a significant cost reduction. It is usually more important to improve uniformity of tool life than to extend the average life length of the tool, and preventive maintenance should be considered (if applicable) in all production processes.

7.1.2 Tools with Longer Lives

Another method for reducing quality cost per product in a production process is to increase the time intervals between successive adjustments, $\bar{u}$, by employing cutting or manufacturing tools with longer lives. Example 7.2 illustrates this point.

Example 7.2. A manufacturer uses turret lathes to bore the housings of four-way solenoid valves. The cutting tool used is made of HSS (high-speed steel). Two types of defective products occur after the boring is complete; among all defectives, reworkable defectives occur 20 percent of the time, and nonreworkable defectives occur 80 percent of the time. The cost of reworking a defective housing is \$6 and the cost of scrapping a nonreworkable defective is \$50. Diagnosis cost is \$1.50 and adjustment cost is \$980. The monthly production is 8500 valves. Two adjustments are performed per month, the tool cost within the adjustment cost is \$250 and the time lag is 4 units.

A new tool with longer life has been introduced in the market with a cost of \$1200. Find the minimum ratio between the expected life of the new tool and the expected life of the current tool that will make it profitable to use the new tool.

Solution. The parameters of the boring process are

$$A = 6 \times 0.2 + 50 \times 0.8 = \$41.2$$

$$B = \$1.5$$

$$C = \$980$$

$$\bar{u} = \frac{8500}{2} = 4250 \text{ units}$$

$$l = 4 \text{ units}$$

The optimal diagnosis interval $n*$ is

$$n* = \sqrt{\frac{2(4250 + 4) \times 1.5}{41.2 - 980/4250}} \approx 18 \text{ units}$$

and the present quality cost per unit is given by

$$L = \frac{1.5}{18} + \frac{19}{2} \times \frac{41.2}{4250} + \frac{980}{4250} + \frac{4 \times 41.2}{4250}$$

$$= \$0.44$$

Consider the new tool. Let the average number of units between successive adjustments be $\bar{u}$. Since l is much smaller than $\bar{u}$, and $C/\bar{u}$ is much smaller than A, $n*$ can be estimated by using the approximation of Eq. 6.6:

$$n* = \sqrt{2\bar{u}\frac{B}{A}}$$

and substituting the equation above into Eq. 6.5, we obtain

$$L = \sqrt{\frac{2AB}{\bar{u}}} + \frac{\frac{1}{2}A + C + lA}{\bar{u}} \tag{7.2}$$

Equations 6.5 and 7.2 are equivalent.

Substituting A, B, l, and C for the new tool ($C = 980 + (1200 - 250) = \$1930$) in the above equations yields

$$L = \sqrt{\frac{2 \times 41.2 \times 1.5}{\bar{u}}} + \frac{\frac{1}{2} \times 41.2 + 1930 + 4 \times 41.2}{\bar{u}} \tag{7.3}$$

$$= \sqrt{\frac{123.6}{\bar{u}}} + \frac{2115.4}{\bar{u}}$$

If the cost L in Eq. 7.3 is less than \$0.44, then it is profitable to use the new tool. Therefore, $\bar{u}$ in Eq. 7.3 must be determined so that

$$\sqrt{\frac{123.6}{\bar{u}}} + \frac{2115.4}{\bar{u}} \leq 0.44$$

or

$$0.44\bar{u} - \bar{u}\sqrt{\frac{123.6}{\bar{u}}} - 2115.4 \geq 0$$

Substituting $x = \sqrt{\bar{u}}$ in the above equation gives

$$0.44x^2 - \sqrt{123.6}\,x - 2115.4 \geq 0 \tag{7.4}$$

The roots of Eq. 7.4 are

$$x = \frac{\sqrt{123.6} \pm \sqrt{123.6 + 4 \times 2115.4 \times 0.44}}{2 \times 0.44}$$

$$x = \frac{11.11 \pm 62.02}{0.88}$$

$$x = 83.10 \text{ or } -57.85$$

Since x must be positive, $x = 83.10$, and the average number of products between successive adjustments is

$$\bar{u} = x^2 = (83.10)^2$$

$$\bar{u} = 6906$$

The required ratio between the average life of the new tool and the present tool is

$$\frac{6906}{4250} = 1.624$$

That is, when the average life of the new tool is at least 1.624 times the average life of the current tool, it becomes profitable to replace the current tool with the new one.

If the new tool's average life is twice as long as the present one's, namely, $4250 \times 2 = 8500$ units, the optimal diagnosis interval becomes:

$$n^* = \sqrt{\frac{2 \times 8504 \times 1.5}{41.2 - 1930/8500}} \approx 25 \text{ units}$$

and the quality cost per product, L, is given by

$$L = \frac{1.5}{25} + \frac{26}{2} \times \frac{41.2}{8500} + \frac{1930}{8500} + \frac{4 \times 41.2}{8500}$$

$$= \$0.37$$

This is a cost reduction of \$0.07 per product from the present quality control cost. Thus, tool life plays an important role in the cost of quality per product, and it may be more economical to use tools with longer lives, even though their costs are higher. Of course, a more significant reduction in quality cost might be attained when periodic tool changes are performed for those tools with longer lives.

Example 7.3. Assume that the new tool introduced in Example 7.2 has an average life of 8500 units and that a periodic tool change is made after every 8000 units of production. With the new tool, the probability of producing a defective product before producing 8000 units is 0.10. Assuming $C = C'$, what would the quality cost be?

Solution. After combining the use of longer-life tools with periodic tool changes, the process production parameters are

$$u' = 8000 \text{ units}$$

$$C' = \$1930$$

$$A = \$14.20$$

$$B = \$1.50$$

$$C = \$1930$$

$$\bar{u} = \frac{8000}{0.10} = 80,000 \text{ units}$$

$$l = 4 \text{ units}$$

The optimal diagnosis interval is

$$n^* = \sqrt{\frac{2(80,004) \times 1.5}{41.2 - 1930/80,000}} = 76 \text{ units}$$

and L is obtained by substituting the above parameters in Eq. 7.1:

$$L = \frac{1930}{8000} + \left(\frac{1.5}{76} + \frac{77}{2} \times \frac{41.2}{80,000} + \frac{1930}{80,000} + \frac{4 \times 41.2}{80,000} \right)$$

$$= 0.24 + 0.066 \approx \$0.31$$

This loss is less than the loss (\$0.37) obtained in Example 7.2.

Because the cost of periodic tool changes in this equation is much greater than the combined costs of process diagnosis and process adjustment, it would be wise to find new methods for reducing excessive periodic tool changes. Such methods can be investigated experimentally by either reducing the cost of toolings or by using tools with different tool lives.

7.1.3   Automatic Process Diagnosis and Production Process Adjustment

This section introduces an alternative approach for improving the process parameter $\bar{u}$ by considering the use of automatic devices in process diagnosis, process adjustment, and inspection.

In recent years, the use of the digital computer in process monitoring, inspection, adjustment, and control applications has been expanded to include many production areas. Computer use has led to changes in production processes, and to the introduction of a variety of process diagnosis, adjustment, and control strategies.

Other control systems are also used. In systems such as feed-forward control systems, potential disturbances are measured before they disturb the process, and anticipatory corrective action is taken. Ideally, the corrective action compensates completely for the disturbance, thus preventing any deviation of the production process from the desired values.

In addition to process monitoring and adjustment systems for disturbances, much of the production equipment now available has sophisticated diagnosis and maintenance systems. When malfunctions or breakdowns occur, it is often difficult for a maintenance crew to immediately identify the source of trouble. Computers and sensors are often used to assist in diagnosing the problem and determining which machine component is malfunctioning. For example, current sensors can be used to detect current draw on motors in order to predict either motor failure or some other consequence. A current sensor, with output to a logic system, can help eliminate costly motor repairs by slowing a machine down or otherwise relieving stress on the motor (Death, 1986). This type of breakdown analysis may significantly reduce equipment downtime, thus increasing machine efficiency.

Diagnosis of the production process can also be performed by using automatic measuring devices attached to (or part of) the production equipment. Such devices permit automatic recording and calculating functions with the gauging of each single piece, thereby producing statistical evaluation virtually simultaneously with the gauging of individual parts. Both activities are executed without human action. There are many varieties of such devices and gauges; however, their detailed descriptions are beyond the scope of this book. The following example shows the effect of the introduction of automatic control systems on quality loss per unit of production.

Example 7.4. A manufacturer is considering the introduction of an automatic inspection device for helical gears. Each gear is inspected for concentricity, pitch, tooth profile, tooth thickness, and gear-tooth shape. The device can inspect all gears and detect 90-percent of all of the defective products. The purchase price of this device is $30,000 and its annual operating cost is 50 percent of its purchase price. The annual production of the process is 600,000 gears and the loss caused by producing a defective gear is $7. The present production process setup requires an operator to perform diagnosis at a cost of $8 per diagnosis. The adjustment cost of the process is $120 and the average number of gears produced between successive adjustments is 4800. The time lag caused by the current practice of the diagnosis method is 5 products, while the time lag of the automatic device is zero. Determine whether it is profitable to introduce the automatic inspection device.

Solution. The parameters of the present setup are:

$$A = \$7$$

$$B = \$8$$

$$C = \$120$$

$$l = 5 \text{ units of production}$$

$$\bar{u} = 4800 \text{ units}$$

The optimal diagnosis interval n^* is

$$n^* = \sqrt{\frac{2(\bar{u} + l)B}{A - C/\bar{u}}}$$

$$= \sqrt{\frac{2(4800 + 5) \times 8}{7 - 120/4800}}$$

$$= 105$$

Using Eq. 6.5, we obtain the quality loss per product:

$$L = \frac{8}{105} + \frac{106}{2} \times \frac{7}{4800} + \frac{120}{4800} + \frac{5 \times 7}{4800}$$

$$= \$0.185$$

The diagnosis cost of the automatic inspection device B' is

$$B' = \frac{\text{annual operating cost}}{\text{annual production}} = \frac{30,000 \times 0.5}{600,000} = \$0.025$$

The device can only detect 90 percent of all of the defective gears. In order to estimate $\bar{u}$ for adjusting the process after finding the defective products, it can be assumed that the operator makes the diagnosis to find the remaining 10 percent of the defective products that are ejected by the automatic inspection device. Thus, it is appropriate to give $\bar{u}$ a value of 10 times the present $\bar{u}$. Therefore, the diagnosis and adjustment cost associated with the remaining 10 percent of the defective gears is calculated as follows:

$$n^* = \sqrt{\frac{2(48,005) \times 8}{7 - 120/48,000}} = 331$$

$$L = \frac{8}{331} + \frac{332}{2} \times \frac{7}{48,000} + \frac{120}{48,000} + \frac{5 \times 7}{48,000}$$

$$= \$0.052 \tag{7.5}$$

The diagnosis and adjustment cost of the automatic device L' is obtained in the following way: The adjustment interval of the device, assuming that the automatic inspection device inspects one unit of product at a time, is

$$\bar{u}' = \frac{4800}{0.9} = 5333$$

and
$$L' = B' + \frac{1 + 1}{2} \times \frac{A}{\bar{u}'} + \frac{l'A}{\bar{u}'}$$

where
$$B' = \$0.025$$

and
$$l' = 0$$

Therefore,
$$L' = 0.025 + \frac{1 + 1}{2} \times \frac{7}{5333} + \frac{120}{5333} + 0$$

$$= \$0.0488 \tag{7.6}$$

The total cost of diagnosis and adjustment per product after the introduction of the automatic inspection device is the sum of Eqs. 7.5 and 7.6. Thus,

$$L = 0.052 + 0.0488 = \$0.1008 \approx \$0.1$$

The reduction of quality cost per product when the inspection device is introduced is $0.085. Economic justification of the device should include the cost of capital investment, life of the device, interest rate, and its controlling cost.

7.2 PROCESS DIAGNOSIS IMPROVEMENT METHODS

Improvement of diagnosis and inspection methods as well as their location in the production process may lead to reductions in total quality cost per product, as illustrated in the following examples.

Example 7.5. Example 6.3 showed that the optimal process diagnosis interval of the spot-welding machine was 183 units and the quality cost per product was

$0.0242. The current inspections of the welded parts involve testing the parts by checking their appearance and by using a tensile test to determine the tensile strength of the welded joints. The inspection process consumes 8 minutes from the time a part is sampled until results are obtained and a decision is made with respect to the quality of the welding process. The tensile test is destructive. Thus, parts that undergo the tensile test are scrapped with no recoverable costs. The cost of the diagnosis is $1.60, and the time lag is 30 parts. Consider replacing the current inspection method with a nondestructive ultrasonic method that uses high-frequency vibrations to detect all types of flaws in welds. The diagnosis cost is $0.4, and the time lag l, is 2 parts. What is the effect of the ultrasonic inspection method on the quality cost per part?

Solution. The parameters of the ultrasonic inspection process are

$$A = \$0.5$$
$$B = \$0.4$$
$$C = \$20$$
$$\bar{u} = 5250 \text{ parts}$$
$$l = 2 \text{ parts}$$

The optimal diagnosis interval is

$$n^* = \sqrt{\frac{2(5252)(0.4)}{0.5 - 20/5250}} = 92 \text{ parts}$$

Using Eq. 6.5:

$$L = \frac{0.4}{92} + \frac{93}{2} \times \frac{0.5}{5250} + \frac{20}{5250} + \frac{2 \times 0.5}{5250}$$

$$= \$0.0128$$

With the ultrasonic inspection method, the optimal diagnosis and adjustment cost per part becomes $0.0128. This is a realization of $0.0242 − $0.0128 = $0.0114 per part, or a monthly cost reduction of $479.

Generally, production process diagnosis is done immediately after processing; however, there are situations where it is preferable to diagnose a process after information from later stages of production (e.g., assembly, shipping, and customer service) has been gathered. Consider the following situation:

Example 7.6. A production process's diagnosis is currently done at the assembly station. Because any defective part is readily found at the assembly station, the diagnosis cost is assumed to be negligible. The loss caused by a defective part, A, is $0.50. Adjustment cost C is $50, and time lag is 800 parts. During the last three months, 300,000 parts were produced, and 20 adjustments were made to the production process.

The manufacturing department is considering moving the diagnosis process from the assembly area to an area where it will be done immediately after the production process. The associated costs of this decision are as follows: Diagnosis cost B = $1.00; time lag l decreases to 5 parts; and the cost incurred by the production of a defective product, A, decreases to $0.40 (reduction in the value-added loss caused by a defective product at subsequent production stations). The adjustment cost is the same as the present cost ($50.00).

(a) Discuss the impact of changing the location of the diagnosis process on the quality cost per product.
(b) Assume that a periodic tool change is made at u' = 10,000 parts and that the probability of producing a defective product (part) is 0.02. Discuss the combined effect of moving the diagnosis process and introducing the tool change on the total quality cost (assume that $C = C'$).

Solution.
(a) In order to discuss the effect of moving the diagnosis process, the quality cost per product for the present system must be determined. The parameters of the present diagnosis process are:

$$B = \$0$$

$$A = \$0.5$$

$$C = \$50$$

$$n = 1 \text{ part}$$

$$\bar{u} = \frac{300,000}{20} = 15,000 \text{ parts}$$

$$l = 80 \text{ parts}$$

The loss for the present system is

$$L = \frac{B}{n} + \frac{n+1}{2} \times \frac{A}{\bar{u}} + \frac{C}{\bar{u}} + \frac{lA}{\bar{u}}$$

$$= \frac{0}{1} + \frac{2}{2} \times \frac{0.5}{15,000} + \frac{50.00}{15,000} + \frac{800 \times 0.5}{15,000}$$

$$= \$0.0300 \tag{7.7}$$

When the diagnosis process is performed immediately after the production process, the parameters become

$$B = \$1.00$$

$$A = \$0.4$$

$$C = \$50.00$$

$$\bar{u} = 15,000 \text{ parts}$$

$$l = 5 \text{ parts}$$

Now the optimal diagnosis interval is

$$n^* = \sqrt{\frac{2 \times 15{,}005 \times 1.00}{0.4 - 50.0/15{,}000}} = 275 \text{ parts}$$

The loss for the new system is

$$L = \frac{1}{275} + \frac{276}{2} \times \frac{0.4}{15{,}000} + \frac{50}{15{,}000} + \frac{5 \times 0.4}{15{,}000}$$

$$= \$0.0108 \tag{7.8}$$

When Eqs. 7.7 and 7.8 are compared, it can be concluded that performing process diagnosis immediately after production results in a cost reduction of $0.0192 per part, or $1920 per month.

(b) Next, the effect of both changing the location of the diagnosis process and introducing periodic tool changes is investigated. Since $u' = 10{,}000$ and the probability of the processing becoming faulty is 0.02,

$$\bar{u} = \frac{10{,}000}{0.02} = 500{,}000 \text{ parts}$$

The loss after the introduction of periodic tool change and without a relocation of the diagnosis process is

$$L_1 = \frac{C'}{u'} + \left(\frac{B}{1} + \frac{1+l}{2} \times \frac{A}{\bar{u}} + \frac{C}{\bar{u}} + \frac{lA}{\bar{u}} \right)$$

$$= \frac{50.00}{10{,}000} + \left(0 + \frac{1+80}{2} \times \frac{0.5}{500{,}000} + \frac{50.00}{500{,}000} + \frac{80 \times 0.5}{500{,}000} \right)$$

$$= \$0.0052 \tag{7.9}$$

The combined loss caused by the relocation of the diagnosis process to a position immediately after the production process and the introduction of the periodic tool change is calculated as follows:

$$n^* = \sqrt{\frac{2(500{,}000 + 5) \times 1.00}{0.4 - 50.00/500{,}000}} = 1582 \text{ parts}$$

$$L = \frac{C'}{u'} + \left(\frac{B}{n^*} + \frac{n^*+1}{2} \times \frac{A}{\bar{u}} + \frac{C}{\bar{u}} + \frac{lA}{\bar{u}} \right)$$

$$= \frac{50.00}{10{,}000} + \left(\frac{1.00}{1582} + \frac{1583}{2} \times \frac{0.4}{500{,}000} + \frac{50.00}{500{,}000} + \frac{5 \times 0.4}{500{,}000} \right)$$

$$= \$0.0064 \tag{7.10}$$

The combined effect of periodic tool changes and relocation of the diagnosis process increases the quality cost per part by $0.0012, or $120 per month, over the loss achieved by periodic tool change alone.

In general, when the average time between successive adjustments is short, diagnosis immediately after the production process is recommended. When the average interval between adjustments is long, it is less costly to diagnose the process at later processing stages where the diagnosis cost is usually nil.

7.3 PROCESS ADJUSTMENT AND PROCESS RECOVERY IMPROVEMENT METHODS

Methods for improving the production and diagnosis processes in order to minimize the quality control cost per product have been discussed in previous sections of this chapter. The recovery process (which involves bringing a production process to normal production after a stoppage) is the third kind of process that has a direct impact on quality control cost. This process, and methods for improving it, will be discussed in this section.

Although there are many improvement methods for the recovery process, this discussion is limited to two of the most commonly used methods. These methods are: (1) use of redundant (spare) machines; and (2) the implementation of an automatic diagnosis-recovery system.

Consider the cost of recovering a process, C. This cost is composed of two elements: the direct cost of recovery, and the cost incurred by the interruption of the production process while the adjustment is being made. This can be expressed as follows:

$$C = C_r t + C_d \qquad (7.11)$$

where C = cost of recovery
C_r = cost incurred by the interruption of the production process per unit time
t = average interruption time
C_d = direct recovery cost

Equation 7.11 indicates that the cost of recovery can be reduced by decreasing the cost of interrupting the system to perform the recovery, by reducing direct recovery cost, or by reducing both costs together. The average interruption time can be decreased by using redundant machines that can immediately continue production when a machine in the production line produces defective products. This decrease can also be accomplished by using automated facilities that can complete the recovery process in a shorter time. The use of redundant machines and the use of automatic recovery methods are discussed below.

7.3.1 Use of Redundant Machines

One of the major problems associated with automated flow production lines (production machines arranged in series) is reliability. Since the line often operates as a single mechanism, failure of one operating machine often results in stoppage of the entire line. Two methods that can improve the reliability of the production line are the provision of buffer storage between production stages and the use of redundant machines at some of the production stages.

This discussion concerns the use of redundant machines as a means of reducing production loss caused by the recovery process. Redundant machines are usually assigned to critical stages of the production system, as well as to bottleneck stages (a bottleneck stage has a cycle time as long as the cycle time of the entire production system). Redundant machines are also assigned to production stages that experience frequent machine failure. Redundant machines are grouped under three classifications:

1. *Hot standby:* a spare machine operating parallel to another similar machine. If one machine fails or needs adjustment and recovery procedures, the other machine continues production without interruption of the entire production system, reducing the time lag for recovery to zero.
2. *Cold standby:* a spare machine is available to start production as soon as the operating machine requires recovery procedures. The time lag for recovery may not necessarily be zero because start-up or setup time is needed to bring the spare machine on line.
3. *Warm standby:* This is similar to a hot standby with the exception that the portion of the production output of the spare machine at the production stage is always less than 50-percent of the total production output of that specific production stage. When the principal machine (machine producing more than 50-percent of production) requires repairs, the spare machine increases its production output to compensate for the portion of production lost while the principal machine is adjusted. In this case, the production loss caused by the time lag for recovery of the principal machine is zero.

The following example illustrates the use of redundant machines in reducing production loss (the quality cost per product) caused by the recovery process.

> **Example 7.7.** An injection molding process is used for the production of print heads for high-speed printers. A mold that contains the pattern of the print heads is set up at the beginning of the production period. The mold must be checked for cleaning at an interval of 2500 units of production with an average cleaning time of 5 minutes and cleaning cost of $6.00. The cost of interrupting the production process is $4.00 per minute. In addition, the average interval of trouble occurrence is 20,000 items, and setting the machine up for resumed production after trouble occurs requires 8 hours at a direct cost of $500. The parameters of the current process are
>
> $$A = \$6$$
>
> $$B = \$5$$
>
> $$l = 1 \text{ product}$$
>
> In order to decrease the quality cost per product, the manufacturing engineering department introduced a redundant machine in a cold standby state: the

redundant machine would carry on production only when the mold required either cleaning or replacement. The cost of the redundant machine is $200,000. The total annual cost is $10,000 per year, and the financing interest is 15 percent. It takes 5 minutes to prepare the redundant machine to resume production.

Assume that the annual production is 3,000,000 print heads. What is the effect (on total quality cost per product) of introducing the spare machine?

Solution.
   Current process. Two types of adjustments are required for the current process. Their parameters and costs are shown in Table 7.2.
   Since type 2 adjustment requires checking the process, the average number of units between successive troubles, $\bar{u}$, is

$$\bar{u} = \bar{u}_2 \qquad (7.12)$$

$$\approx 20{,}000$$

The optimal diagnosis interval $n*$ is

$$n* = \sqrt{\frac{2(20{,}000 + 1) \times 5}{6 - 2420/20{,}000}} \approx 184 \text{ products} \qquad (7.13)$$

The optimal diagnosis interval obtained by using Eq. 7.13 is based on the assumption that diagnosis is performed without interruption of the production process. If the process must be stopped and interrupted for diagnosis, the loss incurred by interrupting the process should be included as part of the diagnosis cost B. The diagnosis cost including cost of interrupting production ($l = 1$ product or 0.5 min) is

$$B = 5 + 1 \times 0.5 \times 4 = \$7$$

The corresponding optimal diagnosis interval is 218 products. The quality cost per product for $n* = 218$ is given by Eq. 7.14:

$$L = \frac{7}{218} + \frac{219}{2} \times \frac{6}{20{,}000} + \frac{2420}{20{,}000} + \frac{1 \times 6}{20{,}000} = \$0.19 \qquad (7.14)$$

TABLE 7.2
Parameters of the injection molding process

Type of adjustment required	Average interruption time	Direct adjustment cost	Number of units between adjustments	Total adjustment cost
1. Reset of mold	5 min	$6	$\bar{u}_1 = 2500$	$C_1 = 4 \times 5 + 6$ $= \$26$
2. Repair or replacement of mold	8 hr	$500	$\bar{u}_2 = 20{,}000$	$C_2 = 4 \times 480 + 500$ $= \$2420$

The adjustment cost is the component of Eq. 7.14 that can be most significantly reduced by the introduction of a redundant machine. The total quality cost for each product after the introduction of the spare machine is estimated below.

New process. The annual interest for financing the machine is $30,000. The annual cost of the machine is $10,000. The total annual cost of the redundant machine is $40,000. The increased cost per product incurred as a result of the introduction of the new machine is $40,000/3,000,000 = \$0.013$.

Thus, the introduction of the redundant machine results in a cost increase of $0.013 per product, as well as continuous production of products, because the redundant machine replaces the principal machine whenever the mold requires cleaning or replacement. When the principal machine is down, preparation time for the redundant machine to start production is 5 minutes (that is, the production process is interrupted for 5 minutes). Therefore,

$$C_2 = 4 \times 5 + 500 = \$520 \qquad (7.15)$$

It should be noted that the redundant machine may not necessarily be used to replace the principal machine when type 1 adjustments are performed. (Table 7-2 shows that the time of type 1 adjustment equals 5 minutes, the same amount of time needed to prepare the redundant machine to start production.)

The optimal diagnosis interval is

$$n^* = \sqrt{\frac{2(20,000 + 1) \times 7}{6 - 520/20,000}} \approx 216 \text{ units}$$

The quality cost per product is obtained as

$$L = \frac{7}{216} + \frac{217}{2} \times \frac{6}{20,000} + \frac{520}{20,000} + \frac{1 \times 6}{20,000}$$
$$+ \text{(cost of spare machine per product)}$$

$$= 0.091 + 0.013$$

$$= \$0.104 \qquad (7.16)$$

The introduction of the redundant machine reduces quality cost by $0.086 for each product, or $258,000 per year.

7.3.2 Automatic Diagnosis: Adjustment and Recovery Systems

The total cost of adjustment and recovery as given by Eq. 7.10 can also be reduced by the introduction of automated diagnosis-recovery systems. Increasingly, such systems are being widely used in many automated production systems because of their economic viability and flexibility. Presently, there is a large variety of automated diagnosis and adjustment systems available that are capable of sorting defective parts, and controlling and adjusting the production process.

Typical applications of automatic inspection and process control systems are similar to those described below. After each production process, an automatic inspection and diagnosis device inspects dimensional and electrical characteristics of the product, and then takes the following action:

1. Control of process: If the value of inspected characteristics deviates from the nominal by the control limit, the control factor level of objective characteristics is changed automatically to ensure that the next unit will be near to nominal.

2. Automatic stoppage: If the actions described above are followed and if the next product is found defective, that is, out of specification limit, the automatic inspection device stops the production process and calls for operator attention.

Recent developments in computer technology, artificial intelligence, and expert systems have resulted in the introduction of advanced diagnosis and adjustment systems capable of diagnosing the causes of defective products and isolating the sources of the problems. In addition, such systems are capable of instituting necessary adjustment and recovery procedures so that the production process is minimally interrupted. The following example illustrates the economic justification for the introduction of automatic diagnosis-adjustment and recovery systems in a production line.

Example 7.8. Assume that it is technically feasible to use an automatic diagnosis-adjustment system for a production process. The cost of such a system is Q, and its annual operating cost is $0.5Q$. The parameters of the current diagnosis-adjustment system are

$$A = \$50$$

$$B = \$160$$

$$C = \$2000$$

$$\bar{u} = 5250 \text{ products}$$

$$l = 30 \text{ products}$$

$$n = 184 \text{ products}$$

$$\text{Annual production} = 504{,}000 \text{ products}$$

What must the cost of the diagnosis-adjustment system be, to make it profitable to introduce it into the production process?

Solution. The cost of quality per unit before the introduction of the automatic diagnosis-adjustment system is

$$L = \frac{160}{184} + \frac{185}{2} \times \frac{50}{5250} + \frac{2000}{5250} + \frac{30 \times 50}{5250}$$

$$= \$2.42 \tag{7.17}$$

The annual cost of the automatic-adjustment system per unit is given by:

$$\frac{0.5Q}{504{,}000} \tag{7.18}$$

Assume that this automatic system continuously diagnoses the unit, and that once a defective unit is found, it adjusts the production process so that the characteristics of the ensuing units are within their specified limits (the time lag is zero). The cost of quality incurred by the introduction of the automatic adjustment system becomes

$$L = \frac{0.5Q}{504,000} + \frac{1 + 1}{2} \times \frac{50}{5250}$$

$$= \frac{0.5Q}{504,000} + 0.01 \qquad (7.19)$$

It is economically feasible to introduce the automatic diagnosis-adjustment system when L in Eq. 7.19 is less than or equal to \$2.42. That is,

$$\frac{0.5Q}{504,000} + 0.01 \leq 2.42$$

or $$Q \leq \$2,429,280 \qquad (7.20)$$

It has been assumed so far that the automatic diagnosis-adjustment system has no time lag and that the automatic system itself has no failures or adjustments. Consider a case where the automatic system finds a defective unit, stops the production process, and makes an adjustment with a time lag of 50 units. In effect, defective units would not be produced; rather, the production process would be interrupted for a production period equal to 50 units.

Consider an automatic diagnosis-adjustment system that costs \$2,000,000 and has a time lag of 1 unit. The cost of quality per unit is obtained by substituting the process parameters in Eq. 7.1.

$$L = \frac{0.5 \times 2,000,000}{504,000} + \frac{1 + 1}{2} \times \frac{50}{5250} + \frac{1 \times 50}{5250}$$

$$= \$2.00$$

A saving of \$0.42 per unit, or \$211,680 per year, is realized.

7.4 SUMMARY

This chapter examined methods for improving product quality during production. Methods for improvement of production processes included periodic tool changes, automatic diagnosis and recovery of the production process, process diagnosis improvement, and the scrap and disposition of defective products. Employing any of these methods separately, or in combination, causes significant improvements in the quality of products. Obviously, the cost of employing any of the methods presented must be considered economically in terms of the increased improvement in product quality. Numerous examples were cited to evaluate the economic consequences of introducing the methods mentioned above.

PROBLEMS

7.1 A production line produces 1000 printed circuit boards (PCBs) per day. Inspection of the boards is conducted after the last production process. If a board is found defective, it is scrapped at a cost of $50 per unit. The process is diagnosed once every 200 units of production at a cost of $100 (this cost includes diagnosis, review, and evaluation of the process). In addition, the diagnosis procedure requires 10 minutes.

If diagnosis determines that the production systems or machines require adjustment, it is immediately performed at a direct cost of $100 per adjustment. The average number of PCBs produced between successive adjustments is 6000 units.

(a) What is the current quality cost per unit?

(b) What will the quality cost per unit be if the diagnosis interval is optimized?

7.2 An injection molding machine is diagnosed at every 100-shot interval (12 products are produced in every shot). The number of units produced per day is 800 shots (250 working days per year). Diagnosis cost B is $2, and the time lag l is 2 shots. The loss per defective unit, A, is $6, and the average number of shots produced between successive adjustments is 4000.

(a) Find the optimal diagnosis interval. What are the annual savings because of the adoption of the optimal interval?

(b) Assume that it takes 5 minutes for each diagnosis and 30 minutes for adjustment. What are the staff-hours required for the following quality control systems? (i) Existing system; and (ii) quality control system when using only the optimal diagnosis interval.

7.3 Suppose the parameters of the diagnosis-adjustment system for a production process are $A = \$8$, $B = \$1.5$, $C = 120$, $\bar{u} = 6000$ units of production, $l = 2$ units. The distribution of the number of units produced before failure, for the last 50 process failures, is shown below:

Number of units produced	0–1000	1001–2000	2001–3000	3001–4000	4001–5000	5001–6000
Number of occurrences	1	2	3	5	6	33

Currently, the diagnosis is performed immediately after the injection process. It can also be performed at the assembly process, and the parameters for this case are $A_0 = \$10$, $B_0 = \$0$, $C_0 = C = \$120$, $\bar{u}_0 = \bar{u} = 6000$ units, and $l_0 = 1200$ units. A periodic tool change can be implemented at a cost of $C' = 100$, with any of the replacement intervals $u' = 1000, 2000, 3000, 4000$, or 5000.

Design quality control systems with the following combinations:

(a) present diagnosis system without tool changes

(b) new diagnosis system with periodic tool changes, using $u' = 1000$, $u' = 2000$, $u' = 3000$, $u' = 4000$, and $u' = 5000$

(c) new diagnosis system without tool changes

(d) new diagnosis system with tool changes as in (b)

Compare the quality control systems in (a), (b), (c), and (d).

7.4 A manufacturer of LVDTs (linear variable differential transducers), used for the inspection of linear dimensions of products, inspects the transducers at the final stage of production. If a transducer is found defective, it is discarded at a cost of $25. The parameters of the production process are

$$B = \$3$$

$$C = \$500$$

$$\bar{u} = 800 \text{ units}$$

$$l = 20 \text{ units}$$

(a) What is the optimal diagnosis interval of the process? What is the quality cost per unit?

(b) In order to minimize the cost of defective units, the quality control department recommended that a check should be made at the third production process. Implementation of this recommendation would reduce the cost of a defective unit to $10. In addition, the present method of inspection should be upgraded at an increased cost of $4 per unit. Determine the cost of quality per unit if these recommendations were implemented. (Annual production is 10,000 units.)

7.5 A manufacturer of light bulbs uses an accelerated life test to determine the average life of the bulbs. The light bulbs are tested at the final production stage with inspection costs of $10 per bulb. (Because of the destructive nature of the test, only samples of the bulbs are subjected to the accelerated life test.) If the average life of bulbs in a sample is less than 750 hours, the production process is interrupted for adjustments for a duration of 90 minutes. The direct cost of adjustment is $50, and the cost of interrupting production is $20 per minute.

The checking process can be improved by using an electron microscope capable of detecting 80 percent of the defects in a bulb filament, at a cost of $0.70 per unit. The following costs are associated with the checking process:

Inspection process	A	l	$\bar{u}$
Accelerated life test	$1/sample	200	2500
Electron microscope	$1/unit	10	—

Assume that annual production is 2,000,000 units. Is it economical to introduce the new inspection and diagnosis process?

7.6 The parameters of a stamping process are as follows:

$$A = \$12$$

$$B = \$2$$

$$C = C_r t + C_d = \$2 \times 180(\text{minutes}) + \$60$$

$$\bar{u} = 5000 \text{ units}$$

$$l = 10 \text{ units}$$

(a) Find the optimal diagnosis interval, and obtain the quality cost per year, assuming a yearly production of 300,000 units.

(b) What are the savings (if any) in quality cost per year if a redundant stamping machine with operating cost of $150,000 per year is acquired, and the interruption time of the production process is reduced to 2 minutes instead of 180 minutes?

7.7 A producer of fiber optic filaments to be used for optical transmission of communications signals, television programs, and telephone calls developed an inspection system for the filaments. The fiber optic filament consists of a single filament of glass drawn to 1 mm in diameter and 3000 ft in length. Maintaining a consistent diameter over 3000 feet is difficult with the filament constantly in motion, making physical-contact measuring methods impossible to use.

    The producer uses a 2-mW laser, scans the laser beam across the moving fiber optic filament, and focuses the reflected laser light into a photo receiver. Any change in the filament diameter can be detected by comparing the signal of the photo receiver with data stored in a comparator. Any increase in diameter will cause a draw motor control impulse to increase the speed of the draw; if there is a decrease in diameter, the processed signal provides a draw motor signal to reduce the speed of the draw. The diameter of the filament is continuously measured. If it is found to be out of the 1 ± 0.05 mm specification, a control system adjusts the speed of the draw motor. However, there is a 1-minute delay, causing a loss of $8.00. The control system is adjusted every 4 hours at a cost of $73.00. The cost of inspection is $5.00 per 1000 feet. Assuming that the production rate is 10,000 feet per hour, calculate the quality loss per unit of production (1 foot).

    In order to increase the production rate of the system, the manufacturer intends to introduce a new inspection system. The cost of the new inspection system is $80,000, and the average time between adjustments is 6.5 hours. However, the inspection cost is $3.00 higher than that of the current system. As a result of the introduction of the new system, the production rate would be 20,000 feet per hour. What are the optimal parameters of the new system? Compare the quality losses for both current and new systems.

7.8 An assembly plant for light and heavy truck axles requires accurate torque on 20,000 bolts per day. Every torque on an axle requires a precise torque value. Application of excess torque results in teeth stripping of the bolt thread, and insufficient torque results in bolt loosening and axle disassembly.

    The operator uses a tool to apply the required torque. The tool is periodically calibrated in order to ensure the quality of the torquing operation. The required torque specification for every bolt is 1200 ± 20 lb · ft. The bolt-tightening operation is continuously monitored. When the torque limits are exceeded (by insufficient torque or excessive torque), the axle is diverted to another assembly station for adjustments at a cost of $10 per axle. The torque monitoring system has an accuracy of ± 10 lb · ft. This may cause the diversion of axles having torque within specification limits to the adjustment station. Also, it may not divert axles that have torque values outside the specification limits. However, the monitoring system is always calibrated to ensure that the probability of not diverting axles with proper torque is 0.999.

    The two processes under study are the torque application process and the monitoring process. If an axle is shipped without having proper torque, it causes a $300 loss. Every 500 bolts, the tool is calibrated at a $5 cost. The cost of calibrating the monitoring system every 2000 bolts is $100. An axle has approximately 50 bolts.

    Determine the tolerance limits for the torque to ensure that no axle is shipped without having the proper torque applied to its bolts. Suggest methods to improve the current system. Compare the performance of the improved systems with the current one.

7.9 Microfinishing, the final operation before assembly on crankshafts, camshafts, and plain bearing journals, achieves surface finishes of 2 μin. The microfinishing process uses a noncompressible, film-backed abrasive that is held in a precision-machined toolholder. The toolholder consists of two halves that conform to the shape of the workpiece, which is held between centers, rotated, and oscillated. The parameters of the process are the following: contact pressure between the toolholder and the workpiece, rpm (revolutions per minute) of the workpiece, degree of oscillation, and heat generated by friction between the toolholder and the workpiece.

It is extremely important to keep tight control on the part's dimensions. This is achieved by measuring, before finishing, the part's dimensions and temperature. The system's in-process controller uses this information to determine the amount of material to be removed and to bring the part within size tolerance. Temperature is measured because during processing, friction generates heat, affecting the size of the part. The data obtained during gauging are fed back to the controller, which constantly compares it with the required size. Once the correct size is reached, the tool is automatically released.

A manufacturer uses the microfinishing process to achieve diameters of plain journal bearings with tolerances of ± 0.004 in. Two critical factors have direct impact on the quality of the process (quality is measured by the percentage of bearings having diameters within the specified tolerance). These factors are temperature between the bearings and the toolholder, and the holding pressure of the workpiece. The temperature is kept at 30°C, with the pressure at 100 lb/in^2. A 1°C change in the temperature results in a 0.0001-in change in the bearing diameter. A 5-lb/in^2 change in the pressure will result in a 0.0002-in change in the diameter. The temperature is controlled by adjusting the amount of the coolant; the pressure is controlled by adjusting the distance between the two halves of the workpiece.

Delays exist from the moment gauging takes place until the required parameter is changed. Because of the demand requirements, each bearing spends 10 minutes in the microfinishing process. Afterwards, its diameter is measured. If it is found that the diameter is smaller than the lower specification limit, the bearing is discarded at a loss of $175. However, if the diameter is greater than the upper specification limit, the bearing is reworked at a cost of $25. The controller is checked after the production of 200 bearings at a cost of $110. The costs for temperature and pressure adjustments are $10 and $15, respectively. Four sets of bearing tolerance measurements are taken after the microfinishing process and are as follows:

Set 1:
Temperature = 30.5°C
Pressure = 103 psi
Bearing tolerances:

+0.0001	−0.0003	+0.0004	−0.0003
−0.0002	+0.0004	+0.0002	+0.0001
−0.0003	−0.0005	+0.0003	+0.0006
+0.0001	+0.0001	−0.0001	−0.0004
−0.0003	+0.0002	+0.0004	−0.0005

Set 2:
Temperature = 30.5°C
Pressure = 105 psi
Bearing tolerances:

+0.0002	−0.0004	+0.0003	−0.0004
+0.0001	+0.0005	+0.0005	+0.0002
+0.0004	−0.0003	−0.0003	−0.0005
+0.0005	−0.0002	+0.0006	−0.0004
+0.0004	−0.0001	+0.0003	+0.0003

Set 3:
Temperature = 31°C
Pressure = 104 psi
Bearing Tolerances:

+0.0003	−0.0001	−0.0006	+0.0002
−0.0005	+0.0003	−0.0004	−0.0001
−0.0004	+0.0005	+0.0005	−0.0003
+0.0006	−0.0004	+0.0003	+0.0001
−0.0003	+0.0002	−0.0004	−0.0005

Set 4:
Temperature = 29.5°C
Pressure = 104 psi
Bearing tolerances:

+0.0002	−0.0003	+0.0003	−0.0003
+0.0002	+0.0002	+0.0001	−0.0002
+0.0001	+0.0001	−0.0001	+0.0004
−0.0003	−0.0004	−0.0002	+0.0001
+0.0001	+0.0001	−0.0004	−0.0005

Determine the controller's optimal adjustment intervals for both temperature and pressure. If the two adjustment intervals are different, can you replace them by one interval? If so, what are the quality losses per bearing?

7.10 A military ammunition plant produces hand grenades. The quality control system for the grenades involves inspecting grenade caps and testing parts for dimensional accuracy and cracks. The dimensional accuracy of the parts is checked by using linear variable differential transducers (LVDTs). As soon as the grenade body arrives at the inspection station, the LVDTs move from their reference positions to touch the part. The amount of travel is electronically compared to preprogrammed limits in the microprocessor. All LVDTs return to their reference positions after each measurement is taken. Sensors detect an LVDT's failure to return to its reference position, indicating that the tolerances of the dimension being measured have exceeded their limits.

After the check for dimensional accuracy, the cap is inspected for proper installation. If a cap is missing or improperly installed, a limit switch is tripped, which in turn directs the grenade to a reject conveyor. The final inspection of the grenade involves the detection of cracks in the grenade's shell. This is done in the following way: After the grenade is positioned it is spun $360°$ in proximity to a pair of eddy-current crack transducers. If a crack exists, indicating a defective grenade, the transducers detect the eddy currents. Cracked grenades are automatically transferred to an eject conveyor.

Thus, the inspection station for the grenade conducts three types of inspections: dimension accuracy, which is a variable case; proper installation of the cap, which is an attribute case; and crack existence, which is also an attribute case. The parameters of these processes are as follows:

Dimensions accuracy:

$$l = 3 \text{ parts}$$
$$A = \$18.00$$
$$B = \$1.00$$
$$\bar{u} = 100 \text{ parts}$$
$$\text{Tolerance of the dimensions} = \pm0.002 \text{ in}$$
$$C = \$25.00$$

Cap installation:

$$l = 2 \text{ parts}$$
$$A = \$25.00$$
$$B = \$0.50$$
$$\bar{u} = 200 \text{ parts}$$
$$C = \$40.00$$

Crack detection:

$$l = 5 \text{ parts}$$
$$A = \$29.00$$
$$B = \$3.00$$
$$C = \$20.00$$
$$\bar{u} = 80 \text{ parts}$$

What are the optimal parameters of the inspection system for each of the above characteristics?

Given the following information for a new system capable of all the functions of the three current systems, what are the optimal parameters of the new system?

$$l = 1$$
$$A = \$26.00$$
$$B = \$4.00$$
$$C = \$80.00$$

Compare the new system with the existing ones.

REFERENCES

Berry, S. A. "Techniques in the Application of Computers to Industrial Monitoring." In *CAD/CAM and the Computer Revolution*, Society of Manufacturing Engineers, 1974, pp. 221–239.

Besterfield, D. H. *Quality Control*. Englewood Cliffs, NJ: Prentice-Hall, 1979.

Death, M. "Sensors: Keys to Automation." *Manufacturing Engineering*, June 1986, pp. 53–57.

Farago, F. T. *Handbook of Dimensional Measurement*. New York: Industrial Press, 1982.

Feigenbaum, A. V. *Total Quality Control*. New York: McGraw-Hill, 1983.

Kirkpatrick, E. G. *Quality Control for Managers and Engineers*. New York: John Wiley and Sons, 1970.

Peters, M. H., and W. W. Williams. "Location of Quality Inspection Stations, an Experimental Assessment of Five Normative Heuristics." *Decision Sciences*, vol. 15, 1984, pp. 389–408.

Pryor, T. R., and W. North, eds. *Applying Automated Inspection*. Dearborn, MI: Society of Manufacturing Engineering, 1985.

Stout, K. *Quality Control in Automation*. Englewood Cliffs, NJ: Prentice-Hall, 1985.

Taguchi, G. *On-line Quality Control during Production*. Tokyo: Japanese Standards Association, 1981.

CHAPTER 8

INTRODUCTION
TO PREVENTIVE
MAINTENANCE

In Chaps. 4 through 7, we discussed on-line real-time quality control systems during production. We also showed that there are many factors that affect the quality of products during production. One of these factors is the production machine itself. The production machine's accuracy and breakdown rate may directly affect product quality. From the viewpoint of the machine producer, a poorly functioning machine has a quality problem.

Similarly, in a communication system where the quality level of information, measured by the signal-to-noise ratio, is poor, an on-line quality control system may be required. There is no great conceptual difference in the quality control systems applied to communication and production systems.

In this chapter, the effect of preventive maintenance on the product characteristics is discussed, and optimal preventive maintenance schedules that minimize the quality loss per unit of production are introduced. Relationships between tolerances of the product characteristics and optimal preventive maintenance schedules are also introduced.

Preventive maintenance involves repairs, replacement, and maintenance of equipment and products before their failures in order to avoid unexpected failures during their use. The objective of preventive maintenance is to minimize the downtime of equipment. However, excessive preventive maintenance results in unnecessary repair and maintenance costs. Therefore, an optimal preventive maintenance schedule exists that minimizes the total cost of repair and downtime of equipment.

Preventive maintenance as it affects on-line quality control systems may involve two areas of applications. The first is the quality control of characteristics of the products. The second is the reduction of the expected failures of the machine during the production operation. A machine may fail in that it is not able to produce products that meet the quality requirements. A machine failure may also be a sudden breakdown of the machine during operation. Failures of either type can be reduced by employing preventive maintenance schedules. This chapter focuses on the development of preventive maintenance schedules for the first type of machine failures. Preventive maintenance schedules for the second type are discussed in detail in the reliability, replacements, and maintenance literature (e.g., Jardine, 1973).

The purpose of the following discussion is to develop a relationship between functional limit values and the average time consumed before a production process produces products having deviations equal to the upper or lower functional limits.

Assume that the loss due to a product failure (when deviations of the product characteristics are greater than the functional limits) is proportional to the amount of downtime of the process.

Let t = average amount of downtime

   P = loss due to product failure per unit of time

   c = repair cost of the process

   u = average time between product failures (mean time between failures, MTBF)

The total loss per failure, C^*, is

$$C^* = Pt + c \qquad (8.1)$$

The total loss of product failure per unit time, assuming there is no preventive maintenance, is

$$L = \frac{C^*}{u^*} \qquad (8.2)$$

where u^* is the long-term average time between product failures.

As presented in Chap. 3, there are two cases of product deviations from the target value. First, the deviations (drifts) can be on both sides of the target value. Second, the deviations can only be on one side of the target value, such as the wear of mechanical parts.

In the first case, we can use a random walk model as an approximation to determine the average time to reach the upper or lower limit of a product characteristic, at which point failure will occur. When using the random walk model, the average time u^* is assumed to be proportional to the square of distance between the target value and the upper or lower limits (the functional limit, Δ^*, is equal for both upper and lower limits of the target value). Thus, u^* is

$$u^* = \lambda(\Delta^*)^2 \tag{8.3}$$

where λ is the constant of proportionality, determined by observing the average time u_0 to reach a predetermined deviation Δ_0. Thus, the value of u^* can be obtained using Eq. 8.3 as follows:

$$u^* = u_0 \frac{(\Delta^*)^2}{\Delta_0^2} \tag{8.4}$$

In the second case, where the average time to reach the functional limit Δ^* is proportional to the amount of deviation from the target value, u^* is

$$u^* = u_0 \frac{\Delta^*}{\Delta_0} \tag{8.5}$$

In the following sections, we discuss the use of preventive maintenance schedules in reducing the loss caused by the deviations in product characteristics from the target values. Maintenance schedules will be determined for products when deviations occur on one or both sides of the target values.

8.1 PREVENTIVE MAINTENANCE SCHEDULES: DEVIATIONS ON BOTH SIDES OF TARGET VALUES

In this section, we consider the occurrence of deviations on both sides of the target values. The preventive maintenance schedules discussed below apply when a product experiences deviations caused by extended use of the operations. The schedules also apply when the parameters of a production machine deviate from their target values, thus causing deviations in quality characteristics of the products being produced. The preventive maintenance schedules that will be discussed below are based on the rule: *Perform preventive maintenance when the amount of deviation in the product characteristic being monitored reaches Δ.* We define the following parameters:

$\Delta^* =$ functional limit of a product or of a parameter of the production machine

$C^* =$ loss per failure due to deviations greater than Δ^*

$u^* =$ average time between product (or machine) failures when no preventive maintenance is performed

$n =$ checking interval (to check the amount of deviation)

$B =$ checking cost

$\Delta =$ preventive maintenance limit (the amount of deviation or drift at which preventive maintenance should be performed)

C = preventive maintenance cost

u = average preventive maintenance interval

l = time lag of the production process, if any

n_0 = current (or initial) checking interval

Δ_0 = current (or initial) maintenance limit

u_0 = current average preventive maintenance interval

Following the derivation of Eq. 4.12, we derive the loss function of the current maintenance schedule as follows:

$$L_0 = \frac{B}{n_0} + \frac{C}{u_0} + \frac{C^*}{u^*} \times \frac{1}{(\Delta^*)^2}\left[\frac{\Delta^2}{3} + \left(\frac{n}{2} + l\right)\frac{\Delta^2}{u}\right] \qquad (8.6)$$

The first two terms of the above equation are straightforward. The third term represents the loss caused by the use of the current preventive maintenance schedule and is derived in the following way:

Assume that the time required for the parameter of the production process to reach Δ is proportional to the squared distance from the target value, and that the time required to reach the maintenance limit is

$$u_0\frac{\Delta^2}{\Delta_0^2}$$

We also assume that the parameter of the production machine being measured follows a uniform distribution within the range $\pm\Delta$. No preventive maintenance is done as long as the value of the parameter is within this range. The mean squared deviation of the parameter of the production machine within $\pm\Delta$ is

$$\frac{[(m + \Delta) - (m - \Delta)]^2}{12} = \frac{\Delta^2}{3} \qquad (8.7)$$

Since the parameter of the production machine is checked at intervals of n units of time, then the average time the parameter is outside the control limit Δ is $n/2$. When the time lag l is considered (not negligible), then the average time the parameter is outside the maintenance limit Δ is $(n/2 + l)$. So, the mean squared deviation becomes

$$\frac{\Delta^2}{3} + \left(\frac{n}{2} + l\right)\frac{\Delta^2}{u} \qquad (8.8)$$

When Δ in Eq. 8.8 becomes Δ^*, failures will occur at intervals of u^*, causing a loss C^*. Thus, the expected loss as a result of preventive maintenance (using a checking interval n and a preventive maintenance limit Δ) is

$$\frac{C^*}{u^*} \times \frac{1}{(\Delta^*)^2}\left[\frac{\Delta^2}{3} + \left(\frac{n}{2} + l\right)\frac{\Delta^2}{u}\right] \qquad (8.9)$$

The following example illustrates how the checking interval, the loss function, and the optimal preventive maintenance interval are determined for a microwave transmission system.

Example 8.1. A microwave transmission system is checked once every three months. The system consists of five smaller systems, and a sixth one, to be used when one of the five primary systems fails. Average repair frequency of the system is once a year, with an average repair time of 3 hours. During repair, another system may fail, causing a transmission failure and a loss of $P' = 5600$ (channels per system) $\times$ \$1.5. The transmission failure rate is one failure per minute. So the expected loss P when failure lasts for 1 hour is

$$P = 5600 \times \$1.5 \times 0.25(\text{working ratio}) \times 60(\text{min}) \times \frac{5}{365 \times 24}$$

$$= \$71.9 \tag{8.10}$$

The cost of checking a system is \$60. The current control (maintenance) limit is 39.5 dBm (decibel margin) against functional failure limit 12.6 dBm. Maintenance cost is \$220, and the average maintenance interval observed is once a year. Determine the optimal checking interval n and optimal limit D, assuming that the parameters of system are

$$\Delta^2 = 12.6 \text{ dBm} = 10^{1.26} = 18.2$$

$$P = \$71.9$$

$$B = \$60$$

$$C = \$220$$

$$D_0^2 = 39.5 \text{ dBm} = 10^{3.95} = 8913$$

$$n_0 = 90 \text{ days} \times 24 \text{ hr/day} = 2160 \text{ hr}$$

$$u_0 = 365 \text{ days} \times 24 \text{ hr/day} = 8760 \text{ hr}$$

Solution. Since the principle "the larger the margin, the better the system" applies here, the the current loss function is

$$L = \frac{B}{n_0} + \frac{C}{u_0} + P\Delta^2 \left(\frac{1}{3D_0^2} + \frac{n_0 + 1}{2} \times \frac{1}{u_0 D_0^2} \right)$$

$$= \frac{60}{2160} + \frac{220}{8760} + 71.9 \times 18.2 \left(\frac{1}{3 \times 8913} + \frac{2161}{2} \times \frac{1}{8760 \times 8913} \right)$$

$$= 0.028 + 0.025 + 0.049 + 0.018$$

$$= \$0.120 \tag{8.11}$$

This represents quality loss per hour. When there are 1500 stations, each having 15 channels, total loss per year becomes

$$\$0.120 \times 24 \times 365 \times 15 \times 1500 = \$23.7 \text{ million}$$

The optimal checking interval n and optimal maintenance limit D are

$$n = \sqrt{\frac{2u_0 B}{P} \times \frac{D_0^2}{\Delta^2}}$$

$$= \sqrt{\frac{2 \times 8760 \times 60 \times 8913}{71.9 \times 18.2}}$$

$$= 2678 \rightarrow \text{once in four months} \qquad (8.12)$$

$$D_2 = \left(\frac{P}{3C} \times u_0 \times D_0^2 \times \Delta^2 \right)^{1/2}$$

$$= \left(\frac{71.9}{3 \times 220} \times 8760 \times 8193 \times 18.2 \right)^{1/2}$$

$$= 11{,}926 \rightarrow 40.8 \text{ dBm} \qquad (8.13)$$

The loss function for optimal maintenance system, L, is then

$$L = \frac{B}{n} + \frac{C}{u} + P\Delta^2 \left(\frac{1}{3D^2} + \frac{n+1}{2} \times \frac{1}{uD^2} \right) \qquad (8.14)$$

and using
$$u = u_0 \times \frac{D_0^2}{D^2}$$

$$= 8760 \times \frac{8913}{11926}$$

$$= 6547 \text{ hr} \qquad (8.15)$$

the following is obtained:

$$L = \frac{60}{120 \times 24} + \frac{220}{6547} + 71.9 \times 18.2 \left(\frac{1}{3 \times 12{,}022} + \frac{2881}{2} \times \frac{1}{6547 \times 12{,}022} \right)$$

$$= 0.021 + 0.034 + 0.036 + 0.024$$

$$= 0.115 \qquad (8.16)$$

The improvement $0.005 is not much, nor is the current maintenance system near optimal. However, the yearly gain is expected to be

$$0.005 \times 365 \times 24 \times 15 \times 1500 = \$985{,}500$$

Example 8.2. Assume that the temperature of the cooling water in an atomic power station causes a major failure when it deviates from the nominal value by as much as 150°C, and that the corresponding loss is $30 million. The current control limit Δ_0 is 20°C, and the average maintenance interval u_0 is once every 15 days (360 hours). The temperature is checked once every 8 hours at a cost of $6. The average preventive maintenance cost for adjusting the control system is $400. The effect of time lag is almost nil. Calculate the total loss of the current system.

Solution. The predicted average time between failures (assuming there is no preventive maintenance) is obtained by using Eq. 8.4.

$$u^* = u_0 \times \frac{(\Delta^*)^2}{\Delta_0^2}$$

$$= 360 \times \frac{150^2}{20^2}$$

$$= 20,250 \text{ hr}$$

The parameters for Eq. 8.6 are

$$B = \$6$$

$$n_0 = 8 \text{ hr}$$

$$C = \$400$$

$$u_0 = 360 \text{ hr}$$

$$C^* = \$30,000,000$$

$$u^* = 20,250 \text{ hr}$$

$$\Delta^* = 150°C$$

$$l = 0$$

Substituting the above values in Eq. 8.6, we obtain the following total loss per hour.

$$L_0 = \frac{B}{n_0} + \frac{C}{u_0} + \frac{C^*}{u^*} \times \frac{1}{(\Delta^*)^2}\left[\frac{\Delta_0^2}{3} + \left(\frac{n_0}{2} + l\right)\frac{\Delta_0^2}{u_0}\right]$$

$$= \frac{6}{8} + \frac{400}{360} + \frac{30,000,000}{20,250} \times \frac{1}{(150)^2}\left[\frac{20^2}{3} + \left(\frac{8}{2} + 0\right)\frac{20^2}{360}\right]$$

$$= 0.75 + 1.11 + 8.78 + 0.29$$

$$= \$10.93 \tag{8.17}$$

It is apparent in the above loss function that the first term is greater than the fourth term, indicating that more checking is being performed than what optimally should be. Also, the second term is much smaller than the third, implying that narrower maintenance limits should be used. The optimal checking interval and the optimal maintenance limit are obtained as follows:

Following Eq. 8.6, the loss function expression is given below.

$$L = \frac{B}{n} + \frac{\Delta_0^2 C}{u_0 \Delta^2} + \frac{C^*}{u^*} \times \frac{1}{(\Delta^*)^2}\left[\frac{\Delta^2}{3} + \left(\frac{n}{2} + l\right)\frac{\Delta_0^2}{u_0}\right] \tag{8.18}$$

The optimal n and Δ can be obtained by taking the partial derivatives of Eq. 8.18 with respect to n and Δ, and equating the results to zero. Thus,

$$\frac{\partial L}{\partial n} = -\frac{B}{n^2} + \frac{C^*}{u^*} \times \frac{1}{(\Delta^*)^2} \times \frac{(\Delta^*)^2}{2u^*} = 0$$

whence
$$n = u^* \sqrt{\frac{2B}{C^*}} \qquad (8.19)$$

and
$$\frac{\partial L}{\partial \Delta} = \frac{2(\Delta^*)^2 C}{u^* \Delta^3} + \frac{C^*}{u^*} \times \frac{1}{(\Delta^*)^2} \times \frac{2}{3}\Delta = 0$$

giving
$$\Delta = \Delta^* \left(\frac{3C}{C^*}\right)^{1/4} \qquad (8.20)$$

Example 8.3. What are the optimal checking interval and preventive maintenance limit of the control system described in Example 8.2?

Solution. Using the parameters given in Example 8.2, and Eqs. 8.19 and 8.20, we obtain the optimal checking interval

$$n = u^* \sqrt{\frac{2B}{C^*}}$$

$$= 20{,}250 \sqrt{\frac{2 \times 6}{30{,}000{,}000}}$$

$$\approx 12 \text{ hr (twice per day)}$$

The optimal preventive maintenance interval is

$$\Delta = \Delta^* \left(\frac{3C}{C^*}\right)^{1/4}$$

$$= 150 \left(\frac{3 \times 400}{30{,}000{,}000}\right)^{1/4} \approx 12°C$$

The total loss after the implementation of the optimal checking interval and the optimal preventive maintenance interval is obtained as follows:

$$u = u_0 \times \frac{\Delta^2}{\Delta_0^2}$$

$$= 360 \times \frac{12^2}{20^2} = 129.6$$

and
$$L = \frac{6}{12} + \frac{400}{129.6} + \frac{30{,}000{,}000}{20{,}250} \times \frac{1}{150^2}\left[\frac{12^2}{3} + \left(\frac{12}{2} + 0\right)\frac{12^2}{129.6}\right]$$

$$= 0.5 + 3.09 + 3.16 + 0.44$$

$$L = \$7.19 \qquad (8.21)$$

Annual savings when the optimal checking and preventive maintenance intervals are implemented (assuming there are 6700 hours per year) are

$$(10.93 - 7.19) \times 6700 \approx \$25,000$$

8.2 PREVENTIVE MAINTENANCE SCHEDULES FOR FUNCTIONAL CHARACTERISTICS

In many instances, the tolerance for a functional characteristic of a product is expressed as a percentage of the functional target value. In this situation, the preventive maintenance limit can also be expressed as a percentage of the functional target value, and the optimal preventive maintenance schedules can be determined using the same equations given in the previous section.

Example 8.4. The characteristic y of a unit used in airplanes is immediately checked before every takeoff at a cost B of $2.50. Should the value of y deviate by 60 percent of its nominal value m, the airplane will have a 0.01 probability of a failure that would cost \$180 million. The current maintenance limit is 10-percent of m and the repair (preventive maintenance) cost is \$800, including the loss caused by a delayed takeoff. The average maintenance interval is once every 120 takeoffs, and the average flight time is 6 hours. Time lag between testing and repairing the defective unit is negligible. Determine the optimal checking interval, optimal preventive maintenance limit, and the total loss per unit time.

Solution. The parameters of this system are

Functional limit Δ^*	$\pm 60\% \, m$
Loss due to failure C^*	\$1.8 million
Current control limit Δ_0	10%
Current checking interval n_0	6 hr
Current average maintenance interval u_0	$6 \times 120 = 720$ hr
Checking cost B	\$2.50
Maintenance cost C	\$800
Time lag l	0

The loss of the current preventive maintenance is obtained using Eq. 8.6:

$$L = \frac{B}{n_0} + \frac{C}{u_0} + \frac{C^*}{u^*} \times \frac{1}{(\Delta^*)^2} \left[\frac{\Delta_0^2}{3} + \left(\frac{n_0}{2} + l \right) \frac{\Delta_0^2}{u_0} \right] \tag{8.22}$$

where u^* is the expected mean time to airplane failure when no maintenance is used; u^* can be determined as follows:

(1) When y deviates on both sides of the target value,

$$u^* = u_0 \frac{(\Delta^*)^2}{\Delta_0^2} \tag{8.23}$$

(2)   When y deviates only on one side of m,

$$u^* = u_0 \frac{\Delta^*}{\Delta_0} \tag{8.24}$$

In this example, we assume that deviations occur on both sides of m. Thus,

$$u^* = 720 \times \left(\frac{60}{10}\right)^2$$

$$= 25,920 \text{ hr}$$

Substitution in Eq. 8.22 results in:

$$L = \frac{2.50}{6} + \frac{800}{720} + \frac{1,800,000}{25,920} \times \frac{1}{60^2}\left[\frac{10^2}{3} + \left(\frac{6}{2} + 0\right) \times \frac{10^2}{720}\right]$$

$$= 0.417 + 1.111 + 0.643 + 0.008$$

$$= \$2.179$$

The optimal checking interval n and the optimal control limit Δ are

$$n = u^* \sqrt{\frac{2B}{C^*}}$$

$$= 25,920 \sqrt{\frac{2 \times 2.5}{1,800,000}}$$

$$= 43.2 \text{ (once every 7 flights)}$$

and

$$\Delta = \Delta^* \left(\frac{3C}{C^*}\right)^{1/4}$$

$$= 60\left(\frac{3 \times 800}{1,800,000}\right)^{1/4}$$

$$\approx 12 \ (\%)$$

The total loss corresponding to the optimal maintenance schedule is

$$L = \frac{2.50}{42} + \frac{800}{5184} + \frac{1,800,000}{25,920} \times \frac{1}{60^2}\left[\frac{12^2}{3} + \left(\frac{42}{3} + 0\right) \times \frac{12^2}{5184}\right]$$

$$= 0.059 + 0.154 + 0.926 + 0.008$$

$$= \$1.147$$

Assuming the total number of airplanes is 200, and each airplane makes 600 flights yearly, then the annual savings resulting from the implementation of the optimal preventive schedule are

$$(2.179 - 1.147) \times 600 \times 6 \times 200 = \$743,040$$

When the functional limits of a product characteristic are equal and are expressed as a percentage of the functional target value, the procedure outlined in Example 8.4 can be used to obtain the preventive maintenance schedules for the production machine that produces the unit. On the other hand, when a product's functional limits are not at equal distances from the target value of the product characteristic (e.g., the functional limits are $m + \Delta_1$ and $m - \Delta_2$), two preventive maintenance checking intervals are determined independently for Δ_1 and Δ_2. The preventive maintenance schedule for the production machine is then based on the minimum of the preventive maintenance checking intervals for Δ_1 and Δ_2.

Example 8.5. The internal gear of the planetary reduction gears for a marine medium-speed diesel engine is 3 m in diameter. The gear is produced by a hopping machine with extreme accuracy. Because of noise and wear-out factors, the tolerances of the diameter are $+0.2$ mm and -0.3 mm. The checking interval is 20 hours, and the cost of checking the gear is $300. If the diameter of the gear deviates from the nominal diameter by $+0.2$ or -0.3 mm, the gear may cause failure of the system where it will be placed, resulting in a loss of $200,000 when Δ_1 is exceeded or $300,000 when Δ_2 is exceeded. The current maintenance limit for the hopping machine is ± 0.05 mm, and the repair and adjustment cost is $250. The average maintenance interval is 400 hours. Neglecting the time lag of the checking process, determine the optimal preventive maintenance control limit for the hopping machine and the optimal preventive maintenance schedule.

Solution. The parameters of the system are

Functional limit Δ_1^*	$+0.2$ mm
Functional limit Δ_2^*	-0.3 mm
Loss due to failure when Δ_1^* is exceeded, C_1^*	$200,000
Loss due to failure when Δ_2^* is exceeded, C_2^*	$300,000
Current control limits Δ_0	± 0.05 mm
Current checking interval n_0	20 hr
Checking cost B	$300
Current maintenance interval u_0	400 hr
Maintenance cost C	$250
Time lag l	0

In order to determine the optimal checking interval and the optimal preventive maintenance limit, we first determine the interval and the limit for Δ_1^* and Δ_2^* independently, as follows:

Preventive maintenance for Δ_1^*:

$$L_1 = \frac{B}{n_0} + \frac{C}{u_0} + \frac{C_1^*}{u_1^*} \frac{1}{(\Delta_1^*)^2} \left[\frac{\Delta_0^2}{3} + \left(\frac{n_0}{2} + l \right) \frac{\Delta_0^2}{u_0} \right]$$

Since the characteristic deviates on one side by Δ_1,

$$u_1^* = u_0 \frac{\Delta_1^*}{\Delta_0}$$

$$u_1^* = 400 \times \frac{0.2}{0.05} = 1800 \text{ hr}$$

$$L_1 = \frac{300}{20} + \frac{250}{400} + \frac{200{,}000}{1600} \times \frac{1}{(0.2)^2} \left[\frac{(0.05)^2}{3} + \left(\frac{20}{2} + 0 \right) \times \frac{(0.05)^2}{400} \right]$$

$$= 15.62 + 2.78$$

$$= \$18.40$$

The optimal checking interval n_1 and the optimal control limit Δ_1 are

$$n_1 = u_1^* \sqrt{\frac{2B}{C_1^*}}$$

$$= 1600 \sqrt{\frac{2 \times 300}{200{,}000}}$$

$$= 87.6 \text{ hr}$$

$$\Delta_1 = \Delta_1^* \left(\frac{3C}{C_1^*} \right)^{1/4}$$

$$= 0.2 \left(\frac{3 \times 250}{200{,}000} \right)^{1/4}$$

$$\Delta_1 = 0.0494 \text{ mm}$$

Preventive maintenance for Δ_2^*:

$$u_2^* = u_0 \frac{\Delta_2^*}{\Delta_0}$$

$$u_2^* = 400 \times \frac{0.3}{0.05} = 2400 \text{ hr}$$

The loss for the current control system is

$$L_2 = \frac{300}{20} + \frac{250}{400} + \frac{300{,}000}{2400} \times \frac{1}{(0.3)^2} \left[\frac{(0.05)^2}{3} + \left(\frac{20}{2} + 0 \right) \times \frac{(0.05)^2}{400} \right]$$

$$= 15.62 + 1.24$$

$$= \$16.86$$

The optimal checking interval n_2 and the optimal control limit Δ_2 are

$$n_2 = u_2^* \sqrt{\frac{2B}{C_2^*}}$$

$$= 2400 \sqrt{\frac{2 \times 300}{300{,}000}}$$

$$= 107.3 \text{ hr}$$

and
$$\Delta_2 = \Delta_2^* \left(\frac{3C}{C_2^*} \right)^{1/4}$$

$$= 0.3 \left(\frac{3 \times 250}{300,000} \right)^{1/4}$$

$$= 0.067$$

The optimal control limit for the hopping machine is ± 0.0494 mm, and the optimal preventive maintenance interval is $\min\{87.6, 107.3\} = 87.6$ hours.

8.3 PREVENTIVE MAINTENANCE SCHEDULES FOR LARGE SCALE SYSTEMS

In this section, we shall develop preventive maintenance schedules for large-scale systems, such as telephone communication networks, power transmission lines, and manufacturing systems. Consider, for example, the case where a preventive maintenance schedule is to be developed for electric power lines used for pantographs (devices for transferring current from an overhead wire to a vehicle, usually consisting of two parallel, hinged, double-diamond frames). This electric power wire is subject to wear. If the wear is even all over the wire, then only periodic replacements are needed for the wire. However, due to many external factors, such as temperature change from one location to another, and from time to time, the wear rate is nonuniform over the wire length. Therefore, periodic checking of the wire is needed in conjunction with a preventive maintenance schedule, which is developed as follows.

Suppose that the optimal periodic maintenance interval is found to be 3 years, and that the total loss L' is given by

$$L' = \text{preventive replacement cost} + \text{loss due to wire breakdown} \quad (8.25)$$

Let us also assume that the replacement cost of the total length of 350 miles of electric wire used for a bullet train is $22 million, and the average loss per wire breakage is $2.5 million. The average number of wire failures during a three-year period of operation is

$$\frac{22}{2.5} = 8.8 \quad (8.26)$$

(assuming that maintenance cost and quality loss are balanced at nominal wearing rate). If the actual number of wire failures is one or two during the three-year life period of the wire, it becomes apparent that the wire is "over-designed," and another wire should be used instead.

Assume that the starting thickness of the wire is m and the allowed amount of wear during three years is 30 mm. The average wear rate b is

$$b = \frac{\text{estimated wear during three years}}{\text{total operating hours during three years}}$$

$$b = \frac{30}{3 \times 365 \times 18 \,(\text{hours per day})} = 0.001522 \text{ mm/hr} \qquad (8.27)$$

Let Δ^* be the functional amount of wear; that is, when the value of the thickness y becomes $m - \Delta^*$, wire breakage occurs. The expected wire breakage per mile per hour, N, is

$$N = \frac{8.8}{350 \times 3 \times 365 \times 18} = 0.000001275 \text{ failures/hr} \cdot \text{mi}$$

Thus, the average time between failures (assuming constant failure rate), u^*, is

$$u^* = \frac{1}{N} \approx 784{,}000 \text{ hr}$$

Preventive maintenance is achieved by first checking the wear of the wire at different locations. The following 20 observations of wear (mm) are taken:

0.03	0.20	0.07	0.23	0.06
0.13	0.22	0.01	0.37	0.15
0.20	0.16	0.02	0.14	0.03
0.02	0.07	0.45	0.23	0.24

The mean rate of wear is 0.152 mm, and its standard deviation is 0.120 mm. Because the value of the standard deviation is comparable to the mean, the use of periodic replacements will only result in high quality loss (many failures will occur between replacements).

If the wire is checked once every 18 hours at a cost of $0.5 per mile, preventive maintenance is not done, and periodic maintenance is done at three-year intervals, the loss function for the entire length of the wire (after deleting maintenance terms from Eq. 8.6 and substituting $\Delta^2/u = (\Delta^*)^2/u^*$) becomes

$$L = \frac{B}{n} + \frac{C^*}{u^*}\left(\frac{n}{2} + l\right)\frac{350}{u^*} \qquad (8.28)$$

The minimization of Eq. 8.28 with respect to n yields

$$n = u^* \sqrt{\frac{2B}{350 \times C^*}} \qquad (8.29)$$

or

$$n = 784{,}000 \sqrt{\frac{2 \times 0.5}{350 \times 2{,}500{,}000}}$$

$$= 26$$

Thus, the optimal checking interval is approximately once a day. The loss function of the current checking and maintenance system, L_0, is

$$
\begin{aligned}
L_0 &= \frac{B}{n_0} + \frac{C^*}{u^*}\left(\frac{n_0}{2} + l\right)\frac{350}{u^*} \\
&= \frac{0.5}{18} + \frac{2,500,000}{784,000}\left(\frac{18}{2} + 9\right)\frac{350}{784,000} \\
&= \$0.0278 + 0.0256 \\
&= \$0.0278 + \$0.0256 \\
&= \$0.0533 \text{ per mile}
\end{aligned}
$$

The annual savings resulting from the implementation of the optimal checking interval are nil.

8.4   SUMMARY

This chapter introduced the concept of employing preventive maintenance schedules to improve the quality of products. It also introduced optimal preventive maintenance schedules that minimize the quality loss per unit of production. Relationships were developed between the tolerances of product characteristics and optimal preventive maintenance schedules. Finally, optimal checking schedules for large-scale systems were offered to help minimize total quality loss.

PROBLEMS

8.1 One of the manufacturing processes of printed circuit boards (PCBs) is solder masking, performed by an automatic mask-dispensing machine. This keeps solder out of the areas where hardware is attached. The thickness of the solder mask is critical. If it is too thick, it can crack or seep through the board material into holes that should be open. Thin or uneven application may allow solder to fill the open areas. The nominal value of the solder thickness is 2 mm, and the loss caused by deviation from the nominal value is $120. The current control limit Δ_0 is 1.5 mm, and the average maintenance interval of the mask-dispensing machine is once every 5 days (120 hours). The solder thickness is checked once every 5 hours at a cost of $10, and the average preventive maintenance cost to adjust the machine is $50. Time lag is not considered. What are the optimal checking interval, the preventive maintenance limit, and the loss per unit time? If you were to design a different masking system, what type of parameters would you consider?

8.2 A coordinate-measuring machine (CMM) is used to measure the diameter of gold-coated shafts. The coat thickness is $m \pm 0.02$ in. Assume that the coating process produces coated shafts with diameters within the specification limits; however, the coordinate measuring machine may reject products because of measurement errors. The CMM is checked every 20 hours for the amount of measurement error by measuring a standard gauge block. If the amount of errors is equal to or greater than

0.0001 in, preventive maintenance is performed to eliminate the sources of error. The cost of checking the CMM is $20, and the preventive maintenance cost is $120. The current preventive maintenance limit is 0.00005 in, and the average maintenance interval is 200 hours. Determine the optimal preventive maintenance schedule of the CMM. Define new methods to improve this measuring system.

8.3 A manufacturing facility for electroplating processes uses an independent electric power source, since regulated and filtered power is an important element that contributes to the uniformity of the electroplating process. The electric cables (50 miles long) that provide power for the process are checked for wear once every 90 days. The maximum allowable wear of the cable diameter is 10 mm in a four-year period. The replacement cost of the total cable system is $5 million. Cable failure will result in a loss of $1.9 million. There are 18 operating hours per day. The following 20 observations are taken of the wear (per 100 hours of operations):

0.02	0.03	0.14	0.17	0.10
0.06	0.14	0.07	0.19	0.04
0.09	0.12	0.06	0.17	0.14
0.13	0.14	0.17	0.06	0.15

The cables are checked once every 2 days at a cost of $0.40 per mile. Determine the optimal checking intervals (in hours) and the loss per hour for both current and optimal maintenance policies.

8.4 Solve Prob. 8.2, assuming that the current preventive maintenance limit is 0.0001 in and the average maintenance interval is 250 hours.

8.5 Solve Prob. 8.3, assuming the cost of checking is $0.50 per mile and a cable failure will result in a loss of $3.5 million.

8.6 An optical transmission system is used for transmitting electrical signals via an optical fiber. Its components are an electro-optic transducer as the light transmitter at the beginning of the route, the actual fiber optic transmission route, and the opto-electric transducer as the light receiver at the end of the route. The quality of transmission is affected by the uniformity of the diameter of the optical fiber cable. The nominal value of the diameter is 1 mm, and the loss caused by deviation from the nominal value is $100 per 1000 feet of cable length. The current control limit, Δ_0, is 0.98 mm, and the average maintenance interval of the drawing machine (it draws the cable to the required specifications) is 10 days (24 hours per day). The diameter of the cable is checked once every 4 hours at a cost of $4, and the average time lag of the system is 2 minutes (production rate is 10,000 feet per hour). The cost of machine adjustment is $70.00. What is the preventive maintenance cost for the drawing machine that results in minimal quality losses? What are the optimal parameters of the system such as checking interval, preventive maintenance limit, and the loss per unit time?

8.7 Solve Prob.8.6, assuming a maximum allowable quality loss per unit of $0.10 per foot.

REFERENCES

Berry, S. A. "Techniques in the Application of Computers to Industrial Monitoring." *In CAD/CAM and the Computer Revolution*, Society of Manufacturing Engineers, 1974, pp. 221–239.

Jardine, A. K. S. *Maintenance, Replacement, and Reliability*. New York: John Wiley and Sons, 1973.

"Robotic PCB Masking Gives Fast ROI, Doubles Production." *Manufacturing Engineering*, vol. 98, April 1987, p. 57.

Stout, K. *Quality Control in Automation*. Englewood Cliffs, NJ: Prentice-Hall, 1985.

Taguchi, G. *On-line Quality Control during Production*. Tokyo: Japanese Standards Association, 1981.

A

AREAS
UNDER
THE
NORMAL
CURVE

Proportion of the total area under the curve that is under the portion from $-\infty$ to $(X_i - \overline{X}')/\sigma'$. ($X_i$ represents any desired value of the variable X.)

$\dfrac{X_i - \overline{X}'}{\sigma'}$	0.00	0.01	0.02	0.03	0.04	0.05	0.06	0.07	0.08	0.09
-3.5	0.00023	0.00022	0.00022	0.00021	0.00020	0.00019	0.00019	0.00018	0.00017	0.00017
-3.4	0.00034	0.00033	0.00031	0.00030	0.00029	0.00028	0.00027	0.00026	0.00025	0.00024
-3.3	0.00048	0.00047	0.00045	0.00043	0.00042	0.00040	0.00039	0.00038	0.00036	0.00035
-3.2	0.00069	0.00066	0.00064	0.00062	0.00060	0.00058	0.00056	0.00054	0.00052	0.00050
-3.1	0.00097	0.00094	0.00090	0.00087	0.00085	0.00082	0.00079	0.00076	0.00074	0.00071
-3.0	0.00135	0.00131	0.00126	0.00122	0.00118	0.00114	0.00111	0.00107	0.00104	0.00100
-2.9	0.0019	0.0018	0.0017	0.0017	0.0016	0.0016	0.0015	0.0015	0.0014	0.0014
-2.8	0.0026	0.0025	0.0024	0.0023	0.0023	0.0022	0.0021	0.0021	0.0020	0.0019
-2.7	0.0035	0.0034	0.0033	0.0032	0.0031	0.0030	0.0029	0.0028	0.0027	0.0026
-2.6	0.0047	0.0045	0.0044	0.0043	0.0041	0.0040	0.0039	0.0038	0.0037	0.0036
-2.5	0.0062	0.0060	0.0059	0.0057	0.0055	0.0054	0.0052	0.0051	0.0049	0.0048
-2.4	0.0082	0.0080	0.0078	0.0075	0.0073	0.0071	0.0069	0.0068	0.0066	0.0064
-2.3	0.0107	0.0104	0.0102	0.0099	0.0096	0.0094	0.0091	0.0089	0.0087	0.0084
-2.2	0.0139	0.0136	0.0132	0.0129	0.0125	0.0122	0.0119	0.0116	0.0113	0.0110
-2.1	0.0179	0.0174	0.0170	0.0166	0.0162	0.0158	0.0154	0.0150	0.0146	0.0143
-2.0	0.0228	0.0222	0.0217	0.0212	0.0207	0.0202	0.0197	0.0192	0.0188	0.0183
-1.9	0.0287	0.0281	0.0274	0.0268	0.0262	0.0256	0.0250	0.0244	0.0239	0.0233
-1.8	0.0359	0.0351	0.0344	0.0336	0.0329	0.0322	0.0314	0.0307	0.0301	0.0294
-1.7	0.0446	0.0436	0.0427	0.0418	0.0409	0.0401	0.0392	0.0384	0.0375	0.0367
-1.6	0.0548	0.0537	0.0526	0.0516	0.0505	0.0495	0.0485	0.0475	0.0465	0.0455
-1.5	0.0668	0.0655	0.0643	0.0630	0.0618	0.0606	0.0594	0.0582	0.0571	0.0559
-1.4	0.0808	0.0793	0.0778	0.0764	0.0749	0.0735	0.0721	0.0708	0.0694	0.0681
-1.3	0.0968	0.0951	0.0934	0.0918	0.0901	0.0885	0.0869	0.0853	0.0838	0.0823
-1.2	0.1151	0.1131	0.1112	0.1093	0.1075	0.1057	0.1038	0.1020	0.1003	0.0985
-1.1	0.1357	0.1335	0.1314	0.1292	0.1271	0.1251	0.1230	0.1210	0.1190	0.1170
-1.0	0.1587	0.1562	0.1539	0.1515	0.1492	0.1469	0.1446	0.1423	0.1401	0.1379
-0.9	0.1841	0.1814	0.1788	0.1762	0.1736	0.1711	0.1685	0.1660	0.1635	0.1611
-0.8	0.2119	0.2090	0.2061	0.2033	0.2005	0.1977	0.1949	0.1922	0.1894	0.1867
-0.7	0.2420	0.2389	0.2358	0.2327	0.2297	0.2266	0.2236	0.2207	0.2177	0.2148
-0.6	0.2743	0.2709	0.2676	0.2643	0.2611	0.2578	0.2546	0.2514	0.2483	0.2451
-0.5	0.3085	0.3050	0.3015	0.2981	0.2946	0.2912	0.2877	0.2843	0.2810	0.2776
-0.4	0.3446	0.3409	0.3372	0.3336	0.3300	0.3264	0.3228	0.3192	0.3156	0.3121
-0.3	0.3821	0.3783	0.3745	0.3707	0.3669	0.3632	0.3594	0.3557	0.3520	0.3483
-0.2	0.4207	0.4168	0.4129	0.4090	0.4052	0.4013	0.3974	0.3936	0.3897	0.3859
-0.1	0.4602	0.4562	0.4522	0.4483	0.4443	0.4404	0.4364	0.4325	0.4286	0.4247
-0.0	0.5000	0.4960	0.4920	0.4880	0.4840	0.4801	0.4761	0.4721	0.4681	0.4641

σ	0.00	0.01	0.02	0.03	0.04	0.05	0.06	0.07	0.08	0.09
+0.0	0.5000	0.5040	0.5080	0.5120	0.5160	0.5199	0.5239	0.5279	0.5319	0.5359
+0.1	0.5398	0.5438	0.5478	0.5517	0.5557	0.5596	0.5636	0.5675	0.5714	0.5753
+0.2	0.5793	0.5832	0.5871	0.5910	0.5948	0.5987	0.6026	0.6064	0.6103	0.6141
+0.3	0.6179	0.6217	0.6255	0.6293	0.6331	0.6368	0.6406	0.6443	0.6480	0.6517
+0.4	0.6554	0.6591	0.6628	0.6664	0.6700	0.6736	0.6772	0.6808	0.6844	0.6879
+0.5	0.6915	0.6950	0.6985	0.7019	0.7054	0.7088	0.7123	0.7157	0.7190	0.7224
+0.6	0.7257	0.7291	0.7324	0.7357	0.7389	0.7422	0.7454	0.7486	0.7517	0.7549
+0.7	0.7580	0.7611	0.7642	0.7673	0.7704	0.7734	0.7764	0.7794	0.7823	0.7852
+0.8	0.7881	0.7910	0.7939	0.7967	0.7995	0.8023	0.8051	0.8079	0.8106	0.8133
+0.9	0.8159	0.8186	0.8212	0.8238	0.8264	0.8289	0.8315	0.8340	0.8365	0.8389
+1.0	0.8413	0.8438	0.8461	0.8485	0.8508	0.8531	0.8554	0.8577	0.8599	0.8621
+1.1	0.8643	0.8665	0.8686	0.8708	0.8729	0.8749	0.8770	0.8790	0.8810	0.8830
+1.2	0.8849	0.8869	0.8888	0.8907	0.8925	0.8944	0.8962	0.8980	0.8997	0.9015
+1.3	0.9032	0.9049	0.9066	0.9082	0.9099	0.9115	0.9131	0.9147	0.9162	0.9177
+1.4	0.9192	0.9207	0.9222	0.9236	0.9251	0.9265	0.9279	0.9292	0.9306	0.9319
+1.5	0.9332	0.9345	0.9357	0.9370	0.9382	0.9384	0.9406	0.9418	0.9429	0.9441
+1.6	0.9452	0.9463	0.9474	0.9484	0.9495	0.9505	0.9515	0.9525	0.9535	0.9545
+1.7	0.9554	0.9564	0.9573	0.9582	0.9591	0.9599	0.9608	0.9616	0.9625	0.9633
+1.8	0.9641	0.9649	0.9656	0.9664	0.9671	0.9678	0.9686	0.9693	0.9699	0.9706
+1.9	0.9713	0.9719	0.9726	0.9732	0.9738	0.9744	0.9750	0.9756	0.9761	0.9767
+2.0	0.9773	0.9778	0.9783	0.9788	0.9793	0.9798	0.9803	0.9808	0.9812	0.9817
+2.1	0.9821	0.9826	0.9830	0.0834	0.9838	0.9842	0.9846	0.9850	0.9854	0.9857
+2.2	0.9861	0.9864	0.9868	0.9871	0.9875	0.9878	0.9881	0.9884	0.9887	0.9890
+2.3	0.9893	0.9896	0.9898	0.9901	0.9904	0.9906	0.9909	0.9911	0.9913	0.9916
+2.4	0.9918	0.9920	0.9922	0.9925	0.9927	0.9929	0.9931	0.9932	0.9934	0.9936
+2.5	0.9938	0.9940	0.9941	0.9943	0.9945	0.9946	0.9948	0.9949	0.9951	0.9952
+2.6	0.9953	0.9955	0.9956	0.9957	0.9959	0.9960	0.9961	0.9962	0.9963	0.9964
+2.7	0.9965	0.9966	0.9967	0.9968	0.9969	0.9970	0.9971	0.9972	0.9973	0.9974
+2.8	0.9974	0.9975	0.9976	0.9977	0.9977	0.9978	0.9979	0.9979	0.9980	0.9981
+2.9	0.9981	0.9982	0.9983	0.9983	0.9984	0.9984	0.9985	0.9985	0.9986	0.9986
+3.0	0.99865	0.99689	0.99874	0.99878	0.99882	0.99886	0.99889	0.99893	0.99896	0.99900
+3.1	0.99903	0.99906	0.99910	0.99913	0.99915	0.99918	0.99921	0.99924	0.99926	0.99929
+3.2	0.99931	0.99934	0.99936	0.99938	0.99940	0.99942	0.99944	0.99946	0.99948	0.99950
+3.3	0.99952	0.99953	0.99955	0.99957	0.99958	0.99960	0.99961	0.99962	0.99964	0.99965
+3.4	0.99966	0.99967	0.99969	0.99970	0.99971	0.99972	0.99973	0.99974	0.99975	0.99976
+3.5	0.99977	0.99978	0.99978	0.99979	0.99980	0.99981	0.99981	0.99982	0.99983	0.99983

FEED-FORWARD
CONTROL

Let $\mathbf{y} = (y_1, y_2, \ldots, y_h)$ be an objective characteristic vector having target $\mathbf{y}_0 = (y_{10}, y_{20}, \ldots y_{h0})$, $\mathbf{x} = (x_1, x_2, \ldots, x_m)$ be given conditions which affect output $\mathbf{y}$, and $\mathbf{z} = (z_1, z_2, \ldots, z_l)$ be a vector of process parameters.

For example, in the steel industry, quality characteristics of iron ore and other materials are observed. The quality characteristics of iron will be affected by the quality of raw materials, including ore. When material conditions are at nominal, standard process conditions are used to produce iron to meet target $\mathbf{y}_0$. When the material conditions are not at nominal, the quality of iron will deviate from nominal. In order to minimize the deviation, process parameters $\mathbf{z}$ are changed by solving the following equation:

$$f(\mathbf{z}, \mathbf{x}) = \mathbf{y}_0 \tag{B.1}$$

where $\mathbf{x}$ = material conditions
          $\mathbf{z}$ = process parameters to adjust in order to satisfy the above
               equation
$f(\mathbf{z}, \mathbf{x})$ = prediction function of $\mathbf{y}$

Using Eq. B.1, y_i's can be predicted. Denote the difference between predictions and nominal values by

$$y_{ip} - y_{i0} \qquad i = 1, \ldots, h \tag{B.2}$$

where y_{ip} is the predicted value obtained for process condition z, and material condition $\mathbf{x}$, and y_{i0} is the target value of the ith quality characteristic. The feed-forward quality control focuses on the search for the right adjustment

168

of $\mathbf{z}$ from $\mathbf{z}_0$, the nominal values of process parameters, in order to minimize the loss. That is,

$$\underset{\mathbf{z}}{\text{Min}} \sum_{i=1}^{h} \frac{A_i}{\Delta_i^2} \big[\beta (y_{ip} - y_{i0}) \big]^2 \tag{B.3}$$

where y_{ip} is the predicted y_i using $f(\mathbf{z}, \mathbf{x})$, and β_i is the shrinkage or damping factor, commonly used in control engineering.

SHRINKAGE FACTOR. Suppose y is the true (unknown) value of a characteristic having target y_0, and suppose y_p is the prediction with an error variance σ_p^2. How much should this characteristic be adjusted? If the adjustment is as much as

$$-(y_p - y_0) \tag{B.4}$$

then error variance σ^2 after adjustment is

$$\sigma^2 = E[\underbrace{y - (y_p - y_0)}_{} - y_0]^2 = \sigma_p^2 \tag{B.5}$$

True value
after adjustment

If adjustment is made with a shrinkage factor β, then

$$\sigma^2 = E[\underbrace{y - \beta(y_p - y_0)}_{} - y_0]^2 = (1 - \beta)^2 (y - y_0)^2 + \beta^2 \sigma_p^2 \tag{B.6}$$

True value
after adjustment

Here it is assumed that y_p has the error variance σ_p^2 around the true value of y.
Minimizing mean square error σ^2 in Eq. (B.6) with respect to β:

$$\beta = \frac{(y - y_0)^2}{(y - y_0)^2 + \sigma_p^2}$$

$$= 1 - \frac{\sigma_p^2}{\sigma_p + (y - y_0)^2}$$

$$= 1 - \frac{1}{F_0} \tag{B.7}$$

where

$$F_0 = \frac{\sigma_p^2 + (y - y_0)^2}{\sigma_p^2} \tag{B.8}$$

This means the adjustment of y should be as much as

$$-\beta(y_p - y_0) \tag{B.9}$$

where $\beta = 1 - 1/F_0$. Note that F_0 is always ≥ 1, and hence $0 \leq \beta \leq 1$.

However, since the true value of y is not known, F_0 has to be estimated. Suppose y_p is an unbiased estimation of y having error variance,

$$E(y_p - y_0)^2 = (y - y_0)^2 + \sigma_p^2 \qquad (B.10)$$

Then $(y_p - y_0)^2$ may be used as an estimator of $\sigma_p^2 + (y - y_0)^2$, and

$$F_0 \approx \frac{(y_p - y_0)^2}{\sigma_p^2} \qquad (B.11)$$

In the case of a vector, we have to calculate

$$F_{0i} = \frac{(y_{ip} - y_{i0})^2}{\sigma_{pi}^2} \quad (i = 1, 2, \ldots, h) \qquad (B.12)$$

and we take

$$\beta_i = \begin{cases} 0 & \text{when } F_{0i} \leq 1 \\ 1 - \dfrac{1}{F_{0i}} & \text{when } F_{0i} > 1 \end{cases} \qquad (B.13)$$

Note that it is possible for the estimated F_{0i} to be less than 1; but since the true value must be ≥ 1, we take $\beta_i = 0$ in such a case.

INDEX